CONFLICT IN THE FAR EAST

CONFLICT IN THE FAR EAST

AMERICAN DIPLOMACY IN CHINA
FROM 1928—1933

BY

JAMES WILLIAM CHRISTOPHER

D. PHIL. (OXON), FORMERLY PROFESSOR OF
HISTORY ST. JOHN'S UNIVERSITY, SHANGHAI, CHINA

LEIDEN
E. J. BRILL
1950

WITH GRATITUDE AND AFFECTION
THIS BOOK IS DEDICATED TO

PROFESSOR N. W. POSTHUMUS,
                    AMSTERDAM

PRINTED IN THE NETHERLANDS

CONTENTS

FOREWORD

Much of the difficulty of writing a history of recent times in the field of international relations lies in the length of the period during which even those governments which eventually publish their diplomatic archives keep them inaccessible to historians. Much may be known or inferred about national policies from the actual course of events, from public statements and speeches, from contemporary reporting by journalists and from subsequent memoirs of political leaders and diplomats. But it is not until the documents of a nation's diplomacy are fully and unreservedly placed at the disposal of the historian that it is possible to observe in detail how policy was made and on what information — or the lack of it; by what arguments it was sustained or criticized behind the scenes; and what moves were made to put it into effect.

Fortunately there are now several fields of recent diplomatic history for which an adequate documentation exists, and one of them is the story of American policy towards China and Chinese affairs during the five years 1928—1933. This period corresponding roughly to the tenure of office of Secretary Stimson, is covered by a series of State Department publications which include consular, as well as diplomatic, reports from China. The documents thus made available have been used, together with other sources, for a study of the Far Eastern policy of the United States in relation to two major international crises by Dr. James Christopher, a former pupil and assistant of the late Professor Harley MacNair of Chicago, and after the war holder of a professorial post in St. John's University, Shanghai. The book he has now written is based on a thesis which was awarded the degree of D. Phil. in the University of Oxford in the autumn of 1948. It was during his residence in Oxford that I had the opportunity of working with him in the study of his material and of discussing with him the problems involved in an appraisal of Secretary Stimson's conduct of American foreign policy.

The period with which Dr. Christopher's book deals begins with the American (and general international) diplomatic recognition in 1928 of the Kuomintang regime in Nanking as the lawful Government of China and ends with the commencement of Roosevelt's Presidency, which practically coincided with the completion of the Japanese construction of 'Manchukuo' by the conquest of Jehol and Japan's notice of withdrawal from the League of Nations. The period thus covers both the two Manchurian crises, the Sino-Russian conflict of 1929 and the Sino-Japanese conflict of 1931—'33. The sequence and balance of the narrative are of special value, because they serve to correct the disproportionate emphasis on the crisis of 1931 which is usual in studies of Far Eastern affairs between the Washington Conference and Pearl Harbour. As the Japanese aggression of 1931 not only created 'Manchukuo' and dealt a crippling blow to the League of Nations, but also led on to the further Japanese invasion of China and ultimately to the Pacific war, it is indeed natural to regard the notorious 'Mukden Incident' as the turning-point of the Manchurian story. But the events of 1929, though now almost forgotten and never adequately treated in previous surveys of the diplomatic history of the period, were nevertheless of decisive importance. The clash over the Chinese Eastern Railway was the sequel to Chang Hsueh-liang's decision to adhere to the cause of the Kuomintang; Manchuria, where both Russia and Japan had so seriously encroached on China's sovereignty without excluding it, was the region where tension was most likely to be produced by any heightening of Chinese nationalist spirit, but the circumstances were such that it was against Russia rather than against Japan that the challenge was first directed. But the manner of Russia's response to the challenge undoubtedly had a great influence on the action subsequently taken by the Japanese in their sphere of interest in Manchuria. For the Russians settled their dispute with China over the railway by a military invasion of north-western Manchuria and rejected any intervention or mediation by other nations. Because there was no declaration of war or permanent military occupation or annexation of territory, and because the world in 1929 did not want to believe that there had been a successful act of military aggression by one of the signatories of the Briand-Kellog Pact on the morrow of the signing of it, there was an almost universal pretence that no war had taken place. But the Manchurian border campaign of 1929 was a real war, though only a little one; the very fact that the success of Russian arms was so quick and easy made it all the more dangerous a precedent. The leaders of the Japanese army saw that, given sufficient strength of will, it was a simple matter to coerce China and defy the world to interfere, and within two years they had followed the Russian example on a larger scale and with a more far-reaching intention.

The Russo-Chinese border war of 1929 showed conclusively, for those who were willing to apprehend facts, the futility of the Kellogg Pact by itself as a restraint on war. But Stimson used the Pact in connection with the crisis of 1929 as a basis for a new diplomatic procedure — the move for parallel representations by the signatories to call the attention of the parties in the dispute to their obligations under the Pact. This was a method which might have been of value in checking a nation meditating aggressive military action, provided it had been supported by some hint of more material forms of pressure. But Stimson never tried to pass beyond purely moral suasion and the appeal to world opinion. In 1931 China's appeal to the League and the obligation laid on League members by the Covenant to apply economic sanctions against a power found guilty of aggression provided an opportunity for the United States to expand the Kellogg Pact renunciation of war into a policy of economic measures against an aggressor in co-operation with the League. But, for whatever reason — and the reader of Dr. Christopher's chapters on the Sino-Japanese crisis can judge for himself what reasons determined the decisions made by Hoover and Stimson at that time — the members of the League never received any assurance of more than verbal American opposition to Japan, and without evidence of American resolve to stop Japan by more than words, they dared not risk by themselves the task of coercing Japan which the League Covenant bound them to undertake. Thus the League was exposed as powerless to protect one of its members subjected to military invasion and the principal nations of the League revealed themselves as ready to repudiate their obligations if their performance might bring them into danger. The system of collective security

constructed to fulfil the hopes of mankind at the end of the First
World War collapsed like a house of cards, and the way was
cleared for a new epoch of aggressions and conquests.

It is instructive to compare Stimson's dealings with Japan during
the Manchurian crisis with British policies towards Nazi Germany
in the Chamberlain period. The skill of the Japanese Ambassador
in Washington in playing for time and making excuses for every
Japanese military move; the prevalence on the American side of
the notion that firmness would only strengthen the extremists and
weaken the moderates in Tokyo; the idea that in the cause of
world peace it is possible endlessly to pass the buck so that the
business of all becomes the business of none — all these things
belong to the case-history of appeasement. To day, after Britain
and America have fought together in a second great war, and with
the memory of the unforeseen bombs on Pearl Harbour still
haunting the consciousness of the American people, the nations
of the West are standing together in an unprecedented unity of
purpose to withstand a new menace to their independence and way
of life. But the new wisdom of timely resistance is all too recent,
and the old habits die hard. Isolationism and appeasement are not
dead; the psychological conditions for their re-emergence continue
to be widespread in the English-speaking world. There is perhaps
no certain prophylactic against fresh epidemics of wishful thinking,
but one means to health is certainly to be found in the study of
British and American foreign policies between the signing of the
Kellogg Pact and the beginning of the Second World War.

All Souls College, Oxford   G. F. HUDSON

October 3, 1949

The disadvantages of writing on the contemporary field are many, one of the greatest is perhaps the question of interpretation. We are too close to the event to see it in perspective, to know what its place and importance in history will be. But one could almost say with certainty that a study of America's Foreign Policy from 1928—'33 could lead to only one conclusion—disaster. This was the opinion of experienced men in the field at the time. Pearl Harbour and its aftermath added point to their earlier interpretation. We, the Americans and British, by our selfish, shortsighted and inept policy made Pearl Harbour inevitable—just as we are today making domination of China by Russia inevitable.

Prophecy has no place in history, it is true, but is does not require prophecy nor a prophet to tell that domination of China by Russia is the beginning of Russian domination of the remainder of Asia and the beginning of a war of extermination between the Communist Empire and European civilization. We did not learn a lesson from our education leading to Pearl Harbour. The price was awful. We can see our policy in perspective and see that our diplomacy was intelligent compared to our recent and present course. Is a war of extermination inevitable? Is it impossible for America to be realistic in her diplomacy? Is it too late to stop Russia yet, without war? At what point was it too late to stop Japan before Pearl Harbour? These points are of the most vital importance to the world today. What can we do? What will we do? What could we have done in Manchuria in 1931—'33? What did we do?

The author must apologise to the scholar for the journalese used in this book. He must apologise to the popular reader for the documentation. An attempt has been made to produce a work which would satisfy both but probably, as in most compromises, it will satisfy neither.

Unfortunately a spate of works were issued, or became available to the author, only after this manuscript was completed or in the hands of the publishers. The book which would have had more value than any other was Stimson's *On active duty in Peace and War* of which I have not yet seen a copy. There is almost no source material available at Oxford on this subject and the materials used have been kindly loaned to the author by Mr. Price, Director of the U.S.I.S. Library in Paris and Mr. Sargent B. Child, Director of the U.S.I.S. Library at the embassy in London. Unfortunately none of the pertinent congressional documents were available.

I wish to thank my very good friends Geoffry Hudson and A. L. Rowse of All Souls College, Oxford, for their kindness and encouragement. I am deeply grateful to Dr. Adams and Sir Arthur Salter, for their kindness and suggestions. Sir John Pratt has been most kind, and while we differ greatly on the subject of this book, I wish to express my admiration and gratitude to him for his kindness and courtesy. I am particularly indebted to Dr. and Mrs. William Cohn, of Oxford, for their understanding and assistance of many kinds. I must thank Miss Jean Sotcliffe and Mrs. Rosemary Howe for their patience in seeing this manuscript through the final reading and typing. And last but not least I must thank Mr. Peter de Ridder, corrector of Brill's for his great tact and patience, and for reading the final proofs when it was not possible for me to do so.

However, for any interpretation or mistakes I alone am responsible. Many of the opinions and interpretations were objected to by one or more of those mentioned above. Whatever merit this book may have is due to my late Professor, Harley F. MacNair of the University of Chicago and to Geoffry Hudson, but they are not responsible for the faults, the style or the final form.

JAMES WILLIAM CHRISTOPHER

Magdalen College, Oxford

June 18, 1948

CHAPTER I

THE CHINESE BACKGROUND

In order to understand the situation in China in recent times it is necessary to know something of her historical background, and first of all to realize her vast size. China at the present day, including Tibet, but excluding Outer Mongolia, covers nearly four million square miles. Her territory extends, from the Pamirs east to the Yalu, over four thousand miles, and from the Amur south to Hainan, more than two thousand miles. These would be immense distances even today, if there were good lines of communication, which there are not. In former times there was practically no means of travel except by water, by mule cart in the northern plains, by sedan chair and barrow in other parts of China, the rivers being used as stages, or by camel in the Mongolian deserts. The Chinese have rarely been a sea-going people, and there are only a few periods when a navy has played an important part in their history, though they indeed coasted by junk in travelling from the capital to the provinces of the south and south-west after having traversed the Grand Canal from Peking to Hangchow. If travel is so difficult even today, when there are some modern means of transport and communication, it is easy to realize what it was like throughout most of China's history.

Over and above its sheer extent, China is for the most part a mountainous country. All Chinese history has been greatly affected by the geographical environment. "Mountains", writes a geographer, "dominate the land forms of China. Level land is present in various deltas and in Mongolia, but elsewhere human activities are restricted by unfavorable topography, so that large areas are sparsely populated". [1] One may think of the mountain systems as fingers radiating out from the palm, which would be the Tibetan plateau.

"...the Tien Shan... enclose(s) the Tarim basin of Sinkiang

---

[1] Cressy, G. B., *China's Geographic Foundations*, (N. Y., 1934) pp. 37—8.

to the south ... continuing eastward into China are the ranges of the Nan Shan and Kun Lun Mountains separated by the Tsaidam swamp and the azure lake of Kokonor; these may be represented by the first and second fingers. In between the second and third fingers would be the Red Basin of Szech- wan ... combine the third and fourth fingers to indicate the extensive but low and indefinite Nanling which extend across China eastward and northeastward to the Pacific ... the little finger might indicate the mountains south of the Si Kiang which reach eastward to Canton and are the shortest of the various mountain chains, just as those represented by the middle finger, the Tsing-ling, are the most important.

Greatest of all the mountains of China is the eastward extension of the Kun Lun, known in China collectively as the Tsingling Shan, which reach eastward from Tibet nearly to the Pacific. These mountains divide China into two major geo- graphic regions, characterized by striking contrasts in climate, agriculture and human activities ... In southern Kansu and along the borders of Szechwan the system is known as the Min Shan and is snow-clad and alpine". [1]

Many parts of China are wild, uninhabitable and almost im- passable, necessitating a long and circuitous journey between two places which may be quite close together. A journey from Peking to the far outlying provinces of the south and west was, in centuries past, a serious undertaking, and particularly for the government officials, as they were scholars and gentlemen of culture and re- finement, and were usually accompanied by their large families and retinues. The dangers of travel were many and great.

China has never had a highly centralized government. She has never been a nation, as we in the West understand the word. Her cohesion has been social and cultural, rather than political. What cohesion there has been in the past was largely due to the tre- mendous respect which the Chinese have had for literary learning and scholarship associated with the Confucian philosophical tra- dition. The administrative officials have, for the past several cen- turies at least, been chosen on a basis of competition in examinations on the Chinese classics, or, using the classics, primarily the Confucian classics, as a point of departure. Since the Han epoch the Chinese

---

[1] *Op. cit.*, p. 38.

have had this great reverence for learning and for scholars, and since, theoretically at least, almost every man in the country had an equal opportunity to compete, and was judged solely upon the basis of the examination, the system established respect for the government officials, all of whom had qualified by the examination system.

The Chinese are nothing if not a cultured people. Culture does not necessarily mean education, wealth, high social position or "manners". One of its hallmarks might be said to be consideration for the dignity and human rights of other people, aside from technical legal rights. It is possible to find culture among illiterate, poverty-stricken people. This is so with the Chinese. A Westerner is often amazed at the natural ease, tolerance and gracious manners which he finds everywhere in the interior among all people from the privileged classes to the peasants, who are lacking in all the external trappings of culture. It is not an exaggeration to say that an uneducated Chinese peasant, using education in its usual western connotation, frequently shows, in a meeting under mutually friendly circumstances, more innate culture and charm and more signs of good breeding than many so-called gentlemen in the west.

The Chinese have learned the art of living together harmoniously as no other people have done. They have had millenia of continuous cultural development, the growth of an original and autochthonous culture, cross-fertilized by other influences from which they have borrowed, but always assimilating intrusive elements, making them typically Chinese, regardless of their source. Furthermore the Chinese, with their dense population in restricted plains areas, have for many centuries had to live cheek by jowl and have been forced to learn how to live together with the least friction, have, in fact, developed this living together into the highest art of Chinese civilization. It makes no difference to what part of China one goes, "face" is the most important thing to all, from the mandarin to the lowest coolie. The Chinese always leave a way open by which one can back down gracefully, without too obvious loss of "face". The man who failed to do this would be the man who lost face, not the man whom he humiliated. The fact is pregnant with significance that the greatest humiliation and loss of face which one Chinese can inflict upon another is to commit suicide in front of his door. Every Chinese knows how to, and that he must, play the game in the traditional way. They have been so steeped for many centuries in Confucian ethics that these ethics have become the social and cultural law of the land. The proper relations between father and son, ruler and subject, husband and wife, in short, between man and man in all social relations are understood by all and he who defies this system of relations makes of himself an outcast. No human achievement, of course, is of absolute value, and it is not meant to imply that China is a social heaven on earth; far, far from it. In war and revolution these rules tend to be honored in the breach rather than the observance, as is only human, and the Chinese are human above all things. Perhaps the very strength of these rules is that they are so pliable; they bend without breaking. It is often said by Westerners that all the old rules have gone by the board since the revolution in 1911, that the old ways are things of the past in China. It is true, indeed, that there is a great flux and fluidity of custom at the present. But, even today, one has to go only a few hundred miles inland from Shanghai to find the fiercely conservative heart of China, and how much more true was this in the years between 1928 and 1933, before the awful agony of the rape by Japan! China evolves and changes progressively, and may even seem to discard completely all old habits and traditions, but that is only because we are looking at the Chinese scene here and now. The changes since 1911 are not the most drastic and revolutionary in China's long history, and if we would understand modern China we must study her in her historical perspective. She has survived many invasions and disruptions and each time, after a period lasting from years to centuries, emerged stronger than before, to enter, in accordance with the Chinese theory of historical rhythm, on the next cycle of development, ripening, decay and regeneration. [1]

---

[1] How true this would be under Communism it is impossible to foretell. It is probable that unless America awakens and goes to China's aid in the very near future, the corrupt "Soong Dynasty" will be overthrown, along with the dictatorship of Chiang Kai-shek. The Communists aim particularly at altering, if not smashing, the old system or institution of social and family relations in the villages. Will there be another "liquidation of the *Kulaks*" under the Communist behemoth or has Stalin learned a lesson in the Russian liquidation?

In order to understand the great respect for, and influence of, the scholar-administrators, who were the government of China in former times, it will be well to consider the background of the examination system and its importance. [1] How it first started is largely a matter of speculation, but it was certainly an institution in a crude form as early the Anterior Han Dynasty (206 — actually 202 — B.C. to 8 A.D.). In the fully developed form of the system every pupil who prepared for it began at the age of five or six. He had to pursue a schedule of studies which was very rigorous for such a young child. After he had progressed to the satisfaction of his teachers and had passed an examination held by the county magistrates, he was ready for his first official trial in the great examination which led to fame, honour, power and wealth (wealth unfortunately, in the main, was acquired through "squeeze", though this ancient practice has in the past, on account of the insufficiency of the salary, been extra-legal and expected, rather than illegal and unexpected).

The first test was the *hsien* or county examination, in which an average of two thousand competed in each county; some 99 % were eliminated. Those who passed were awarded the first degree, *hsiu-ts'ai*, which meant "budding genius". They were fortunate people indeed, for, having once passed this examination, they received many special privileges and were held in high esteem in

Should the familiar pattern of Communist disruption and destruction be followed in China, it is possible that they would again fail, as they did in the twenties. One cannot predict the reaction of the Chinese peasants, should such a plan be followed again. It is more likely the Chinese advisors to the Communist government would advise against antagonizing the masses too soon. It is safe to assume that they would leave the peasants alone for a time. In fact, they will probably redivide the land and thus woo the peasantry. It is questionable, whether or not they would ever be able to put through the "reforms" they did in Russia, even if they gave the peasant land and security. Such an attempt would more than likely lead to another revolution.

One cannot believe for a moment there will be an independent Chinese government under Mao Tse-tung, Chou En-lai and Chu Teh or any other Chinese rulers. The government would be at least a Russian satellite.

[1] For an excellent description of the examination system in a brief form see Chapter I, Han Yu-shan, *Moulding Forces,* in *China,* edited by MacNair, H. F., (Cal., 1946) pp. 3—18.

the local community. They were exempted from taxes and from corporal punishment, and though residing within the area ruled by county magistrates, they were outside this jurisdiction; and could not be punished unless they had first been tried by a Government Educational Commissioner and stripped of their degree.

The next step was a provincial examination, usually held triennially. Some fifty thousand students, on an average, enrolled annually and were permitted to study in the district academies, where they were rigidly disciplined for three years in preparation for the provincial examination. Here in the academy further classification took place through examination, dividing the students into two groups of which the higher, the *Lin-sheng* (salaried student), received a subsidy.

The provincial examination was divided into three sessions each of which lasted for three days; on each occasion the student was locked in a small cell until he had completed the examination. His future depended not only on his knowledge but also on his discipline and powers of concentration and not least on his health. Most scholars worked so hard during their youth that they had no time for proper physical exercise, and, unless they had naturally robust constitutions, were weak and in poor health by the time that they sat for the examinations; many ruined their health, or impaired it permanently, by the strain of preparation. Early and high mortality was common among the scholars.

The number sitting for the provincial examination ranged from three thousand to seventeen thousand, and the number chosen for the degree of *chü-jen* (promoted man) ranged from 52 to 184 persons. The third and final degree of *chin-shih* (achieved scholar) was awarded as a result of the palace examination held triennially at the capital of the Empire. There was only one session, but the standard required was so high and the emotional tension so great that few were successful. In this examination, calligraphy was of extreme importance, as was the rigid observance of traditional forms and usages of composition.

The question of impartiality in the examiners was obviously very important in such an event, and more particularly since a family, or a group of related families, would practically bankrupt themselves to give a promising candidate the education necessary to pass the examination. "Each paper", says Dr. Han Yü-shan, "was marked with a cipher copied by an official clerk; thus no examiner could discover a candidate's identity". [1] Actually this was not always true. There have been famous cases where officials or Emperors had a successful candidate marked down in order to advance a favourite. [2] But with rare exceptions the examinations were, by and large, very fair; considering the sacrifice made by families to prepare the candidate, it could not well have been otherwise. The Chinese people who ordinarily seemed inarticulate became very voluble about such things. They have often in the past taken action about a seemingly trivial matter after letting great injustice of other kinds pass for years without retaliation.

When it is remembered that this examination system has existed intermittently for at least two thousand years, or longer, and has extended into every province and county, perhaps it is easier to understand why the people were bound to respect the men chosen by the system. It is a revealing commentary on Chinese traditional culture that instead of a national football pool, or horserace sweepstake, the most absorbing popular speculative event in old China was a scholar pool in which all comers could back their favourite brain for the examinations, and form was closely studied by the man in the street.

Spoken Chinese is differentiated into varieties which can be regarded as separate languages: the so-called "Mandarin", which is spread through most parts of northern, north-western and western China and much of the basin of the Yangtze; the Wu language, spoken throughout most of Chekiang and Kiangsi Provinces; and the Yüeh language, spoken in southern, south-eastern and south-western China. Actually the Yüeh language is broken up into a number of dialects which are very difficult for people living only a few miles apart to understand; especially is this true in Fukien. The fact that China had so many spoken dialects or languages did not, however, imply that she had also an equal number of written dialects. China had only one written language. It has been called

---

[1] Op. cit., p. 12.

[2] In 1898 the Empress Tz'u-hsi had the successful candidate ploughed for spite and in 1899 one of the presiding examination judges did the same — to cite only two cases.

a sub-continental written esperanto. This phrase may be adequate to describe Chinese to people who have no general knowledge of Chinese or of languages, but the analogy is false and misleading in so far as Esperanto is an artificial, synthetic language, whereas written Chinese is the product of an evolution covering several millenia. The written characters have developed in meaning through a slow process during many centuries; there have been no sharp breaks, and no new ideography has been formed and put into national use, nor has any alphabetic script ever been adopted. The written Chinese of the Han is much more readily understood by modern Chinese than Anglo-Saxon by us. The characters have, for the most part, very much the same meaning today as then, or perhaps it would be correct to say that a great many characters retain their Han meaning, together with other meanings which have grown up as accretions. The greatest difference is the syntactical. The language of the Han was concise to the point of being almost unintelligible to anyone with knowledge of modern Chinese but without special training in classical or Han Chinese. It becomes less and less concise as time passes, but always remains, even today, almost enigmatically terse to a Westerner.

Since this written language has been used in all parts of China, as these regions were added to, and assimilated to, China, the evolution has been the same everywhere; the script, not being alphabetic, was independent of the variations of speech and in historical times there has been only one written language. Since the spoken languages have never been identical, they have evolved independently; even assuming that they may have sprung from a common mother tongue, they have diverged, the differences becoming wider and wider as centuries passed, whereas the literary written language was always a unity.

Despite the fact that officials (who were never in theory — though, as in all things Chinese, there is no absolute rule in practice — appointed to administrative office in the provinces in which they were born) often could not communicate in speech with those whom they must govern and employ in government, they could communicate in writing. This made for a loose unity, a peculiar, but vitally important, cultural and political cohesion, which helps to explain how it was possible to govern such a huge country and such a linguistically diversified people by predominantly peaceful means.

It must by now be apparent that the government of China in the past had to be, not a strong centralised control, but rather a loose co-ordination. The Westerners, to their own and to China's sorrow, were unable to realise this for half a century. It was this failure which must, in part, be held to account for the so-called injustices done by the Westerners to China. If they had realised that the Chinese Empire, was like a huge pyramid of sand instead of one of solid substance, they would have realized that by putting pressure on the Emperor or on the central government, they could not exert pressure downward to the local authorities for, to follow the metaphor, the sand pyramid was simply flattened out by pressure and collapsed into a formless incoherence.

Another factor making for decentralization and weakness of the state authority was the "big family" system, one of China's most characteristic institutions. The Chinese ideal is "five generations under one roof". Respect for old age and for conventional authority undoubtedly arise from this institution, under which the father is the unquestioned superior and, in theory at least, makes all important decisions for the family and controls the welfare and up-bringing of not only his own, but of all his male descendant's children. This is, of course, reckoning without the influence of the lady of the house, who in theory has little voice, but who in practice wields very great authority.

It is often pointed out that this system has been one of the principal causes for China's conservatism, which is held to be responsible for her material backwardness. Unquestionably it has evil consequences, leading to nepotism, indolence and exploitation in many cases, but on the other hand it has been one of the great stabilizing influences in Chinese history. It is a very potent force, socially and economically. It provides for the young and old, the infirm and ill. It is the equivalent of a combination of most of our social services in the west. The tight cohesion of the family group has always made for local stability. This institution is the social and political pattern of China; the state in Confucian theory is simply the family on an enlarged scale.

The loyalties of members of the family are concentrated within it. No sacrifice is too great to make for its welfare. Filial Piety, the most honored emotion (or, one could almost call it, institution) in Chinese society, demands that all obligations and duties are owed first to the family, and to the father as the head of the family. Next to the family, but with greatly diminished intensity, there is loyalty to the village, then a more attenuated attachment, growing weaker at each stage, to the *hsien*, the province and the empire. One might well compare the traditional loyalties of a Chinese to the effect of throwing a stone into a lake. The immediate splash is forceful and strong, but the waves spreading out are weaker and weaker until the ripple dies away altogether. So in China, by the time the sentiment of loyalty reaches to the emperor and the empire, it is like the outermost ripple of the splash. In this also there would be a great potential difference under Communist rule.

A further result of the family system, which has been a great obstacle to the modernization of China's state administration in recent years, was the almost universal prevalence of graft in official life. The official was expected to provide well for his family and relatives, and as official salaries were never substantial, it was always customary to make up with bribes, perquisites and "squeeze". This was not regarded as wrong as long as it was not carried to excess and its conventional limits were well understood. But when the attempt was made to set up a civil service on the modern Western model, it was found hard indeed suddenly to change the habits of centuries, and the breakdown of traditional ethical standards has brought an increase, rather than a reduction, of official corruption in China.

China's is the oldest civilization existing today with a continuous tradition and is perhaps the most highly developed and complex which has ever survived over such a long span of time. Chinese civilization has expressed its genius most completely in the sphere of the arts. Her bronze art, reaching back into what is still Chinese pre-history, was by the 15th century B.C. so highly developed that it had already reached its apogee. No nation developed ceramic art superior to China's, and no people has developed one equal to it in the Christian era. The ceramics of the T'ang period were superb, and no porcelain has ever been produced comparable to that of the Sung for sheer beauty of form and glaze. In the field of painting, China has developed a unique art, and what is surprising is that, although utterly different from Western painting, it has a universal appeal. Its depth, quiet meditative serenity and profound spirituality bestow an experience of beauty of a kind which no other art affords. In its highest development this painting is the result of Buddhism and of the ripeness of Chinese culture in the age of Sung in the twelfth and thirteenth centuries A.D. The artists absorbed landscape into their minds and distilled it in their painting so as to create a spiritual significance which transcends race or creed, a deep inner meaning which one feels, and sometimes grasps, but finds extremely difficult to express. These arts are the essence of the civilization which produced them.

China has at several periods in history been one of the greatest powers on earth. Under the Han dynasty it was perhaps the equal of the Roman empire in extent and population. In the seventh and eighth centuries of the Christian era it was rivalled in imperial greatness only by the Moslem Caliphate. In the late thirteenth century, under Kublai Khan, it was the center of the most extensive empire the world has ever seen, and in the seventeenth and eighteenth centuries it was still one of the strongest and richest states in existence.

This nation, which many Westerners have been wont to dismiss with a shrug or with some statement about its queerness and backwardness, has indeed been accustomed in the past to consider itself the hub of the universe, as is shown by the standard Chinese name for their own land — Chung Kuo, the Central Country. As Chinese culture was so largely autochthonous, so highly developed and so extremely isolated by geographical factors, and was for very long periods out of contact with other cultures of comparable quality, the Chinese developed a marked superiority complex towards all other peoples. As they were accustomed to having close relations only with peoples of inferior culture, they came to think of all non-Chinese as being barbarians and themselves as superior. They considered China to be the central body round which all other nations ought to revolve as humble satellites. They could not and would not admit the equality of any other nation.

The Chinese idea that the emperor was the Son of Heaven, who ruled and held his mandate from heaven, goes back to very early times. But the Chinese did not long retain, like the Japanese, the

idea that the imperial family was divine by dynastic descent from
a God. They developed too rational an outlook for this. They held
that the emperor held his mandate to rule from Heaven, conceived
as a semi-personal divine power, to which he was directly responsible, and held the mandate only so long as he ruled justly. The
political idea of the right of the people to revolt when the emperor
lost the mandate of Heaven is a very old one and is held to be the
teaching of Confucius. Certainly this right of revolution has been
applied by the people periodically for more than two thousand
years. The emperor was not holy in himself; only his mandate from
heaven was inviolable, and he forfeited it by misrule. Calamities
such as invasion, droughts, floods, plagues, internal disturbances
and natural phenomena such as earthquakes and comets, were
usually taken as signs that he had lost the mandate. Then it was
not merely the right but the duty of the people to revolt and
overthrow him.

By the very nature of the Chinese political system and society,
few rulers have been able to establish a really strong central government, and all had to depend upon the loyalty of the civil and
military officials without being able to coerce them with full state
sovereignty as it has existed in theory and practice in the West in
modern times. For this reason, as well as because of the Chinese
claim to superiority, it was extremely difficult for foreign nations to
have diplomatic relations with China. The Emperor was the Son
of Heaven, China was the Central Kingdom, and all other peoples
were barbarians compared to the Chinese; hence other nations could
not approach the Chinese Emperor except at his will and on his
terms. But even if relations were established the Emperor was
hardly in a position to enforce agreements he might make with
foreigners, against the will of the powerful viceroys and provincial
governors. Even if the Emperor had wished to punish an official
for over-riding foreign rights — and it is doubtful whether any
Emperor did wish to do so of his own volition after about 1780 —
it was very questionable whether he had the power. If he was
successful in doing so, there was a grave question whether it was
wise, for he lost the confidence of the very class upon whom he
depended to maintain his position and prestige and that of his
dynasty. It was almost impossible to hold the Central Government

responsible for the actions of the provincial officials of the empire, still less for those of the Tributary States such as Korea or Annam.

It was also a fact of importance for China's foreign relations in the nineteenth century that the reigning dynasty was not of pure Chinese stock but Manchu, and that it was always regarded by many Chinese, especially in the south, as a line of alien usurpers. The army "bannermen" were largely Manchu and Mongol. The principle of government in China has always been authoritarian, but loose and flexible, with no strong military nobility, or martial tradition, as in Japan. Japan's background of social supremacy is one of feudal military nobility, China's of scholarly civilians. China made an end of feudalism in the third century before the Christian era, and from the time of the Sung dynasty soldiers have been despised as a necessary evil. Though the idea that China has never had a military tradition is untenable — for even in the Han and T'ang periods the military profession was held in honour — the old Chinese proverb "One does not make nails out of good iron nor soldiers out of good men" has fairly represented Chinese opinion for many centuries. This unmilitary character was a great disadvantage to China in her early contacts with the Western nations and it also meant that, when China did try to develop military strength, she produced a military class of a very ruffianly type.

There was no preparation in China for parliamentary institutions or for democracy prior to the "Hundred Days" of 1898, and that was only the venture of a clique of reformers depending on the favour of the reigning Emperor. The ideas of popular sovereignty were never the ideas of the masses, and as far as one can observe, are not even now. They came from the West, and were accepted and partially understood by only a small western-educated group. The abolition of the old examination system in the opening years of the twentieth century discredited the scholar class, who were the backbone of Chinese society and government, and there was no substitution of a national education system along Western lines, as in Japan. Education was left mostly in the hands of the missionaries who, according to their lights, and to the best of their ability, did good work. But the education of a nation cannot wisely be left in the hands of foreigners, no matter how good or impartial their intentions may be. The springs of inspiration, the cultural bases, the psychological assumptions and the purpose in view are bound to be more or less unsuitable.

For a short time indeed, it seemed that there were good hopes for a constitutional monarchy and general governmental reform to meet the needs of a new age, under the Emperor Kuang Hsü. But fate decreed otherwise. The whole situation was anomalous in the "Hundred Days" which lasted from June to September 1898. [1] The reform movement was inspired by K'ang Yu-wei, a Cantonese, and supported by southerners, who were traditionally opposed to the Manchu dynasty. However, the reforms which might have both prolonged the life of the Manchu dynasty and at the same time restored much power to the hands of native Chinese, threatened to eliminate the element upon which the success of the movement would ultimately have depended, namely the scholar class. [2] Vested interest and prejudice were stronger among the old-fashioned scholars than their dislike of the Manchus, and threw them into league with the Manchus to prevent constitutional reform. The movement was violently suppressed and the growing discontent in the country became revolutionary, anti-Manchu and, in the end, republican.

The revolution of 1911 set up the republic, but destroyed the last vestiges of central authority based upon China's historical tradition. It threw China into a strife between Sun Yat-sen, the Father of the Republic, and Yuan Shih-kai, who was always a believer in autocracy, though he was ready enough to get rid of the Manchu dynasty when it was obviously no longer capable of governing. He became first President of the Republic, assumed dictatorial powers in 1913, and later tried to make himself Emperor and found a new dynasty. He was frustrated by widespread rebellion and after his death in 1916, China relapsed into a condition of anarchy and continual civil war between provincial army commanders, generally known as "war lords". There was no new integration until the Kuomintang brought in the period of "tutelage" in 1928. This involved a revision of Sun Yat-sen's original idea of direct transition to parliamentary democracy in favour of the theory

---

[1]　Morse–MacNair, *Far Eastern International Relations*, pp. 445—450.

[2]　For an excellent account of the reform movement read Bland and Backhouse, *China under the Empress Dowager*, (London, 1910) pp. 190—210.

of the "three stages": military revolution, "tutelage" by a single party (the Kuomintang), and free democracy as the final outcome. [1]

Economically Chinese society had been based hitherto on intensive agriculture, with large towns and considerable local trade, but with primitive communications and a still more primitive fiscal system. The difficulty of starting the industrialization of China in the late nineteenth century was largely due to the opposition of the conservative scholar-officials and the anti-foreign prejudice of the people at large under their influence. The old vested interests of China were all opposed to any change, and the Chinese failed to understand that what had saved Japan and put her on the road to becoming a world power, despite her relatively small area and scanty resources, was her ability, if not willingness, to adapt herself to the new order.

As the result of this resistance to change the trade and industry of China were concentrated in the hands of foreigners living in the "treaty ports" and foreign settlements and concessions. It was not a wholesome condition, either for the foreigners or for China, that this state of affairs should exist, but it was not so much the avarice of the foreign capitalist and merchant which brought it about as it was the attitude of the Chinese gentry. The Chinese of the present generation are generally unwilling to admit this and have the habit of putting all the blame for China's ills on foreign "imperialism". The combination of the old traditional contempt for foreigners with Western ideas of "anti-imperialism", as introduced to China, especially by the Russian Communists after 1920, have produced the modern Chinese brand of "anti-foreignism" — a state of mind which has parallels in other countries but a quality all its own. The desire to liberate China from what was felt as a foreign yoke, or at least a humiliating status of international inferiority, was the strongest single factor in the revolutionary movement embodied in the Kuomintang party. The domestic reform programme of the Kuomintang was always secondary to its nationalist "rights recovery" aims, and China's grievances against other nations have been proclaimed not less, but more loudly, at times of internal breakdown and confusion.

---

[1] For the best and most complete concise story of this period see MacNair, Harley F., *China In Revolution* (Chicago, 1931).

The Kuomintang began as a party recruited from the bourgeoisie and professional classes in the large towns, especially in Canton and Shanghai, with much support from the Chinese communities overseas, in California, Malaya and the Dutch East Indies. It had, at the outset, little attraction for the peasants or industrial workers, but it needed to stir the masses in order to wrest power from the "war lords", and to this end it entered into an alliance in 1925 with the recently formed Chinese Communist party, which was making rapid progress among the poorest classes in certain areas. The Communists, in accordance with the general principles of the Communist International, supported the programme of national struggle against the "imperialist" powers, as adopted by the Kuomintang, but they were much more interested in social revolution directed ultimately against the classes from which the Kuomintang drew its following. It was not an alliance which could last long, and it did not.

Dr. Sun, the Father of the Chinese Revolution, was not able to control the Government which he set up at Canton, and on three occasions was forced to flee as a refugee to the international settlement at Shanghai. On his last exile there he had met the Soviet envoy Joffe, and worked out a scheme for close co-operation between the Kuomintang and Moscow. They issued a joint communiqué in which Sun said that it was his opinion that China was not *yet* ready for the introduction of communism or of the Soviet system, and Joffe agreed, declaring that China's most important task was internal unity and independence. He said that in these aims, the people of China had the best wishes of the peoples of the Soviet Union.

A short time after the issuance of this declaration Sun returned to Canton, his military opponent having been driven out. He had learned, after much bitter experience, that he was helpless without the assistance of a strong administration and armed force to support him. Accordingly, he invited a group of Russian advisers to help him reorganize the Kuomintang and provide it with an efficient army. He got a number of experts in various fields to help him execute his grandiose plans.

The leading personality in this group was Michael Borodin, a very clever and capable man and an excellent organizer and administrator. He soon realized that 'his main task would be to reorganize the Kuomintang on a much broader and more radical base. He had perceived that there was great internal conflict within the party. He decided that he must weed out the more conservative elements and force those remaining to co-operate unquestioningly. The principal objectives of Borodin and Sun Yat-sen were to reorganize the Kuomintang along communist lines. The members of the new organization would be highly disciplined, and linked with a tightly-knit and intensively trained propaganda shock-corps. The second string to the new bow was to be the creation of a powerful and well-trained army. The first move must be the training of officers. They must not only be taught to fight, but, much more important, must be shown how to develop a mass of illiterate "recruits" into a powerful striking force capable of eliminating all other military factions in China. This latter objective was accomplished by founding the new Whampoa Military Academy under the leadership of Chiang Kai-shek, who was assisted by a group of Russian military advisers. The chief of these advisers was General Bluecher, alias Galens.

As soon as the new Kuomintang was organized, the First National congress was called. At this conference, after much bickering and compromise, a manifesto was adopted and published. It was a gravely significant document from the international point of view. It gave the Kuomintang and the Chinese nationalist movement an anti-capitalistic, anti-imperialistic and anti-foreign (but not anti-Russian) policy. In the first section of this manifesto appeared the accusation that the foreign powers were responsible for the ills of China. "Since the occupation of China by the Manchus there reigned in the hearts of the Chinese race a feeling of injustice for a long time. After the country was thrown open to international commerce, foreign imperialism came like an angry tide. Armed plundering and economic pressure reduced the country to a semi-colonial status and caused her to lose her independence". [1]

The manifesto stated that the revolution had been carried out not

---

[1] Borg, Dorothy, *American Policy and the Chinese Revolution 1925—8,* (New York, 1947) p. 17. Also cf. Woo, T. C., *The Kuomintang and the Future of the Chinese Revolution,* appendix c. (London, 1928).

CHRISTOPHER, Conflict in the Far East   2

only to overthrow the Ch'ing Dynasty but to reunite China, forming
a strong democratic nation in control of its own economy, whose
principal aim would be to throw off the fetters of "semi-colonialism"
and take its place among the powers as a sovereign nation. But the
revolution had failed and China, under Yuan Shih-kai, and later,
under the Northern war lords, had been reduced to anarchy. The
foreigners, taking advantage of the chaos, had served their own
selfish ends and attempted to throttle the political and economic
life of the nation. Now the arbitrary rule of the militarists and 'the
invasion of the Imperialists' were growing worse every day, causing
the nation 'to sink deeper into the hell of a semi-colonial status'. [1]

In this remarkable document one sees a failing which is inherent
in the Chinese and goes as far back as we can trace their history:
the inability to see their own faults and weaknesses, as a race or as
a nation. It almost smacks of a confusion of the real and the unreal.
The best short example one calls to mind is the habit of painting
cannons on the Great Wall and withdrawing other defence, leaving
the painted cannon to strike fear into the heart of the enemy and
cause him to flee, and this even in modern times; comparable devices
are well attested for the period of their wars with the Hsiung-niu,
the Huns, who later overran Europe.

In the statements quoted above we see the typical Chinese psychology of blaming everyone and everything except themselves.
Certainly they did not see fit to blame the impractical idealism of
Sun Yat-sen and his followers or the cupidity of many of the
members of the Kuomintang. Throughout Chinese history it has
always been someone else who was to blame for China's failures.
By assigning all China's misfortunes to the special privileges of
foreigners and to the restrictions placed upon China's sovereignty
by foreign powers, the Kuomintang roused the masses against the
foreigner and furthered its own popularity. This policy had its
natural consequences in anti-foreign outrages.

The Kuomintang took as its platform the abolition of the "unequal treaties" and all they implied, stating that after their cancellation new treaties would be negotiated on a basis of equality.
This first Kuomintang congress was fraught with significance for

---

[1] Borg, *loc. cit.*, quotation and paraphrase.

the future of China. The Communists were accepted as members
of the party after promising to accept its principles, though this
was done against the advice of many old members and with the
misgivings of many more.

Borodin, who was an experienced revolutionary, realized that
Sun Yat-sen was the best and, at the moment, the only asset the
new organization had. He realized the value of capitalizing this
asset and urged Sun to spread his ideas broadcast in every possible
manner. Out of this grew the propaganda of the *San Min Chu I*
of 'Three Principles of the People', — nationalism, democracy and
'people's livelihood'. Sun was an even better instrument than Borodin could have hoped at the outset. In his old age, suffering from
bitterness and disillusionment, coupled with ill health, he became a
venomous bigot. Borodin missed no opportunity to turn this essentially lovable and idealistic old man into the most rabid type of
anti-western propagandist. He used him to undermine the Western
influence and, although Sun did not realize it, to build up the
power of the Communists so that Russia could take over the
direction of affairs when the time was ripe.

It is difficult for one who has not lived in China or one who is
not familiar with their psychology and sociological institutions to
realize just how clever and effective Sun Yat-sen's propaganda
was. He played upon the emotions of the people as he would play
on a musical instrument. He worked them up to a climax of
emotional excitement and then pulled all the stops. As Miss Borg
remarks:

> "Dr. Sun argued that basically China resembled a 'sheet of
> loose sand' because her people were not united by a genuinely
> patriotic feeling: they had developed a loyalty to family and to
> clan but not to the nation as a whole. As a result China was
> unable to withstand the disaster that threatened her from
> without. Oppression by the foreign Powers had reduced her
> to a 'semi-colonial' state — a state lower than that of the
> average colony which was at least able to claim some degree
> of protection from a mother-country. 'Whose semi-colony is
> China?' Dr. Sun asked. 'China is the colony of every nation
> that has made treaties with her, and the treaty-making
> nations are her masters. China is not the colony of one nation
> but of all, and we are not the slaves of one country, but of
> all'. The only reason that China had survived with any degree

of independence was that the powers wanted to avoid war in the Far East and, therefore, checkmated one another by establishing a balance of power. However, it was still the intention of the major Treaty Powers to 'crush China', and this aim could be attained by diplomacy as well as by military force. 'The concentrated thinking of the Powers will certainly evolve some consummate method of overthrowing China.... Just a paper and pen and a mutually satisfactory agreement will spell our ruin. It is only necessary that the diplomats of the different countries meet in one place and make their signatures; in one day the signing of a document, in one day united political action can wipe out China'. And, if by 'some good luck' China should escape military control and diplomatic oppression, she would still be destroyed by the economic tyranny of other nations 'which is day by day pressing in upon us and sucking our very life blood.' " [1]

The dangers and the latent possibilities of tragedy in this type of propaganda were at first not realized by many of the foreign legations and consulates in China, and particularly were they not realized by the foreign governments. The few men who, like Sir John Pratt, did realize the true situation were prophets without honor in their own day among their compatriots.

Dr. Sun soon went north to Peking, to try to make a rapprochement with Tuan Chi-jui's government there. It proved impossible to accomplish this purpose. Already a very sick man, he died in Peking in March 1925. He was to be much more of a power, and much less embarrassing to his followers, as a dead martyr than as a living leader.

His apotheosis was immediate and had great influence on China and on her relations with the world. It is a rather sad commentary on Dr. Sun's career that, having been such a complete failure during his life, he had so much success in death. Of course it can be argued that he was not a failure in life, that he was the fountain-head of the revolution. This is partly true. He was very successful in raising money abroad, and in stirring up the overseas Chinese in support of the revolution, as well as in arousing sympathy for the independence of China among foreigners abroad. But he was a failure as an internal organizer, administrator or executive. He was not a

---

[1] Borg, op. cit., pp. 18—19.

judge of men and was easily fooled and used for the selfish ends of those whom he trusted. Towards the end of his life, the last two years, he embarked upon the course of action which was to prove so disastrous to China, with enduring consequences which have only been apparent in all their ramifications since the close of the war in 1945. That he became so bitter was not, indeed, without reason. He originally looked to the West for a lead, but the Western capitalist nations were too much concerned with their own short-term interests to pay attention. Unfortunately the psychology of the "China Hand", which greatly influenced governments, was often one of considering the Chinese as a sort of sub-human being; the mind of the "China Hand" tended to become so atrophied that he lost all sense of perspective and all ability to evaluate the situation accurately. There were of course exceptions; there were foreign residents such as Mrs. Ayscough, who made it a life mission to try to understand and explain to others the beauty of Chinese life and culture. But there were too many who were sunk in blind prejudice, especially members of the British and French communities with a Colonial or Indian background. There were some Americans who were just as bad, but a much smaller percentage, perhaps because of the different social and political attitude. At any rate it is unhappily true that few foreigners ever took Dr. Sun and his movement seriously. The West at that time was too smug and self-complacent, too sure of itself and its world-wide ascendancy to realize the potential strength of Chinese nationalism. That was left to Russia. She had here the first of many tailor-made situations which she would exploit for her own ends. Whereas the diplomats in Peking ignored the signs of change and kept "China hours", Borodin and his associates realized the possibilities of the situation and no hours were too long for them to work to exploit their opportunity. They were motivated by the religious zeal of communism, and they had a cleverly calculated system of tactics based on their Marxist-Leninist political training. Every move was carefully thought out. The men advising Sun were men who knew exactly what their objective was and how to accomplish it.

Sun Yat-sen is said to have left a political testament which, together with the *San Min Chu I* and the Manifesto mentioned above, became the three sacred things of Chinese nationalism. The authorship of the *San Min Chu I* and the "will" is open to more than a little question. Dr. MacNair writes: "During the last weeks of his life the radicals who surrounded him were busy in preparations for allying his memory with that of Lenin in Russia. Messages *purporting to come from Sun* [1] were sent to Russia, including one commanding his party to continue cooperation with Soviet Russia. In the exchange of messages between Peking and Moscow, that from China declared: 'We, the heirs of Sun Yat-sen, greet you, the heirs of Lenin' ". [2] One of these radicals referred to by Dr. MacNair, a young Chinese in Dr. Sun's confidence, is said to have been responsible for much of the *San Min Chu I* and for the "will". Whether or not this is true we may never know definitely, but there seems to be no doubt that the extremist influence in his entourage was at its height in the period immediately preceding his death.

For several months before the death of Dr. Sun a split had been developing between the moderate wing of the Kuomintang and the left wing with its Communist "tail". The final break did not come, however, until March of 1927.

Shortly after the death of Dr. Sun events in China took an entirely unexpected turn. An accidental clash between Chinese and the foreign police in the international settlement of Shanghai detonated the new explosive force of Chinese Nationalism. The Chinese blamed the British for this incident. Actually the British were not to blame any more than other foreigners, and not nearly as much as the Japanese, since the original trouble which led to the Nanking Road shootings occurred in a Japanese mill where Japanese officials had been trying to break a strike of Chinese employees. But the British, by reason of their position in Shanghai and Hongkong, were inevitably the main target for an anti-foreign agitation centered in South China. As a result of the trouble with the British, and the Russian incitement, the Southern government became more anti-foreign and also anti-Christian. It began persecuting Christians in the interior, seizing, looting and often destroying missionary property, including hospitals. Conditions in China steadily

---

[1] The italics are mine.
[2] Morse–MacNair, *op. cit.*, p. 717.

deteriorated for the foreigners, as one crisis was followed by another. The foreign powers found that in the anarchic political situation prevailing in the country they could no longer ensure the observance of their treaty rights and protection of their nationals without the use of force on a large scale. They were still according *de jure* diplomatic recognition to the government established in Peking, but this government had little authority in the north and none at all in the south. The Peking government was merely the plaything of shifting combinations of provincial military governors; unlike the Canton government it had no basis in an organized political party, and its very lack of anti-foreign speech and action, which made it preferable from the point of view of foreign interests, deprived it of popularity with the rising generation of educated Chinese. By the middle of 1926, after various *coups d'état* and civil wars, Peking was left virtually without a government and lost its political importance. The power now began to pass to the south.

Chiang Kai-shek, the successor to Sun Yat-sen in the leadership of the Kuomintang, with the aid of Galens and Borodin, organized and led an expedition northward from Kwangtung in the spring of 1926. The Whampoa Academy had paid large dividends. With the hundreds of officers trained there Chiang made a drive which carried his army to the Wuhan cities on the middle Yangtze. By October 10th Wuchang had been captured; Hanyang and Hankow had fallen a month earlier. This was an achievement beyond the fondest hope of the Kuomintang. It was almost unbelievable to the foreigners living in China who had not hitherto taken the Canton régime seriously as a power in China or realized that there was a new spirit, a crusading zeal, dominating the Nationalist movement. By the end of March 1927, Nanking was in the hands of the Kuomintang, with all China south of the Yangtze under nominal control except Yunnan, which was friendly to the cause.

Sun Yat-sen had ordained that the capital of China should be moved from Peking back to Nanking, where it had been in the early days of the Ming dynasty. The aim was partly to make a break with the old tradition of officialdom centered in conservative Peking, partly to bring the seat of central authority nearer to the southern provinces where the strength of the Kuomintang lay.

Having captured Nanking, the Kuomintang proclaimed it the capital, but the foreign powers were not yet ready to recognise the new régime, partly because Peking, where the Legations were, was still in the hands of Chang Tso-lin, the despot of Manchuria, partly because of splits and dissensions within the Kuomintang and partly because of the anti-foreign incitement and outrages which marked the progress of the Kuomintang-Communist forces. However, the break with the Communists which took place first in Shanghai (where the Communists for a while controlled the powerful labour unions of the city) made the Western Powers more favourably disposed to the Kuomintang, which seemed at least a lesser evil than Communism and it was soon clear beyond dispute that it was by far the strongest power in China. The capture of Peking was long delayed, mainly because of the local Japanese intervention in Shantung, but when it was finally accomplished in June 1928, there was no longer any reason for refusing to recognise the Kuomintang government in Nanking as the legal government of China, and one foreign nation after another now gave it formal recognition.

CHAPTER II

THE TRADITION OF AMERICAN POLICY
TOWARDS CHINA

Tyler Dennett says [1] there was no early American policy in China, but that, instead, there was a policy of early Americans, which was entirely negative. This appeared only when there was opposition to, or obstruction of, trade. As long as trade was unrestricted, or as Dennett says, "free", there was no policy. Where there was one, it was only in proportion to the desire of the Americans concerned to have the same rights as other nations. Strictly speaking, there was never "free" trade in any modern sense of the word, because of the cumbersome costs and procedure and the arrogant behaviour of the Chinese. But as long as Americans were on the same footing as other nations, it might be said of American policy, as of Topsy, that it just growed.

In the early days of the China trade there were many American merchants who were merely adventurers. There was neither diplomatic nor commercial policy other than that mentioned above, whereas the British East India Company had a definite trade policy, and control over its traders. England had a long history of diplomacy and organised trade behind her commerce in China, while the Americans were raw pioneers with little more than the settled opinion that they were "as good as anybody else and a damned sight better than most." They were lacking in most things which England had to her advantage, except shrewdness and boundless enterprise. Many of them were little better than, and in fact many of them were, privateers and smugglers, though these sins were not confined to them alone in the China Seas. But within a few years the China trade was concentrated in the hands of a few large and wealthy Yankee firms based on the New England coast.

---

[1] Dennett, Tyler, *Americans in Eastern Asia*, (N.Y., N.D.) p. 3, pp. 69 *seq.* Pp. 29—45 are a digest of this work.

Because of the danger of carrying specie and the general inconvenience of trying to settle for their cargoes of exports and imports, it became the policy to substitute a system of exchange bills on London for specie. In the beginning the Yankees were practically carrying traders, that is, they bought what they could sell in China and disposed of it there. On the return trip they bought what they could sell in the West, especially in Europe, and in some cases sold it there, in others taking it to America for transhipment, in the first case bringing only a small part of the China cargo back to the States, since there was at first little market in America for China goods which consisted mostly of tea, rhubarb and silk. The first has never been very popular in America, the second they were soon able to produce to suffice for their wants, and the third was too expensive to demand a wide market in a poor pioneer country. The China traders usually filled up their empty cargo space on the last stage of the return trip to America with European commodities, which they could more easily dispose of at home. Often, however, they did not return to America for long periods, making the voyage back from Europe to China immediately. This was especially true during the Napoleonic wars and after the exhaustion of the fur trade, when they began buying English manufactured goods, primarily cottons, and taking them to China. They were able to undercut the English prices there because of difference of operating costs and because, as the agents of the East India Company complained, they bought inferior goods, rejected by the Company, and chopped [1] them with a mark so closely resembling that of the Company as to be almost indistinguishable from it. [2]

After a time, however, the Americans began to manufacture their own cottons and to take them to China, especially coarse whites and prints, which successfully met the British competition and became very popular in China.

America did not have a consul in the diplomatic sense of the word. The consul was usually a trader or supercargo, appointed by Congress without pay, offices or interpreters. His success depended largely upon his popularity among his fellow-countrymen.

---

[1] Chop — a word used in China for mark or seal.
[2] Dennett, Tyler, op. cit., p. 73.

The principal duties of the consul consisted in caring for distressed Americans, usually seamen, making reports on the tonnage entered and cleared at Canton, administering the estates of the deceased and drawing up contracts, agreements and legal papers required. It was from the fees therefor that he received his sole emoluments as consul.

It was more or less imperative that the consul be a man who could get on well with the Chinese with whom he had to come into contact, because the rights and success of the Americans depended much more largely upon the goodwill of the Chinese than did those of the English. The latter had back of them the support and dignity of the Company, which, for a variety of reasons, the Chinese had cause to fear, actually or potentially. The Company backed the individual British subject and was in turn backed by the might of the crown. The American could depend only on the respect and friendliness of the Chinese, apart from the support which he might receive from the English Company officials on the spot, in exceptional circumstances.

The Englishman had great advantages — but these also entailed disadvantages. He was rigidly controlled by the Company. He could not act independently in any sense of the word, either as an individual or as a trader. If his actions displeased the Company officials, he was not allowed to remain in, or return to, Canton. The policy of the English toward the Chinese was coloured by their policy toward, and experience of, the Indians and Malays. They adopted a superior and arrogant attitude, looking on the Chinese as inferiors. The Americans, on the other hand, were free to buy and sell when and where they could. Being Yankees, they were entirely free of race prejudice and knew no colour-bar; there evidently were few, if any, Southerners in the trade, but even when Southerners did come into contact with the Chinese, except for a very few individuals they rarely seemed to think in terms of colour in relation to the Chinese. The Americans, having only recently won their independence, were essentially a democratic people, inclined to a universal fraternity, except for the American Indians, and in the South for negroes. The English were naturally much more reserved, a nation of older civilisation, and at this time the greatest maritime power on earth; the Englishman in the Far East was certain of the backing of the

Company and at the same time was affected by the colour-bar because of relations with native peoples elsewhere in the Orient.

The American had to make himself *persona grata* to the Chinese, if he wished to hold the trade, to a much greater degree than the Briton, and at the same time it was not so difficult for him to get on to a friendly footing with the Chinese, in so far as this was possible for any foreigner at all. The circumstances of early trade had a great influence on the later policy of America, as a nation, towards China. The policy of the early traders, as later of the American government, was to retain equal rights of trade and economic opportunity with other nations in China. Out of this would grow the policy of the Open Door, linked with respect for the territorial integrity of China. Of course this policy has vacillated and fluctuated, and, as we shall see, America has very often assumed an air of pious and sanctimonious moral superiority, refusing to act in concert with England and France and other European powers in extracting from China rights and privileges which China was unwilling to grant and yet afterwards claiming, under the most-favoured-nation clause, the benefits of those acts which she condemned. Yet it is possible to trace a continuity of principle in the growth of American policy long before the time of the "Hay Doctrine".

The relationship of the U.S. government to its citizens in China in the early nineteenth century was a very attenuated one. For instance, the Consul was supposed to discipline mutinous sailors, and presumably other Americans who required discipline, yet he had no jail and no judicial or executive powers. The chairman of the Select Committee of the East India Company and the French consul, on the other hand, had great judicial and executive powers and kept a much tighter rein on their men than the American consul could. The Americans on the China coast knew no law except that of expediency. Fortunately, however, the more respectable element among them, who had a vested interested in maintaining the good will of the Chinese, made it a point to see that their less careful countrymen did not jeopardize their position. Often the Consul was incompetent or did not reside in China, and delegated his authority to someone else. As time passed the American merchants became less and less satisfied with these conditions and at last in 1815, petitioned Congress for a more efficient consular service; declaring that:

> The consul of the United States residing here has not the means of being sufficiently useful to his countrymen with their intercourse with the Chinese Government, and of supporting the dignity of the flag of which he has charge; in consequence of which it frequently happens that impositions are placed upon the memorialists that are avoided by the citizens or subjects of other nations whose representatives have the means to oppose with firmness and effect the first attempts which, if successfully repelled, are seldom renewed; but when once a new imposition has been submitted to, it is considered an established custom, and demanded as a right from the nation that has yielded. [1]

The petitioners asked for a consul unconnected with the trade, who should receive $ 3,000 a year and a residence. They also requested a physician and a fund to pay for translation of documents. But no action was taken on the petition by Congress.

At the time of the withdrawal of the British from Canton in 1838, the American merchants again petitioned Congress. It is interesting to note from the contents of this memorial how close together the British and Americans were drawing in their aims. The petition called for Government action to obtain: [2]

(1) Permission for foreign envoys to reside near the court at Peking with the usual diplomatic privileges. (2) Promulgation of a fixed tariff. (3) A system of bonding warehouses, or some regulations for the trans-shipment of goods for re-export. (4) Liberty of trading at other port or ports in China as well as at Canton. (5) Compensation for losses caused by stoppage of legal trade and guarantees for the future. (6) A provision that until codified laws should be available, punishment for crimes of foreigners should not be more severe than that for like offences under the laws of the United States or England, and that no punishment should be inflicted upon any foreigner by Chinese before his guilt was fully proved. The petition urged government action in concert with other interested nations:

---

[1] *Op. cit.*, p. 76.
[2] *Op. cit.*, p. 99.

"We would, therefore, with all deference and respect express our opinions that the United States Government should
take immediate measures; and, if deemed advisable, to act in
concert with the governments of Great Britain, France and
Holland, or either of them, in their endeavours to establish
commercial relations with this empire upon a safe and honourable footing, such as exists between all friendly powers;
and by direct appeal to the Imperial Government at Peking, to
obtain a compliance with the following among other important
demands." [1]

Here we see the first emergence of a workable and honourable
American policy, but springing, it must be observed, from private
individuals and not from the government. No immediate action
was taken, but a short time after the signing of the Nanking Treaty,
between China and Britain in 1842, Commodore Kerney negotiated
for America, a most-favoured-nation clause with China, through
Ki-ying, the Viceroy of Canton. As a matter of historical interest, it
should be pointed out here that the credit for the opening of the
Chinese ports to all nations on an equal footing, which has always
been given to Sir Henry Pottinger, belongs in reality neither to Sir
Henry, nor to any other Westerner, but to the Chinese themselves.
The translation of the Chinese text of Article VIII of the treaty of
1843 was found to be somewhat different from the original English
text. This is the translation:

"Formerly the merchants of every foreign nation were permitted to trade at the single port of Canton only, but last year
it was agreed at Nanking, that if the Emperor should ratify
the treaty, the merchants of the various nations of Europe
should be allowed to proceed to the four ports of Foochow,
Ningpo, Amoy and Shanghai for the purpose of trade to which
the English were not to make any objections..." [2]

In the light of this quotation we must revise again many ideas
previously held about the most-favoured-nation clause and the Open
Door. The Chinese themselves introduced the Open Door policy
and have always insisted upon it. This fact has never been stressed

---

[1] *Loc. cit.*
[2] *Op. cit.*, p. 110.

sufficiently by historians. The most-favoured-nation clause as an inviolable treaty agreement is due primarily to Commodore Kerney. It was not included in the treaty of Nanking, but was included in the treaty of the Bogue in 1843, and has been included ever since, in every treaty with a foreign power. The Open Door, which this clause guarantees, is in itself a justifiable and honourable agreement, but when the most-favoured-nation clause began to be used by America and other nations, to gain without the expense or odium of military agression, whatever any nation had obtained from China by force, it became an instrument of extortion.

Caleb Cushing, a man of engaging personality, was sent to China as Commissioner to make the treaty of Wanghsia. He officially determined what would be American policy for decades to come. He carried out one of the most brilliant negotiations in American diplomatic history. By the subtle use of means which were well understood by the Chinese, a combination of threats and flattery, he negotiated the treaty of Wanghsia with little difficulty. This treaty was infinitely superior to that made by Sir Henry Pottinger, so much so, that it became the model for the French and subsequent treaties until that of Tientsin in 1858. America gained through the most-favoured-nation clause all the benefits which England had, while England, on the other hand, through the same instrument also gained the advantages of Cushing's policy. These were some of the peculiar advantages gained by Cushing: (1) Merchant ships might remain in any of the open ports two days without paying duties, provided that they did not discharge cargo. (2) Having paid the duty at one port, they might go on to other ports without again paying such duty. (3) Having landed their cargo and paid the duties, they could re-ship it to another port without duty by means of Customs house certificate. (4) Permission was granted to employ Chinese as teachers, and for Americans to purchase Chinese books. (5) There was a provision for revision after twelve years from the original date.

The first three of these provisions, in reality, created the right for Americans to carry on a coasting trade. This would be an extremely valuable right, while exploring the possibilities of the various newly-opened ports, and would give the Americans a great advantage, with their light and fast ships. Dennett points out that

Britain forced China to cede Hong Kong to her mainly in order to use it as a warehouse from which to send ships to various Chinese ports, and in so doing incurred permanent resentment among the Chinese and gave some ground to those who claimed that her actions were selfish and unjust. Cushing gained the same end without odium, and without assuming responsibility of sovereignty over any territory. On this and on subsequent ocassions American policy was able to gain its desired ends by every device short of war and nevertheless always to pose as the only power which was a true friend to China.

Cushing gained the right of extraterritoriality and amplified it with much greater precision in the treaty of Wanghsia. Pottinger had not included it explicitly in either the treaty of Nanking or that of the Bogue, though he gained it in effect by an ambiguous clause which provided:

> "Regarding the punishment of English criminals, the English Government will enact the laws necessary to attain that end and the Consul will be empowered to put them into force; and regarding the punishment of Chinese criminals, these will be tried and punished by their own laws, in the way provided for in the correspondence which took place at Nanking after the concluding of the peace." [1]

Two articles of the Treaty of Wanghsia, relating to extraterritoriality were:

> „Article XXI. Subjects of China who may be guilty of any criminal act towards the citizens of the United States shall be arrested and punished by the Chinese authorities according to the laws of China; and citizens of the United States who may commit any crime in China shall be tried and punished only by the Consul, or other public functionary of the United States, thereto authorised, according to the laws of the United States." [2]

> "Article XXV. All questions in regards to rights, whether of property or person, arising between citizens of the United

---

[1] *Op. cit.*, p. 162.
[2] *Loc. cit.* and p. 163.

States and China, shall be subject to the jurisdiction of, and regulated by the authorities of their own Government." [1]

In 1858 America acquired through the most-favoured-nation clause the rights won by Britain and France through their war against China, though not without some reluctance on the part of the American Commissioner, Reed. As an interesting sidelight on the respective attitudes of the British and American diplomatic representatives at that time, one may compare a comment of Lord Elgin's with one by Reed on the opening of the interior of China.

> "I sent for the Admiral; gave him a hint that there was a great opportunity for England; that all the powers were deserting me on a point which they had *all*, in their original applications to Peking, demanded, and which they all intended to claim if I got it; that therefore we had it in our power to claim our place of priority in the East, by obtaining this when others would not insist on it. Would he back me? ... This was the forenoon of Saturday, 26th. The treaty was signed in the evening." [2]

On the other hand, even though this was in accordance with American aims, Reed was very uncomfortable about the consequences:

> "This (access to the interior) is provided for in both the English and French treaties, and, of course, with its limitations, inures to us. The provision of the former treaty is very comprehensive for, with the limitation of requiring a passport, the form of which the Consuls and not the Chinese are to determine, any foreigner may go anywhere in China 'for pleasure, or for purposes of trade, and may hire vessels for the carriage of his baggage or *merchandise.*'"
>
> "No routes are specified; no limit to the character or the amount of merchandise which may be taken into the interior, and there is nothing to prevent a foreigner ... from unloading his ship load of cottons or, if he happens to be unscrupulous, of opium, at Shanghai ... and carrying it in one on a fleet of junks, or small craft steamers, to the frontiers of Thibet ...

---

[1] *Loc. cit.*
[2] *Op. cit.,* p. 318.

selling it as he goes along. But this is not all. He carries with him his 'extraterritoriality'; for the article which provides for his transit in the interior also provides for his immunity. 'If', says the British Treaty, 'he shall commit any offence against the law, he shall be handed over to the nearest Consul for punishment, but he must not be subjected to ill-usage in excess of necessary restraint.' This rendered into plain language means that the foreigner who commits a rape or murder a thousand miles from the sea-board is to be gently restrained, and remitted to a Consul for trial, necessarily at a remote point where testimony could hardly be obtained or relied on. These are the abuses and dangers which this new system of unlimited intercourse seems to foreshadow . . ." [1]

It is not the purpose here to condemn or condone, but in passing it may be remarked that the British treaty of 1858 broke the Back of China, and that America, while refraining from participation in the actual military operations, received, in spite of Reed's misgivings, her full share of the spoils under the most-favoured-nation clause. It is not enough to say, though it is so, that China brought her fate upon herself. As Tyler Dennett says, China's fault "mitigates the responsibility neither of Great Britain which had acted with so little regard for the evil consequences of such an opening up of the Empire, nor of the United States which sent an envoy to play the part of Saul holding the coats of those who committed the assault." [2] America, indeed, gained the benefits of the forcible opening of China to foreign intercourse without taking part in the military operations carried out by Britain and France and acquired a common interest with other Western nations in the new system of treaty rights in China, including extraterritoriality. Thus America, together with other holders of these rights, eventually became a target for Chinese nationalist indignation and incitement. On the other hand, America did not, at any time, annex or extort a leasehold of any Chinese territory. There was no American Hong Kong, Kwangtung, Kiachow, Weihaiwei or Kwangchowwan. Nor was there ever any American-administered railway zone or American sphere of influence pivoted on a territorial base within, or on the borders of, China. Until the Philippines were acquired in 1899, the

---

[1] Dennett, Tyler, *op. cit.*, p. 319.

[2] *Op. cit.*, p. 322.

United States had no territory at all in the Far East, and she never had a foothold on the mainland of Asia. The Chinese thus came to regard America as a relatively disinterested and harmless Power, which might even afford some protection against the rapacity of other nations. The tendency of China to appeal to America, when in trouble, was well illustrated in 1894, when she faced complete disaster in her war with Japan. China requested the good offices of the United States, asking her to join with the other Powers in intervention, and Gresham requested Dun, the Minister in Tokyo, to approach the Japanese Foreign Office for the purpose of learning whether or not American good offices would be welcome to Japan. He carefully defined his position in an *aide-mémoire* in which he said:

> "The deplorable war between Japan and China endangers no policy of the United States in Asia. Our attitude towards the belligerents is that of an impartial and friendly neutral, desiring the welfare of both. If the struggle continues without check to Japan's military operations on land and sea, it is not improbable that other powers having interests in that quarter may demand a settlement not favourable to Japan's future security and well-being. Cherishing the most friendly sentiments of regard for Japan, the President directs that you ascertain whether the tender of his good offices in the interests of peace alike honourable to both nations would be acceptable to the Government at Tokyo." [1]

Japan refused these good offices until she had consolidated her victories in November 1894, which gave her control of the seas, the peninsula and Port Arthur, and practically of Liaotung, the doorway to Peking. She then let America know that she would accept mediation. The war was concluded by the treaty of Shimonesëki of April 17th, 1895, followed by the Sino-Japanese Treaty of July 1896. These treaties were disastrous for China. They began the era of the scramble for concessions by the European Powers. The latter staked out spheres of influence for themselves, threatening the dismemberment of China. China began, unwisely, borrowing money from foreign Powers, mortgaging her natural resources and,

---

[1] *Op. cit.*, p. 499.

in fact, her sovereignty. She also began a course of diplomacy, the
final result of which cannot even yet be foreseen. Estranged from
America over the question of Chinese immigration to California
and America's refusal to intervene in the late war, and completely
deserted by Great Britain, who now favoured Japan as a stabilising
influence in the Far East, China turned to Russia. The disastrous
results of her relations with Russia will be dealt with elsewhere.
With the situation rapidly deteriorating, America had no energetic
or consistent policy. It was not only on account of the fact that she
did not wish to see increased foreign influence in China, but also
because of lack of sustained effort, that America lost valuable
railroad-building contracts which had already been signed. Needless
to say, America viewed with increasing alarm the course of
events in China, whereby it seemed that China would now be
partitioned among the European powers and Japan.

As a result of the so-called "Triple Intervention" (of France,
Germany and Russia) Japan had to give up Port Arthur which she
had taken in the war; it was returned to China and leased by Russia
from China, under pressure, three years later, while Germany
obtained the lease of Kiachow on the coast of Shantung. Russia's
position was now indeed powerful because possession of Port
Arthur gave her control of Manchuria, which would lead, in a few
years, to the Russo-Japanese War. Great Britain was left in a
weaker position in relation to China than at any time since the
opening of the country. America was now faced with two possibilities; co-operation with Great Britain, or independent action. She
was in grave danger of being eliminated from any position of
influence in China. Since military aggression was out of the question
for her, she decided that she must co-operate with other powers who
had the same interests and act as a restraining influence on states
pursuing policies of aggression. Had John Hay at this time been
able to do as he would have liked, it is probable that he would have
entered into an alliance with Britain and Japan, but he could not,
under the conditions limiting American foreign policy, do more than
issue a diplomatic note setting forth America's policy of the Open
Door. It is a fallacy to suppose that he invented the "doctrine"; it was
as old as American relations with China. He merely reasserted it
more clearly and formally than it had ever been stated before. The

result of this note was that all the Powers agreed to maintain the
Open Door, thus saving the sovereignty of China, though not
eliminating the spheres of influence. He had barely avoided the
partition of China. As a temporary expedient his policy was a
success. It has subsequently been learned that Great Britain used
the good offices of John Hay to take this step. If the lead had come
from Great Britain, it could not have succeeded because of European
hostility towards her at that time, but coming from America, a
great neutral power, fresh from her conquest over Spain, it had a
much greater effect.

In the Russo-Japanese War, America's sympathy lay openly
with Japan; in fact she assisted her in every way short of war. As
so often previously in the Far East, America really let another
nation accomplish an aim which was of vital importance to her —
the prevention of Russia's expansion which threatened to overwhelm
China from the north. America, under Theodore Roosevelt, took the
lead in bringing the war to an end and seeing that Russia's influence
in Manchuria was strictly limited by the Treaty of Portsmouth.
But hardly had this treaty been signed when America realised that
she had sown dragon's teeth by her strengthening of Japan's
position as a world power. Victorious over a Western Power, Japan
began to show an unexpected arrogance and truculence. American
sentiment immediately turned against Japan, and became very
hostile towards her, the question of Japanese immigration in the
Pacific States, which affected domestic politics, being a contributory
factor.

By 1909, America realised that she was again on the point of
losing her influence in Manchuria and China proper as a result of
the struggle for concessions and spheres of influence there. Japan's
aggressive policy in Manchuria, since 1905, was a matter of great
concern to America, as was also the attempt to eliminate her from
participation in the financial group which planned to float the
Hu-kuang loans to be used for the construction of a railway by that
name. P. C. Knox, Secretary of State at the time, realised that some
reënunciation of Hay's policy was necessary to prevent the closing
of the doors of Manchuria. He therefore proposed to the other
Powers two alternative plans for the "complete commercial neutralisation of Manchuria". The first suggested that the Chinese govern-

ment be assisted to purchase the Russian and Japanese railways in Manchuria by means of a loan floated by the Powers. The alternative plan suggested that Great Britain and the United States should support, by diplomacy, a scheme for the construction of a railway from Chinchow in the south to Aigun in the north of Manchuria, by an international syndicate. The only result of this move was to alarm Russia and Japan and cause them to draw closer together in their efforts to keep Manchuria as a closed preserve for themselves.

America was very sympathetic to the Chinese revolution of 1911. There was great enthusiasm for the new "sister republic". The establishment of a Chinese republic had not only a great sentimental appeal to Americans, but seemed likely to help the American policy of preventing further foreign encroachments on China, eliminating spheres of influence, and re-establishing China's sovereignty. Americans seem to have believed that the mere establishment of a republic in a land, which was less fitted for such a form of government than America was for a monarchy, would solve over-night the problems due to more than a century of domestic misrule and half a century of foreign intervention.

In 1915, America was confronted with a crisis in the Far East which threatened to deprive China of independence once and for all. On January 18th, Japan presented to China the notorious "Twenty-one Demands". These demands were divided into five groups. The first group concerned Shantung and required that China (1) assent in advance to any agreement which might later be made between Japan and Germany as to the German rights in Shantung; (2) agree not to alienate "to a third power" any territory in, or along the coast of, Shantung; (3) permit Japan to build a railway to join Chefoo or Lungkow with the Kiaowchow-Tsinan railway, and (4) open "certain important cities and towns" in Shantung as commercial ports.

Group 2 concerned South Manchuria and East Inner Mongolia where "the Chinese government has always acknowledged the special position enjoyed by Japan." China was to agree to the extension of the leases of Port Arthur and Dairen and of the South Manchuria and Antung-Mukden railways to ninety-nine years, and the control and management of the Kirin-Changchun line were to go to Japan for the same length of time. Instead of expiring in 1923, the lease for the Kwantung Peninsula would not expire until 1997; the South Manchuria railway lease would be extended from 1928 to 2002; the Anking-Mukden railway lease, instead of ending in fifteen years, would last until 2007. This clause went on to enumerate many special privileges which were to be accorded to Japanese subjects. Furthermore it forbade China to employ "political, financial or military advisers or instructors" in these regions without consulting Japan, or to give permission to any other power to build railways there, or to raise loans for this purpose or to pledge local taxes without permission of Japan.

Group 3 concerned the Hanyehping Company at Wuhan, the largest iron ore mining and smelting concern in China. It forbade China to dispose of interests in this company, and demanded that it be made a Sino-Japanese joint enterprise.

Group 4 forbade China to alienate any Chinese territory along the coast to a third party.

Group 5 provided for priority for Japanese civil and military advisers in China, joint police control in certain areas, joint arsenals, options for Japan on several projected railway and harbour projects and other items adding up to the formation of a Japanese protectorate over China.

Japan made what Dr. MacNair calls a twenty-second demand, absolute secrecy. No other power was to be informed of the twenty-one demands. To add point to them, they were written on official Japanese War Office paper, water-marked with machine-guns and battleships. Japan was not successful in keeping the secret, however, for Yuan Shih-kai saw that the American Minister, Reinsch, received the information within three days. When he notified Washington of his information, the Secretary of State immediately questioned the Japanese Ambassador. Japan officially denied it. Soon afterwards the story was published. Japan then said that her claims did not violate China's integrity, and dropped some of the demands, including all of Group Five, but she forced China, by an ultimatum, to sign an agreement including many of them. Much of the future trouble between the two countries was over rights "given" in this treaty, which China subsequently disavowed, as extorted under duress.

America was the only power to object. It must be remembered that Japan was an ally of Britain, France, Italy and Russia in the war against Germany and they were not in a position to quarrel with her. America refused to recognise any agreement which would impair her rights. She protested particularly against the granting of special rights to any power in Fukien, and undertakings for exclusive purchases of munitions, and employment of Japanese specialists and advisers. But she committed the tragic blunder of recognising (in the subsequent Lansing-Ishii Agreement) that in the cases of Shantung, South Manchuria and East Inner Mongolia "territorial contiguity creates special relations between Japan and these districts." In general, America proclaimed that she would not "recognise any agreement or undertaking ... impairing the treaty rights of the United States and its citizens in China, the political or territorial integrity of the republic of China, or the international policy relative to China commonly known as the Open Door policy." She furthermore notified them that she would claim, under the most-favoured-nation clause, any rights given to Japan.

Here America was following, in a blundering fashion, the only policy she has ever consistently held in China, that whatever cut of the cake anyone else got, she would demand an equal slice. [1]

In 1919 China went to the Paris Peace Conference with all the cards stacked against her. Even America, her traditional friend, had, through the stupid and blundering action of a politician-playing-diplomat, signed the Lansing-Ishii agreement, contained in an interchange of notes between Secretary of State Lansing and Viscount Ishii. It must be admitted that Lansing was tricked by the much more clever Ishii. The supposed purpose of the Ishii mission to Washington was to arrange for naval dispositions and "... exchange of ships, to be used as military transports for American steel for Japanese shipyards." [2] The real purpose was to induce Lansing to sign an agreement recognising a Japanese sphere of influence in China. The text began with the usual patter about the Open Door and equality of opportunity for all in China;

[1] The quotations and the entire section on the 21 Demands are paraphrased from Morse–MacNair, op. cit., pp. 580—85.

[2] Morse–MacNair, op. cit., p. 597.

it stated the common opposition of America and Japan to acquisi-
tions of any rights or privileges which would affect China's
independence and sovereignty or deny to the citizen of any country
equal opportunity in China. But Ishii with clear intention and
Lansing without it prefaced the agreement with the concession
Bryan, another politician who mismanaged the State Department,
had made to Japan in 1915: "The governments of the United States
and Japan recognise that territorial propinquity creates special
relations between countries, and, consequently, the government of
the United States recognises that Japan has special interests in
China, particularly in the part to which her possessions are contiguous." [1] On the face of it this does not seem like a sinister
document, since it does not very clearly say anything at all, but
in fact it was the very ambiguity which made it so dangerous, as
time was to reveal.

Despite the fact that the Chinese delegates had no chance at
Versailles, they made a very creditable showing. The settlement
insisted upon by Lloyd George and supported by Italy and France
was a completely dishonest one. [2] Japan got almost everything she
asked for. She brazened out the question of the "Twenty-one
Demands", and rejected China's claim that treaties extorted by
force were not valid. It is remarkable how well China presented
her case through Wellington Koo, San Tseng-tsiang, Alfred Sze,
S. T. Wei and C. T. Wang. None of the other powers conducted
themselves in such an admirable manner.

The Versailles treaty actually settled nothing finally about Shantung, and the whole question would be reopened at the Washington
conference. The Chinese did not come away wholly empty-handed.
The Japanese victory was limited by a promise, which was not
included in the treaty. At the insistence of Lloyd George, all
Germany's rights in Shantung were transferred to Japan by articles
156, 157 and 158 of the Versailles treaty. But Japan had to go
on record with the declaration: "The policy of Japan is to hand back
the Shantung Peninsula in full sovereignty to China, retaining only

---

[1] Loc. cit.
[2] For the best short account of the problems, see Morse–MacNair, op. cit.,
pp. 601—612.

the economic privileges granted to Germany and the right to establish a settlement under the usual conditions at Tsingtau." [1]

The Washington Conference [2] was called primarily because of American interest in the Anglo-Japanese Alliance, which America felt to be tying Great Britain's hands as far as Japanese aggressions on the mainland were concerned. Indeed it looked as though Great Britain might be forsaking the Open Door. One ground for such fear was the Cassel Collieries contract of 1920. [3] The Anglo-Japanese alliance was renewable only for ten years and was due for renewal in 1921. This treaty had been a cause of great tension between America and England, and had put a heavy strain on the unity of the British Empire, due to the resentment of Canada and Australia at the Alliance. The Crown Prince of Japan had gone on a visit to London, shortly before the question of renewal was considered by the conference of Prime Ministers and Representatives of the United Kingdom, the Dominions and India, which took place in the summer of 1921. No decision was reached because information was received that the American Government was about to call a conference.

Again China had to come into a conference of extreme importance to her existence as a sovereign power, under conditions of great weakness. This was due to the chaotic conditions in the country and the virtual absence of a government. But China was most ably represented by the eminent diplomats Doctor S. K. Alfred Sze and Wellington Koo. What became known as the "Root Principles" were unanimously adopted by the conference, and incorporated into Article One of the Nine-Power treaty:

The contracting powers, other than China, agree:

1. To respect the sovereignty, the independence and the territorial and administrative integrity of China;

2. To provide the fullest and most unembarrassed opportunity to China to develop and maintain for herself an effective and stable government;

---

[1] *Op. cit.*, p. 609.
[2] This section largerly based on Morse–MacNair, *op. cit.*, p. 690—714.
[3] *Op. cit.*, p. 690.

3. To use their influence for the purpose of effectually
establishing and maintaining the principle of equal opportunity
for the commerce and industry of all nations throughout the
territory of China;

4. To refrain from taking advantage of conditions in China in
order to seek special rights or privileges which would abridge
the rights of subjects or citizens of friendly states, and from
countenancing action inimical to the security of such states. [1]

Shortly before this article was adopted, Japan admitted that
Manchuria constituted a part of China, confirming Koo's answer as
to the term China, raised in the conference. This was an important
point for China.

The only nation which had hesitated to join the Washington
Conference was Japan. Upon receiving the invitation from the U.S.
she had agreed to send representatives only on the terms that
questions "of sole concern to certain particular powers or such
matters that may be regarded as accomplished facts" should be
'scrupulously avoided' and omitted from the Conference agenda." [2]
These terms were accepted, and she sent her representatives on this
basis. She was, of course, precluding discussion of the Shantung
question and of the Twenty-One Demands.

Balfour got around this reservation nicely by suggesting that
Japan and China negotiate with each other about Shantung. He
and Hughes offered their good offices suggesting that they or
their representatives should be present at any meetings which
might be held. Japan reluctantly agreed to this — finding herself
isolated at the conference, with Britain and America acting together
in full understanding on the main issues of Far Eastern policy.

The question of Shantung was settled amicably in two and a half
months of discussion. It was agreed to leave the details to a joint
Sino-Japanese commission which would meet after the proposed
treaty came into force, the transfer to take place six months thereafter. Japan agreed to turn over to China all important documents
relating to the former leased territory, and agreed not to establish a

---

[1] Willoughby, W. W., *The Sino-Japanese Controversy and the League of
Nations* (Baltimore, 1935), p. 685.
[2] Morse–MacNair, *op. cit.*, p. 691.

Japanese or foreign settlement at Tsingtau. On the question of railways and public properties there was much greater difficulty. In the end Japan managed to salvage as much as possible, relinquishing the railway to China on very favourable terms to herself. She relinquished public properties, but retained extensive commercial interests. Thus ended the struggle over the Shantung question, and thus began China's slow recovery of her rights. She owed this initial victory partly to her own diplomatic skill and partly to the use of the boycott as a weapon by the Chinese people, but above all to resolute Anglo-American pressure on Japan.

China was not to be dissuaded from bringing up the Twenty-one Demands, the sorest point of her recent history. Koo pointed out that the original lease of the Kwangtung territory would expire in 1925 and claimed that the extension obtained by Japan in 1915, as one of the Twenty-one Demands, was not valid because it was extorted by duress. He added the "fact of close proximity of Manchuria to Korea, if it justifies any claim to consideration, can be equitably appealed to only on the condition of reciprocity." Shortly thereafter Wang Chung-hui, after stating that the Twenty-one Demands affected the very fibre of China's being, pleaded that they be cancelled. But on the day after the announcement of the settlement of the Shantung affair, Baron Dan read a statement for Japan in which he said that Japan could not consider the cancellation of those of the Twenty-one Demands with regard to Manchuria which China had accepted. [1] "If it should once be recognised that rights solemnly granted by treaty may be revoked at any time on the ground that they were conceded against the spontaneous will of the grantor, an exceedingly dangerous precedent will be established, with far reaching consequences upon the existing international relations in Asia, in Europe, and everywhere." [2] China was thus left in a weaker position in Manchuria and with regard to Japan generally, since she had unsuccessfully challenged the Twenty-one Demands.

China's request for an agreement providing for gradual abolition of extraterritoriality by a specified date met with an adverse recep-

---

[1] Op. cit., p. 700.
[2] Op. cit., pp. 700—701.

tion. The powers made a vague commitment to investigate the whole question, but specified that no one was to be bound by the results of the investigation. It was agreed to abolish foreign post offices throughout China by January 1, 1923, provided China maintained an efficient postal system and retained the foreign co-director.

The question of the "Open Door" was for the first time openly discussed and analysed by a group of powers assembled in a conference at which China was present. This problem had been implicit in the Twenty-one Demands, which aimed at giving Japan a privileged position in China at least within a "sphere of influence". The Chinese now raised the question of the Open Door for official definition. Wang said that the phrase "sphere of influence" or "sphere of interest" was a vague term "implying that the powers making such claims in China are entitled within their respective 'spheres' to enjoy reserved, preferential, exclusive or special rights and privileges of trade, investment, and for other purposes." [1] The Chinese asked that "the powers represented in this conference disavow all claims to a sphere or spheres of interest or of influence or any special interests within the territory of China." This challenge from China had some effect in bringing about the inclusion of the clause against "special rights or privileges" in the Nine Power Pact. [2]

After the Washington Conference American policy was, broadly speaking, to wait and see what new central power would emerge from the civil wars in China, in readiness to conclude a treaty revision with any government which showed itself able to ensure law and order in China and effectively control the whole country. [3] America had no objection to recognizing the government set up by the Kuomintang as soon as it could make good in fact or claim to be the supreme authority in China. The Kuomintang, however, wanted treaty revision — or rather cancellation — before China put her own affairs in order, and its intransigeance drove America to make common cause with other nations in defending the system of foreign treaty rights in China, even though American

---

[1]   *Op. cit.*, p. 704.

[2]   *Loc. cit.*

[3]   Borg, *American Policy and the Chinese Revolution*, I, pp. 47—68; II, pp. 95—122.

public opinion, led by the missionaries, recognised in principle the validity of China's claim for full sovereignty. Extraterritoriality was seen to be an anachronism, yet America was no more willing than any other nation to expose its nationals to Chinese jurisdiction before China developed an efficient state administration and a modern judicial system. Thus in the years which followed the establishment of the Kuomintang government at Nanking, America tended to have a dual policy — on the one hand to protect China against the aggression or encroachment of other nations, and on the other hand to join in support of foreign treaty rights against Chinese nationalist attempts to override or evade them without properly negotiated revision.

CHAPTER III

THE PROBLEM OF MANCHURIA

Since 1895 Manchuria has been the main focus of trouble in China's foreign relations. This was not so before 1895, for in the years of the early and middle nineteenth century the strongest pressure on China, and the greatest threat of force, had come from the south. Manchuria, as the homeland of the reigning dynasty, was naturally a special concern of the Court in Peking, but there did not seem to be any immediate threat to it; in 1858—60, indeed, China gave away to Russia large territories north of the Amur and east of Ussuri in return for Russian diplomatic mediation, but these areas were so remote, so slightly inhabited and of such little value in the circumstances of that time that their loss was regarded as unimportant — next to nothing in comparison with the cession of Hongkong, the opening of the interior of China to foreign travel or the admission of foreign Ambassadors to residence in Peking.

Manchuria became important through the coincidence of two factors. One was the building of the Trans-Siberian Railway, which made Russia strong in the Far East for the first time, and created Russian pressure to get Chinese permission for carrying the line by a short cut across northern Manchuria to Vladivostok. The other factor was the expansion of Japan through her victory in the Sino-Japanese war of 1894, when Japanese forces occupied Port Arthur and the Liaotung Peninsula. Russia took advantage of China's humiliation and fear of Japan to establish herself in Manchuria under guise of protecting China.

Apart from the desirability of a direct route to Vladivostok, there were very good reasons why Russia should want to start building railways in Manchuria. She wanted to forestall Japan and England in Asia, to stake out her claims first in what was apparently a moribund empire, and to connect Moscow by rail with Peking, which meant ultimately all important Chinese cities. This

Russia might do by building a line connecting Peking with the Trans-Siberian railway. [1]

In the treaty of Shimonoseki in 1895 China, among other things, was forced to cede the Liaotung peninsula to Japan. Russia, because she considered Japan upon the continent a menace to her position in the Far East, got France and Germany to back her up in forcing Japan to take a larger cash indemnity and return the Liaotung peninsula to China. Yakhontoff makes an interesting comment:

> This "timely" interference of Russia, coupled with the good services rendered by her to China in floating a loan of 4,000,000,000 francs through the French bankers (with a guarantee by the Russian Government of the payment of interest on the bonds; a condition *sine qua non* to get money cheaply after a lost war), in order to enable her to pay the indemnity, created for Russia in China the status of a "friend in need". The chance to capitalise this friendship soon arrived.

By the type of face-considering diplomacy which China appreciates, Russia was to get, in the Li-Lobanov treaty, [2] the rights to build railways through Manchuria. This treaty has never yet been fully released, though a telegraphic summary was issued at the Washington conference when the Chinese delegates were asked to present every treaty ever made by China with the Powers. Up until this time it had not been officially issued. It is interesting to note that the Bolsheviks did not publish it when they came to power in 1917, although they made public many other documents which several of the powers would have liked to suppress. Yakhontoff claims to have got hold of the original in the archives of the Ministry of Foreign Affairs at Moscow and copied it. Articles IV and V are interesting to us in this connection.

> *Article IV.* In order to facilitate for Russian land forces access to the points under menace and to assure the means of existence the Chinese Government consents to the construction of a railway across the Chinese provinces of Amur and Kirin in the direction of Vladivostok.

---

[1] Yakhontoff, Victor A., *Russia and the Soviet Union in the Far East* (London, 1932), pp. 24—35.

[2] *Loc. cit.*, pp. 28—29.

The junction of this railway with the railways of Russia shall not serve as a pretext for any encroachment on Chinese territory, nor for an attempt against the sovereign rights of His Majesty the Emperor of China. The construction and exploitation of this railway shall be accorded to the Russo-Chinese Bank.

Article V. It is understood that in case of war foreseen by the Article I, Russia shall be free to use the railway mentioned in Article IV for the transportation and provisioning of her troops. In peace time Russia shall have the same right for the transportation and provisioning of her troops, with the right to stop over for no purpose other than those justified by the necessity of transportation.

Here China put her head in the lion's mouth. But what alternative did she have? She had been very harshly dealt with by the other Western Powers in the past and feared a renewal of Japanese invasion. She was practically defenceless from a military point of view and the promise of protection from a Great European Power, which had not joined in any war against China during the nineteenth century, was naturally attractive.

It was the British who were actually the first in the field in railway construction in Manchuria. In 1880, they began to build a light railway for carrying the output of the Kaiping coal mine situated between Shanhai-kwan and Tientsin, [1] and from 1887 onwards Li Hung-chang worked for the extension of this line into Manchuria as military precaution against Japan; unable to raise native capital, he borrowed foreign money and the British built the line as far as Suichung by 1894 and Hsinmintun by 1903. It was prolonged from Hsimintun to Mukden by 1907, thus completing the line from Peking to Mukden. Russia demanded and obtained from China as compensation "for the German seizure of Kiaow-chow, a leasehold of the extremity of the Liaotung peninsula from which the Japanese had been evicted in the Triple Intervention of 1895." This area, henceforth known as the Kwantung Leased Territory, included the land-locked harbour of Port Arthur suitable for a naval base, and the commercial port of Talienwan, which the Russians called Dalny and the Japanese Dairen. Having got this

---

[1] *Manchurian Yearbook 1932* (Tokyo, 1932), p. 244.

CHRISTOPHER, Conflict in the Far East   4

territory on the shore of the Yellow Sea, Russia now began building
a branch line of the C.E.R. southward from Harbin through Changchun and Mukden down to Dalny and Port Arthur.

In 1898 the British-sponsored North China Railway reached
Yinkow and, when Russia also built a branch line there, the two
systems were connected by rail at the Liao river. Under the
American-sponsored Portsmouth Treaty, which concluded the
Russo-Japanese war of 1904—5, Japan acquired the Russian leasehold of Kwantung and the Russian railway south of Changchun
together with a railway between Antung and Mukden built by
Japan for military purposes during the war. This was a line of 290
kilometres. Japan standardised all the railways in her sphere on a
narrow guage, in contrast to the broad guage of the Russian railways, at a cost of Y 42 million raised by debentures floated in
Great Britain.

An unexpected consequence of the Russo-Japanese war was that
Russia and Japan immediately afterwards found they had a common
interest in Manchuria and began to combine, both to put pressure
on China, and to keep other nations out. The Treaty of Portsmouth
stipulated in Art. VIII that "the Imperial governments of Japan
and Russia, with a view to promote and facilitate intercourse and
traffic, will, as soon as possible, conclude a separate convention
for the regulation of their connecting railway services in Manchuria." This was done in 1907, but there was also at that time
concluded a secret convention between them in which they agreed
to respect each other's rights and spheres, Japan's south of the line
of demarcation and Russia's north of that line. Russia agreed to
recognise Japan's special rights in Korea and not to interfere there
in any way, Japan to extend most-favoured-nation rights until
conclusion of a final treaty. Japan recognised the same rights of
Russia in Outer Mongolia and agreed not to interfere. Article IV
of this treaty is revealing. "The present convention shall be strictly
confidential between the two high contracting parties. This treaty
was signed at St. Petersburg on the thirthieth day of July 1907
by Iswolsky and Motono." In a supplementary article the line of
demarcation was defined.

In 1909 Japan forced new concessions from China concerning
the reconstruction of the emergency line from Mukden to Antung.

which together with construction of a new network in Korea gave Russia a few bad moments and caused a temporary tension and suspicion on the part of Russia. But Knox, at this time Secretary of State in America, advanced a new plan for neutralisation of the Manchurian railways, which was an enlargement on one which he had unsuccessfully advanced for the same project in 1902. It was to have been a development of a gigantic network backed by J. P. Morgan, F.N.B. and Kuhn, Loeb and Co. of New York, using Willard Straight, Consul-General at Mukden as front man. But Japan and Russia reacted immediately and violently while Great Britain refused to join in the scheme and thus wrecked whatever chances it might have had.

This flyer taken by Knox brought Japan and Russia even closer together and made them forget their mutual suspicions. It resulted in the convention of 1910 and in another secret treaty. The first four articles merely elaborate upon and reaffirm the convention of 1907 except that in Art. II appears this rather prophetic statement: "Consequently they recognise the right of each of them within its own sphere, to take such measures as shall be deemed necessary for the safeguarding and protection of these interests." Article V states that the two nations will enter into communication "frankly and honestly on all matters of common concern in Manchuria and agree to decide upon what common action shall be taken or support accorded in defence of these interests."

After the Chinese revolution Russia stirred up the Mongols, even more than she had done in the past, to declare their independence. In 1912 she signed with Japan a further secret convention, this time in regard to Mongolia, in which the two nations agreed that Outer Mongolia should be Russia's sphere of influence together with western Inner Mongolia, giving Japan eastern Inner Mongolia. These spheres were divided by a line of demarcation in Inner Mongolia along latitude 116° 27" E.

In 1916 was signed the last (as far as is known) of the secret conventions between Russia and Japan. This was a definite treaty of alliance. Article II stated that "in the event of either party going to war over these mutual interests the other is bound to come to the assistance of the one engaged." This was not only a treaty, but it was an offensive and defensive alliance and appears to have been directed against possible interference in Manchuria by the United States; the latter had protested against the Japanese policy of the Twenty-one Demands which had received moral support from Russia. However, there was never an occasion for this treaty to be invoked, for within a year the Czar was overthrown and the Bolsheviks, when they came to power, repudiated all the secret treaties which his government had made. The Russian Revolution produced quite a new situation in the Far East, for Japan was left without Russian support, and after the war, Britain, victorious over Germany, allowed the Anglo-Japanese alliance to lapse and joined with America in putting pressure on Japan at the Washington Conference.

Meanwhile the C.E.R. (the name was confined to the Russian-owned system, the part transferred to Japan being known as the South Manchuria Railway or S.M.R.) presented a problem. To whom did it belong? It was the property of a company which was really controlled by the Russian Government. Did the new Soviet Government inherit the rights of the old Russia on Chinese soil? The Bolsheviks, who had confiscated foreign property in Russia, were hardly in a strong moral position for claiming Russian property rights in other countries and in any case up to 1923 none of the principal nations of the world had given their Government *de jure* recognition. On the other hand, there could be no unaminous opinion as to what, alternatively, should to be done with the C.E.R. None of the other nations wanted Japan to have it, but with the Japanese established in South Manchuria and the Russians on three sides of North Manchuria, it would be a great risk for any nation other than Russia or Japan to take responsibility for the C.E.R. As an interim measure it was run by a provisional administration with the old Russian staff, but the question of its legal ownership was left undecided.

The new Russia was soon to step into the shoes of the Czardom in Manchuria, but began by offering to give the C.E.R. to China. This was part of the Russian Communist anti-imperialist propaganda designed to set China against the Western Powers and Japan, and spread Communism, or sympathy for it, among the Chinese. The rebuff to the Chinese case at the Paris Peace Conference in 1919, when Great Britain and France, bound by their secret treaties acting in collusion with Japan, gave the Russians the perfect opening. The Karakhan Manifesto issued in Moscow to "the ministers, civil governors, bureaux and People of the Chinese Republic" was the result. The manifesto declared that "all people, no matter whether their nations are great or small, no matter where they live, no matter at what time they may have lost their independence, should have their independence and selfgovernment and not submit to being bound by other nations". [1] After having denounced all secret treaties, Russia offered to negotiate with China as an equal on the following basis: [2]

1. The territory seized by the former Imperial Russian Government to be returned to you.

2. The Russian Government will restore to you the sovereignty of China, the Chinese Eastern Railway and the mines and forests appropriated by the former Imperial Russian Government, and it will not ask one cent therefor.

3. This government will not accept the Boxer indemnity payments.

4. The special privileges for Russian subjects established by the former Imperial Russian Government, and acting independently or with Japan, or with the Entente powers, with the envoys of China, in which there are unfair points, will be null and void. [3]

Russia saw that many copies of this manifesto were broadcast throughout China, using Shanghai as a base for this propaganda. It was not until after the fall of the Anfu government, however that the campaign began to produce results. This was the most clever Russia could have released in China. It strengthened the determination of the Chinese to settle all outstanding issues with Russia. The next step was to send Karakhan as ambassador to China. Russia was the first nation to give such recognition to China. All other envoys at Peking were Ministers.

The question of the Kwantung Leased Territory was raised by China as a result indirectly of the encouragement given by this Russian diplomacy. The Peking cabinet, on March 10th, 1923, sent a note to Japan demanding the abrogation of the Sino-Japanese

---

1, 2, 3 *Op. cit.*, pp. 670—71.

treaties of 1915, and the return of the Liaotung peninsula. [1] Had it not been for these treaties the Japanese lease would have expired on March 27th, of that year. Japan immediately and emphatically refused the demand, and a new series of student-led anti-Japanese strikes and boycotts started.

There was, at this time, another of those frequent changes of war-lord-controlled rulers in Peking. By the most shameless graft and corruption conceivable, Ts'ao K'un, by spending more than fifteen million silver dollars [2] to buy the votes of the legislators, got himself appointed president, when President Li Yuan-hung, the man who had led the Revolution in 1911 and who had actually been President by the grace of Wu Pei-fu, fled Peking. Wu, Chang Tso-lin and Feng Yü-hsiang were the war-lords who would shortly tangle. Only the danger of foreign intervention over the Lincheng affair, delayed the clash from the spring until the fall.

Karakhan arrived in China in September, 1923, and began negotiations with C. T. Wang. He continued the campaign of vilification of the United States begun by the previous Russian envoy, Joffe. When Wang praised American policy and intimated that China would appreciate it if Russia modelled her behaviour on that of America, Karakhan was quick to turn the Lincheng affair to his account and further to vilify America by replying:

> Russia will never follow the example of America nor put her signature under such a document as the Lincheng note. Russia will never claim the right of extraterritoriality, nor establish her courts or administration. Nothing pleased me more during my recent stay in Harbin than the fact that I saw there a Chinese administration, Chinese laws and the realisation of Chinese sovereignty. [3]

In a footnote to this cynical and platitudinous statement, Dr. MacNair quotes a statement from the China Year Book, 1924, p. 866: "It suffices to walk through the streets of Harbin to see that the Chinese authorities are rather bent upon rendering the lives of the three hundred thousand Russians confided to their care

---

[1] *Manchurian Yearbook 1932,* p. 675.
[2] MacNair, H. F. (ed.), *China* (Cal., 1946), p. 137.
[3] *Loc. cit.,* p. 677.

as disagreeable and inconvenient as possible... The situation in Harbin, so pleasing to the observant eye of the ambassador, was anything but pleasant to his co-nationals who resided there. The Russian press of the city was complaining bitterly of the 'brutalities of intercourse' between the Chinese and the Russians."

Despite the deep concern for China's sovereignty which Karakhan expressed and the deep joy it gave him to see China again fulfilling her destiny, he soon revealed his own designs. He stated that before negotiations could begin it would be necessary for China to accord formal recognition to Soviet Russia. There ensued a long wrangle with each side making claims and counterclaims and reviling the other. Karakhan replied to China's demand that Russia withdraw her troops from Mongolia by complaining of White Russian activities in Manchuria. Russia and China could not agree upon what, exactly, Russia had promised in 1919—20. The diplomatic recognition of the Soviet régime by France and Great Britain strengthened Karakhan's hand. By March 14th, 1924, he had reached a preliminary agreement, but Foreign Minister Koo refused to recognise it, and disavowed it on the ground that Dr. Wang had exceeded his authority in signing an agreement, since he had been authorised to negotiate only. In reply to this refusal to recognise the agreement Karakhan sent an insolent note demanding that China accord formal recognition in seventy-two hours. Koo coldly refused to recognise that the Soviet envoy had any legal right to impose a time limit upon the Chinese Government; [1] and did not at once yield, but finally, on May 31st, two and a half months instead of three days later, the dispute was settled and an agreement was signed. In this agreement Russia relinquished extraterritoriality and surrendered her concessions at Tientsin and Hankow. Russia secured the return of the Peking Legation and the consulates throughout China, and all the property of the Russian Orthodox Church, subject to Chinese laws concerning property in the interior. Russia gave up her claims to the Boxer Indemnity funds, which were to be applied to the education of the Chinese and administered by a board of three, one of whom must be a Russian, appointed by the Soviet Government. China's sovereignty

---

[1] *Op. cit.*, pp. 677—8.

over Mongolia was specifically recognised, and the evacuation of Soviet troops undertaken. On the subject of the Chinese Eastern Railway, however, Russia gained the substance of her demands.

In view of Karakhan's statements about the sacred and inalienable rights of China, and Russia's offers of 1919 and 1920 to hand over the railway to China, his adamant refusal to renounce Russian claims on the C.E.R. must have been a particularly bitter pill for China to swallow. These facts should have confirmed the suspicions of the realistic Chinese about Russia's real intentions. From the first agreement on the C.E.R. in 1896, and despite the propagandist offers of 1919 and 1920, Russia has always refused to surrender the C.E.R. until the present and at the Yalta Conference in 1945 successfully reasserted her original rights in spite of having sold them to Japan and having received payment for them in 1935, contrary to the Portsmouth treaty.

The 1924 Sino-Soviet treaty provided for joint ownership of the C.E.R. by Russia and China — in appearance an improvement for China on the original agreement which made the railway exclusively Russian property. But the real control of the line remained in Russian hands. China agreed to the formation of a new board of ten directors, five Chinese and five Russians, the President to be Chinese and the Vice-President and the General Manager to be Russians, appointed by the Soviet Government. There was no provision for solution of any deadlock which might arise, and since the General Manager, the actual executive head of the railway, was the appointee of the Soviets, and a majority on the board was required to carry out any action over which there was a disagreement, it should have been patent what would have happened in such a case. China was soon to learn to her sorrow just what would happen.

The delayed war between the war-lords was resumed and Karakhan dealt with both sides. Chang Tso-lin was in possession of the territory through which the railway passed, and was in fact dictator of Manchuria; he refused to recognise the agreement with the Peking Government, so Karakhan made a new and secret agreement with him. As MacNair comments:

> The Chihli-Fengtien struggle of 1924 strengthened the position of Ambassador Karakhan, who desired to arrange with

Marshal Chang a *modus operandi* for the Chinese Eastern Railway. Assuming the role of protector of China as soon as the struggle began, Russia announced to the powers a "Hands off China" policy, at the same time beginning quietly to mass her troops on the northern border of Manchuria at Chang's rear. Chang agreed to negotiate the desired agreement, and the document was signed at Mukden on September 20th.

In general the new agreement was similar to that signed in Peking in the preceding May. There were, however, a few important differences. The period of eighty years specified in the agreement of 1896, after which the railway was to pass to the Chinese government free of charge, was now reduced to sixty years. The Peking agreement did not specifically provide for a revision of the 1896 agreement, but that of Mukden provided for such a provision within four months of the signing of the new agreement. The time within which a revision of the Chinese Eastern Railway Company should take place was now reduced to two months. No change was made in the management of the Railway. By the Mukden agreement, another step had been taken by Russia in detaching Chinese dependencies in her southward push. It thus became clear that the China policy of the Union of Soviets, while broadened to include the use of China as a base for world revolution, was in other respects similar to that of Czarist Russia, and that the price of friendship had not been lowered with the passing of years and the Czarist regime. [1]

Article II of the recent agreement provided for a conference to settle all outstanding problems between China and Russia. Karakhan postponed this meeting to August 25th, since he was on the point of leaving for Moscow. But it was not held for more than seven months, because disputes started immediately between the two countries over operation and management of the railway. The Russians refused to attend the meetings of the directors, hence tying the hands of the Chinese, and leaving the Russian manager in control.

One source of the trouble sprang from the fact that Marshal Chang's troops had supplanted the Russians as railway guards in 1920. He demanded that these and others of his troops should be carried over the railway either free or at the expense of the Peking

---

[1]   Morse–MacNair, *op. cit.*, p. 682.

Government. When the bill had reached 11 million dollars, silver, and the Russians realised that he moved his troops too conveniently towards the Siberian border, Ivanov, the General Manager, issued an order forbidding any more of Chang's troops to be moved. Chang argued that the cost was being paid out of China's share of the profits of the railway, and when Ivanov still refused, Chang had him arrested. Karakhan immediately protested to the Peking Government and to Mukden. After some days Chang released Ivanov, but the Chinese sacked him and appointed another Russian in his place.

The trouble had started with Ivanov's dismissal of large numbers of White Russians from their positions immediately after assuming his post. He did this over the protest of Chang and the Chinese President of the Board of Directors. A conference was held in Moscow in November to arrange for schedules for through traffic across Manchuria and Siberia. Russia wasn't having any. She did not want traffic for anyone except the Soviet citizens or those whom she designated. She certainly was not going to allow the railway to be used for world benefit. She was not interested in commercial profit. She was interested in controlling the only means of moving troops overland to the Pacific. It was not a business to be run on a business-like basis. It was a governmental monopoly and was only to be used for Russian convenience, strategy and political infiltration purposes. Needless to say the conference broke up in a stalemate. The differences between the Russians and the Chinese over the policy of the C.E.R. became greater and greater. But Russia just refused to do anything except what pleased her and left the Chinese in impotent rage und frustration.

Karakhan's actions and his type of diplomacy convinced many Chinese that the Soviet Russians were much worse to have to work with than the Czarists. Many saw trouble in the near offing.

When China finds herself dealing with an utterly realistic and unscrupulous power such as Japan and Russia, she is helpless. It is only where the Chinese have a chance to use their charms and grace on people who are sympathetic to China that they are able to make headway in diplomacy in spite of their military weakness.

The troubles over the C.E.R. were not China's only worries in Manchuria in the years just before 1928. As regards the S.M.R.

there could be no disputes similar to those which arose on the
C.E.R., because the S.M.R. was not even nominally jointly owned,
but was a purely Japanese concern. There were, however, disputes
in plenty about branch lines which the Japanese wanted to build
and about the Japanese claim of a right to prevent Chinese railway
competition in south Manchuria.

After the Russo-Japanese war the first new railway to be constructed was one from Kirin to Changchun, built by China, but
half financed by Japan, that is, to the extent of Y 2,150,000; this
line was 128 kilometres long. A light railway 19 kilometres long,
from Tsitsihar, capital of Heliunchang, to Angangki on the Chinese
Eastern was constructed as a purely Chinese line in 1909. The last
line built before the First World War was constructed in 1913; it
was the Hsichien, a mining railway running from Penhsihu to
Niuhsintai with joint Sino-Japanese capital. In 1914 Russia held
the largest share of Manchurian railways with 43 %, while Japanese
ownership came next with 31 %. The purely Japanese holding was
less than 1 % and even that was only a light railway.

Railways built after the First World War and up to the "Manchurian incident" were briefly the following: the so-called five
railways of Manchuria and Mongolia; of which the Ssupingkai-
taonan railway with a branch to Tungliao. This line of 426 kilos
was opened in 1923.

This is one of the five lines mentioned in the Sino-Japanese
agreement for financing and constructing railways in Manchuria.
The rights obtained by Japan were:

(A)   Japan to supply capital when the Chinese government
      constructs the following three railways:
      (1) Ssupingkai-Chenchiatun-Taonan,
      (2) Kaiyun-Hailung,
      (3) Chanchun-Taonan.

(B)   Preferential right to be given to Japanese capital in case
      China requires foreign capital for the construction of
      the following two railways:
      (1) Hailung-Kirin,
      (2) Taonan-Jehol. [1]

---

[1] *Manchurian Yearbook 1932*, p. 247.

Of these roads only the first, [(A) (1)] was finished according to the original contract. In 1918 Japan made a new agreement with China that the remaining four lines and a spur running from the Taonan-Jehol line to a seaport were to be constructed by the Chinese government with loans obtained from Japan. China did not honour this contract or any of its terms, but Chang Tso-lin built his own lines. Japan should not have been surprised, however, because she had expected this since 1905 and had in fact made a treaty with China under which China could not construct any lines parallel to the South Manchurian Railway. Chang questioned not the interpretation, but even the existence and certainly the validity of such a contract. In fact he began to rush construction of new lines, using not only Chinese personnel, but his own capital. The first of these was the Tahushan-Tungliao line, from a station on the Peking-Mukden line to the terminus of the proposed Japanese-financed line, started in 1921 and finished in 1926. Next came the Fenghai and Kihai lines connecting Mukden and Kirin via Hailung and Chaoyangchun. These were opened in 1927 and 1929.

In 1928 the Northeastern Communications Commission attempted to unify all Chinese railways whether built with Chinese or Japanese capital into a powerful network to drain off all haulage and revenue from the South Manchurian, probably hoping by cut-throat competition to force the Japanese to sell it to China.

In 1928 the Hulan-Hailun railway was opened in north Manchuria, running from Tsitsihar to Taian, and several mining railways. These lines were the last built before the Japanese invasion of Manchuria.

There was increasing Sino-Japanese tension due to this construction by the Chinese. The Japanese had control of the life line of southern Manchuria. Their railway traversed the richest area of Manchuria and controlled not only the main areas of natural resources, developed farmland, mines and forests, but also the industrial area, which they had largely developed themselves. The Chinese were developing parallel lines and had opened a competitive port, Hulutao. Their railways were syphoning off much of the freight and passenger traffic from the S.M.R. [1] The strong na-

---

[1] Morse–MacNair, *op. cit.*, pp. 758—9.

tionalist movement, which did not so greatly influence Manchurian Chinese, under the iron control of Chang Tso-lin, as it did the Chinese of the rest of China, nevertheless affected them as Chinese versus Japanese, and the anti-Japanese movement was in many respects more intense and effective here than in the rest of China. Special laws were passed forbidding the sale or lease of land and property to Japanese under extreme penalties. The Japanese saw that the anti-Japanese movement would cripple them, making their hold of the S.M.R. valueless and undermining their entire position in Manchuria. If independent Chinese railway construction continued, the Chinese would consolidate their position, and since the finances and political condition of Manchuria was more stable than elsewhere in China, it would further stiffen the Chinese everywhere and help Chiang K'ai-shek to stabilise conditions in all China, thus depriving Japan of the cornerstone upon which she planned to build an empire. Here Japan had enough coal and iron resources much greater than in her own islands.

Furthermore Japan depended upon Manchuria for essential imports of food commodities, for an outlet for her surplus capital and her technical and white-collar classes. Japan's dream of an empire would be shattered if her hold on Manchuria were to be loosened.

CHAPTER IV

THE KUOMINTANG IN POWER

The United States recognized the independence of China by signing a treaty, on July 25, 1928. During the next five months eleven more powers recognized the new government: Germany (Aug. 17); Norway (Nov. 12); Belgium and Luxemburg (Nov. 22); Italy (Nov. 27); Denmark (Dec. 12); Portugal (Dec. 19); the Netherlands (Dec. 19); the British Empire (Dec. 20); Sweden (Dec. 20); and France (Dec. 22). All the treaties except those of the United States and France were signed at Nanking. [1]

China had finally succeeded in her long fight for tariff autonomy and the Kuomintang in its fight for recognition as the government of China. The events which led up to the recognition were the death of Chang Tso-lin, the war-lord of Manchuria, and the capture of Peking by forces supporting the Kuomintang and Chiang K'ai-shek. The latter had been delayed by Japanese intervention in Shantung in 1927 [2] and again in 1928 by the "Tsinan incident", in which Japan threw troops across the Shantung railway, blocking General Chiang K'ai-shek's march on Peking. Chiang was in alliance with Marshals Feng Yu-hsiang and Yen Hsi-shan. The strategy as planned had been that Chiang was to march north through Anhwei and Kiangsu to Shantung to attack Chang Tso-lin, while Feng, Yen and others were to attack Peking from the west and south. After a number of protests and an appeal to the League of Nations, which were of no avail, the Kuomintang resorted to the old Chinese weapon of an economic boycott. After further delays a settlement was reached and the Japanese permitted part of Chiang's army to proceed north to attack Chang Tso-lin's forces.

It soon became apparent that Chiang would not be in time to

---

[1] Morse–MacNair, *Far Eastern International Relations*, p. 748 (N.Y., 1939, 2nd ed.).

[2] *Op. cit.*, p. 742 *seq.*.

have a decisive influence on the campaign and that Peking would fall to Yen and Feng. It was, indeed, Yen's army which at last entered Peking on June 8, 1928, followed by Yen himself on June 11. The Japanese, in the meantime, warned both Nanking and Peking that they would not tolerate the spread of the civil war into Manchuria and threatened Chang that, if he did not withdraw to Manchuria at once, they would cut off his retreat at Shanhai-kwan, where the mountains which bound Hopei on the north extend to the sea, leaving a narrow coastal pass through which runs the Peking-Mukden railway. This left Chang no alternative and he was forced to give up the capital and flee into Manchuria.

The Japanese were worried about the spread of the war into Manchuria, but they were much more worried about the increasing strength and stability of the Kuomintang. They knew that Chang was negotiating for an agreement with Nanking which would bring Manchuria under Kuomintang supremacy. Chang, for a number of reasons, had never been exactly a puppet for the Japanese. Perhaps one of the strongest reasons was the fact that he realized himself to be only a brigand, looked down upon and despised by the better class of Chinese, and wanted badly to make himself respectable by a show of patriotism. While he had never been too intractable with the Japanese, he had not been as pliant as they desired. If anything happened to him, his heir and successor would be his son, Chang Hsüeh-liang, whom they evidently thought would be just the man for their purposes; hence, when Chang Tso-lin, in pursuance of the Japanese order, evacuated Peking and withdrew to Mukden, his train was bombed as it entered the city. The train was bombed in an area guarded by the Japanese on the night of June 2—3, and the bombing occurred on June 4. His death was announced nineteen days later and he was succeeded in his position and rank by Chang Hsüeh-liang.

It has often been claimed that Chang was murdered by the Japanese, and the evidence available all points in that direction. [1] But if the Japanese thought to serve their interests by the act, they miscalculated. They made a grievous error in their judgment of

---

[1] Young, C. Walter, *Japan's Special Position in Manchuria*, p. 20 (Baltimore, 1931). The fact has subsequently been established in the war-crime trials in Japan.

Chang Hsüeh-liang. He proved much more intractable than his father had, and, instead of placating the Japanese, he defied them in every possible manner. He hoisted the Kuomintang flag on December 31, 1928, throwing in his lot with Chiang K'ai-shek. As an inducement he was given Jehol in addition to the original three provinces of Manchuria. He ruled these provinces as commander of the North-east Frontier Defence force. He was also made a member of the State Council at Nanking.

During 1928 the Nanking incident of 1927 was finally settled with all countries except Japan. Settlements were reached with the U.S. in April, with Great Britain in August, and with France and Italy in October. It was not, however, until May, 1929, that the Nanking and Hankow incidents were settled with Japan.

During this period China was undergoing many stresses and strains. Although Chiang now had *de jure* recognition as "the government" by most of the interested countries, the fact was that he was only precariously perched on top of a heaving mass. He was actually in control of a very small area of China and drew practically his sole revenue from only two provinces, Kiangsu and Chekiang. [1] Nominally twenty-two provinces and special districts claimed allegiance to Nanking, but actually rebellions and defections were brewing in all parts of China at the moment, and would break out in a few months in full scale campaigns. Internally China was in a state of ferment. She was practically exhausted by the almost constant civil wars which had been waged for the past fifteen years. Old ways of life and thought were breaking down, government by Confucian precept was giving way to political and military dictatorship, the classical examination system had given way to the western system of education. The mandarin was replaced by the militarist, the young liberal intellectual and the western-educated politician.

Externally China had succeeded in her battle for tariff autonomy and was now engaged in a struggle for the abolition of extraterritoriality, foreign concessions, settlements and leased territories, inland and coastal navigation by foreign ships and the stationing

---

[1] Department of State, *Papers Relating to the Foreign Relations of the United States, 1929*, vol. II (Washington, 1943), p. 130. As these documents will be quoted constantly they will be hereafter referred to as F.R.U.S.

of foreign troops on Chinese soil. In short, China was out to regain her full sovereignty. The propaganda for this had at first owed much to Russian inspiration. China had received a tremendous impetus from the Communist assistance and from the Russian example, despite Chiang's break with the Communists.

China had seen what Japan was able to do after getting rid of Western interference in the nineties and earlier. She had watched her rise from an unimportant island nation, isolated from the world, to the position of one of the Great Powers. She had also seen Russia go through the Bolshevik revolution with the world against her and re-establish an integrated empire. By her revolution she had seemingly rid herself of centuries of oppression and misgovernment, and had seemingly installed a just government in which the will of the people ruled, a country in which there was no exploitation of any kind, with all its resources belonging to and being controlled by the people, for the benefit of the people.

The Kuomintang would use these arguments to get control of the people and the country just as the ruling clique had in Russia. Many among the people, and some among the leaders, honestly believed all these things. Many were coldly cynical and opportunist and in the game for what they could profit personally. Few probably realized the whole truth about Russia.

It was in Manchuria that the endeavour of the Kuomintang to unify the country, and at the same time to promote and exploit "rights recovery" agitation, was destined quickly to lead to international complications. Chang Hsüeh-liang, having thrown in his lot with the Kuomintang, was determined to show himself the best nationalist of them all and thus to maintain his regional leadership. But first of all he had to deal with trouble among his own subordinates. On January 11, 1929, two of the most important of them, Yang Yu-ting and Chang Yin-huai, who had been invited to Chang's residence for a conference, were seized and summarily executed. It seems that they were plotting to eliminate Chang and take over Manchuria. Chang held a conference of high officials the morning after the execution and had them approve it. [1]

It had long been recognized that there was no great cordiality

---

[1] *Op. cit.*, pp. 123—26.

between Chang Hsüeh-liang and Yang, but since Chang Tso-lin's death there had been outward harmony between Yang and the young Marshal. Undoubtedly Yang Yu-ting, as director of the arsenal of which he had full control with freedom from other duties, was in a powerful position for political conspiracy. Chang Yin-huai, a subordinate of Yang Yu-ting, in his position of Director of the Communications Commission for the Three North-eastern Provinces, controlled media of great political power — telephones, telegraphs and radio. Together these two men were a definite menace to Chang, a disruptive influence in Manchuria and strong bidders for Japanese backing. It is quite likely that, had they lived, they would have overthrown Chang and become the puppets for whom Japan was seeking. It appears [1] that Chang had knowledge of their plans and probable intentions, but had only received what he regarded as definite proof a short time before he liquidated them. It would have been dangerous to arrest them openly, so he simply invited them to his home and forestalled them by execution.

It was generally recognized that Chang had strengthened his personal position by the liquidation of Yang and Chang. In some quarters, however, it was regarded as a dangerous action politically. Meyers, Consul at Mukden, voiced this opinion when he said in a dispatch to MacMurray: "......the elimination of the two most powerful and probably able members of the Fengtien Party...... may later result in the breakup of that party through internal or external agencies". [2] This prophecy did not prove, however, to be true.

Confirming the general impression that Chang had been mis-judged sadly by Japan, the same Consul says: "Outwardly, at least, the Fengtien Party which controls the Three Eastern Provinces and Jehol is closely united under the leadership of Chang-Hsueh-liang who is believed to be more interested in the development of the resources of these provinces than in playing politics south of the Great Wall. Whether or not the General can maintain his position as the head of a united party remains to be seen, but his conduct of affairs since the death of his father ... has been a surprise to

---

[1] Op. cit., p. 124.
[2] Op. cit., p. 133.

many persons". [1] Victor A. Yakhontoff [2] says of the young marshal: "A man of about thirty, with no unusual abilities but with some Western education, Chang Hsüeh-liang was a reformed addict of the opium-smoking habit (a proof of his strong will power)......" At any rate, Chang proved himself a capable administrator and performed a great feat in remaining in power as long as he did, in view of the Sino-Japanese difficulties which were being daily aggravated, not least of all by Chang himself, and the Sino-Soviet crisis which he was soon to precipitate.

Although the year 1929, at the outset, seemed an extremely auspicious one for China, events soon showed that appearances were deceptive. The power still remained in the hands of the provincial rulers in the various parts of China, governing as "war lords", rather than as members or high officials of a central government. There was continuing unrest in the country and the momentary equilibrium did not last long. It was followed by another outbreak of internal strife and dissension among the leaders.

Shantung was the first to go up in flames. For a time it seemed as though all north China would be involved. In fact the great war lords of the north and north-east (according to the claims of General Chang Tsung-chang, who temporarily seized most of eastern Shantung, before "arrangements" were made for a peaceful turnover), including Generals Yen Hsi-shan, Chu Yu-pu, Wu Pei-fu, Pai Chung-hsi, Chi Hsieh-yuan, and some of the Manchurian leaders, but not including Chang Hsüeh-liang himself, were going to carry out a concerted campaign against the "southern Party" of Chiang K'ai-shek. [3] But as things have a way of doing in China, the whole affair died down again, as suddenly as it had started.

Meanwhile fresh trouble had flared up between Nanking and Hankow, which really meant the Kwangsi group. Chiang K'ai-shek, realizing that his position was very insecure throughout the country, decided to create a diversion by striking at his most dangerous opponents. For this purpose he chose the Kwangsi group. He

---

[1] Loc. cit.
[2] Yakhontoff, op. cit., p. 195.
[3] F.R.U.S., 1929, II, p. 143.

started by having Generals Li Tsung-jen, Li Chai-sum and Pai Chung-hsi expelled from the Kuomintang and then having the Third National Congress approve an expedition which he lead in person against those three. It was the usual story so familiar in China in civil war campaigns, with reputed bribes, defections of large forces to Chiang, poor leadership on the one side, and worse on the other, followed by a general debacle ending in victory for Chiang.

The Third National Congress, from which so much had been expected, was packed with party men of the right-wing Kuomintang and all who were *personae non gratae* were excluded. Again the cause of democracy was set back in China. It began to be apparent, however, that the stability of China and the fortunes of Chiang K'ai-shek were inextricably intertwined. By excluding the party members who were against him he saved himself and his government. He was to become more and more adept at this as time wore on. His art has been always to play off one rival against another, having this one crushed and that one appeased. He had been trained in a hard school, and these were times to test and further refine that ability which was to keep him on top.

On several occasions the opposition sprang surprise attacks which caught him completely off base. In one instance the Nationalist forces were out of the Nanking area when a general, Shih Yu-san, newly appointed Chairman of the Anhewi Provincial Government, raised the flag of rebellion across the Yang-tze from Nanking. There was nothing in Nanking to stop him. For one of those unaccountable reasons which one only meets in China, when he had Nanking in the palm of his hand he failed to cross the river and take the city. That it was serious may be gathered from the remark of the Foreign Minister to American journalists: "I might myself be a prisoner now if the Pukow mutineers had shown a little more initiative. When they revolted there was nothing in Nanking to stop them from crossing the river and taking possession of the city". [1] It might be argued that this was unimportant and would have been put down without serious effort by Chiang, but it must be remembered that at this time the Kuomintang was engaged in a

---

[1] *Op. cit.*, p. 185.

desperate struggle with the combined Chang Fa-kwei and Kwangsi forces. A loss here would likely have meant the ousting of Chiang and the establishment by Wang Ch'ing-wei of a more leftist government. In passing, it is interesting to note that as soon as the Nationalist forces had won, "Mr. Wang was expelled from the Kuomintang on December 12th and his arrest ordered". [1] At any rate it was at this crucial moment when Shih Yu-san revolted and had the capital at his mercy. According to the consular report it was estimated that at the time of the revolt there were between ten and fifteen thousand troops of Shih's division, the Twenty Fourth, in Pukow and another ten or twelve thousand stationed at the Tsin-Pu railway not far removed. "The revolt took Nanking utterly by surprise and caused a panic amongst the central government officials. At the time the Capital was without troops other than the small personal bodyguards of the military leaders..." To get an idea of the seriousness with which the revolt was viewed at the time one has to read contemporary reports. Quoting from the above report of Perkins [2] to the Secretary of State: "The revolt at Pukow, occurring in the face of a serious crisis at Canton, was followed by a revolt of part of the 5th Division on the Shanghai-Nanking Railway and by a military disturbance at Hangchow... The month ended with Shih Yu-san balked but still astride the Tientsin-Pukow Railway, near Pengpu, thereby cutting Nanking's communications with the North.... The serious problem of suppressing the rebellion of Tang Sen-chi (T'ang Sheng-chih) in Honan became the uppermost task of the National Government about the middle of the month". Perkins added that most political and military forces were directed to either suppressing him or neutralizing his authority and his menace to national peace. This was most difficult because only recently he had been of great value to the Central Government in its campaign against Feng Yu-hsiang, and although the real cause of the revolt was not known, Perkins suspected that it was a quarrel between the dissident Nationalist generals T'ang and Liu. T'ang wanted Liu to evacuate from Hupeh

---

[1] Op. cit., p. 184.

[2] Chargé in China. The quotations and paraphrase on this page and the next are from F.R.U.S., 1929, II, pp. 185—6.

to Kiangsi, so that he, T'ang, could again occupy the profitable and strategic center of Hankow, Liu's peremptory refusal and the resulting loss of face to T'ang had made him decide to take it by force, in which attempt he almost succeeded. He was checked only by forces beyond his control, among which were a new rally to Chiang, an unexpected increment of Liu's forces, and the deepest snows and coldest weather in Honan of thirty years, which affected T'ang more than Liu because of the former's isolated position. At the time he was being slowly driven back, but, even with an offer of $ 50,000 for his capture or $ 30,000 for his death, he had not been routed.

Had Shih Yu-san taken Nanking and T'ang Sheng-chih come to his aid, it would have forced Chiang to split his forces in the south and rush aid to Nanking; it is more than likely that he would then have lost the battle in the south and that a group of generals in the north would have rebelled against Chiang and joined Shih and T'ang. They were ever, at best, lukewarm in their support of Chiang, and were never trustworthy, as far as he was concerned. He could never rely upon them, and although they were supposed to be his subordinates and allies, he always had to ask himself when he committed himself to battle not only whether he could depend upon their promised aid, but whether they would join his enemies in battle. There is no place for hindsight in history and luck is not a logical or scientific explanation, but in looking at political and military history one cannot fail, on occasion, to be impressed by the seemingly unaccountable success of the careers of certain leaders. One must admit either that Chiang has had much luck along with his skill or that he is one of the most adroit and clever leaders in history. His success at staying in power has indeed been phenomenal.

CHAPTER V

THE CHINESE EASTERN RAILWAY CRISIS:
THE OPENING PHASES

The Sino-Russian crisis and border war of 1929 have generally been given much less than their real importance in studies on international relations between the two world wars. The conflict has been overshadowed in retrospect by the Sino-Japanese crisis of 1931, which involved a challenge to the League of Nations, intruded into the forefront of world affairs, and formally diminished Chinese sovereignty by the creation of the new puppet state of ,,Manchukuo". The crisis of 1929, on the other hand, produced no appeal to the League of Nations, no permanent Russian military occupation of Manchuria and no formal breach of China's sovereignty. In appearance it was resolved by an amicable settlement. In fact, nevertheless, it was settled by force, for Russian troops crossed the border and carried out a real military invasion of China; if there was little fighting, it was only because of the utter collapse of the Chinese armies on the frontier. This little war provided the first test of the recently signed Kellogg Pact and demonstrated its futility to all those who were not blinded by humbug. Since the Washington Conference no foreign power had invaded Chinese territory beyond the limits of the foreign settlements and concessions in order to impose terms on the Chinese government; by being the first to do so, anti-imperialist Soviet Russia showed herself more ready, instead of more reluctant, than the "imperialist" powers to coerce China on account of purely material national interests. Her success in the use of force (with the acquiescence or even approval of the rest of the world) was a major factor in encouraging the Japanese militarists to draw the sword, likewise, two years later and use it in a much larger way.

Chang Hsüeh-liang made his first move against Russia before the end of 1927. On December 29, he raised the Kuomintang flag over the Chinese Eastern Railway property at Harbin and other places in northern Manchuria. Previously the C.E.R. had had its own flag combining the old five-barred flag of the Chinese Republic above and the Soviet flag below. This corresponded to the joint ownership of the railway, but it certainly suggested that it was something more than a merely commercial enterprise. In accordance with the new nationalist idea Chang now prohibited further use of this composite flag and ordered that only the new Chinese sun flag, adopted by the Kuomintang, was to be flown.

The practical implications of this were several. It showed that, as far as foreign affairs were concerned, north and south China were one, that Manchuria, as it was called abroad, and China proper would present a united front. Such unity would have little effect on the internal administration of Manchuria, since most of the appointments were made by Chang, and the rest required his tacit approval. But it would mean a great deal to Chinese sentiment everywhere. It would bolster Chinese self-confidence, which was badly in need of bolstering. It would give the Chinese something to show for the revolution. It would increase their prestige as a sovereign nation and at the same time serve notice on the world that they meant business over "rights recovery". China was faced with issues which, if left to the discretion of the Great Powers, would drag on for years and be settled by piecemeal concessions. The Kuomintang could not stand for this. It must have immediate gains to show the country, to explain the lack of democracy which was long overdue and which Chiang and the party promised in more glowing terms each year. These promises all had a way of petering out and being replaced by new and bigger promises. The people were becoming restive and demanding fulfillment. International gains were the best means of pacifying the people, short of fulfilling the promises. It had become the practice of the revolution to make promises which sounded well but were recognized by all intelligent people, Chinese or Western, as incapable of fulfillment. The seizure of the railway, which was to follow the changing of the flag, was in part a trial balloon, but it was also a challenge to Russia — although a foolish challenge —, for China was hopelessly far behind Russia in actual strength, even though Russia at that time was very weak. Russian intelligence in China knew this. Chinese lack of intelligence in Russia handicapped the government from the beginning. The Chinese authorities seem to have been too ready to take their estimates of Soviet power from the many White Russian exiles in China, who never ceased optimistically predicting the imminent collapse of the Communist régime. In reality, although Russia, then in the throes of the first Five-Year Plan, was quite unready for a major war it was not difficult for her to concentrate enough military strength to deal with China's frontier defence, as the event showed. China probably relied on the hostility of the Western Powers towards the Soviet régime — the U.S.A. had not yet established diplomatic relations with Russia — and thought she would have their goodwill and protection in any conflict with Communist Russia, especially if Communist propaganda and intrigue could be used as a pretext for action. But, as it turned out, the Powers were much more concerned about the threat to the whole treaty system in China which would arise if China were allowed to abrogate, unilaterally, a treaty commitment. Whatever the rights and wrongs of the history behind the law — and what nation in China could afford too close an inspection of the origins of its title-deeds? — Russia had certain legal rights and these were overridden by China. With their own treaty rights in mind the Western Powers were very unwilling to see China establish a dangerous precedent by confiscatory measures, even at the expense of the Soviet Union.

It is interesting to note that France was to take an adamant stand on the question of legal rights and contracts, when, in 1932, the Lytton Commission tried to work out an equitable solution for the Manchurian problem. France steadfastly demanded that judgment be made on the basis of the legal rights as they stood at the time. France, however, was not concerned primarily with her position in China. She was determined to prevent the creation of a precedent which Germany could invoke for revision of the Versailles treaty.

It had long been known in the Foreign Offices of the world that Russia was carrying on subversive activities in China through the best medium available to her. Chang Tso-lin, however, took steps to do something about it. In a raid on the Soviet Embassy in Peking on April 6th, 1927, evidence was found which, had China, and Chang himself, been in a stronger position politically and diplomatically, would have put Russia in the dock before world opinion for gross misuse of an Embassy against the government to which it was accredited. Much of the material was never made public, but was in fact suppressed by a very high Chinese official well known in the West, if not for his own integrity at least for his various family connections, and by two Western advisers. One of the leaders of this raid was a young Chinese officer who had graduated from West Point a short time before. Perhaps some days in the not distant future it will be possible to explain and elaborate upon this rather enigmatic statement in greater detail. It is a fact that enough evidence of subversion and espionage was found to have brought Russia before any body of international justice had that been possible, or to have justified any nation in the most drastic action. Almost immediately after the Peking discovery a raid upon Arcos House, the Russian Trade Delegation's headquarters in London, verified much of the Russian material released by the Chinese Government. The raid on Arcos House took place on May 12, 1927.

After Chang Hsüeh-liang joined the Kuomintang he took his position seriously and, as seen above, soon made others likewise take him seriously. He was well aware of what was in the material seized in the Embassy at Peking, at the order of his father, two years previously. He was also well aware of what Russia and the Communists, both native and foreign, were attempting to do in China. During a regional Communist meeting at the Russian Consulate in Harbin the Chinese swooped down after the delegates had arrived and arrested the lot, in the meantime searching the consulate thoroughly. They found consulate seals of both the United States and Japan which were evidently used for forging and faking documents, visas and passports. The raid was made on May 20, 1929. As already mentioned, the Chinese Eastern Railway flag had been replaced by the Nationalist flag on Dec. 29, 1928, on the personal order of Chang Hsüeh-liang. This had been only the beginning of a series of moves which were to be very costly to China because they were made in such a way that China was deserted for a time by all her former friends. America almost appeared to take the lead in humbling her in the Sino-Russian conflict, which the raising of the flag and a number of subsequent acts quickly brought to a head.

On January 9, 1929, Chang caused the C.E.R. telephone system to be seized without compensation. On February 7, the Russian Consul at Mukden protested to the Mukden Government against the seizure. He delivered the protest to the Commissioner of Foreign Affairs, who later accompanied him to call on Chang Hsüeh-liang. Chang is reported to have answered the protest by saying that the action was in accord with China's sovereign rights and was entirely correct. Melnikoff, Soviet Consul-General at Harbin, then arrived in Mukden about March 26, to negotiate with Chang. His arrival was unexpected and caused general surprise. He stated that he had much broader powers than were usual with Soviet Consuls and had come to iron out all differences.

It appeared that he was actually on a special mission as a Minister Plenipotentiary for this one case. He stated that in order to clear up all misunderstandings he thought it better to negotiate new treaties. Evidently he intended to overawe and dictate to Chang. If so, he was sadly mistaken. Chang retorted that he saw no reason whatever for negotiating a new treaty. When Melnikoff referred to the violation of the Sino-Russian treaty and cited the seizure of the telephone system as an example, Chang replied that the agreement referred to the railway and not to telephones, and that the action had only been taken to prevent impairment of China's sovereignty. Chang pointed out that the Soviet Union had failed to answer three letters regarding the matter, and said he might be forced to take still further steps for the same reason. On each point raised by Melnikoff, Chang showed himself more than a match for him, completely refuting his arguments.

It was quite evident by now that Chang was out to reaffirm the sovereignty of China in every disputed area as far as possible. It was under these circumstances that the Consulate at Harbin was raided during the Communist meeting on May 20. During the raid the Russians burned papers and documents, but the Chinese recovered from a stove a code book, charred about the edges, and other evidence of the activities of the Russians in China.

There was much speculation why Russia at first did nothing as a result of the situation. The general opinion was that she was powerless to do anything under the circumstances. For some time the Moscow press dit not even mention the Chinese activities in

Manchuria. In Harbin it was thought that the evidence against
Russia, seized by the Chinese, was so serious that Russia was
keeping quiet in the hope that the Chinese would not reveal the
evidence, as they surely would if Russia began to make trouble.

Karakhan, a very astute statesman, then Acting Commissar for
Foreign Affairs, soon realized, however, that the Russian silence
would be taken for acquiescence, and that Russia must make some
move. Accordingly he handed to Hsia, the Chinese Chargé d'Affaires in Moscow, a long and surprisingly sophomoric harangue,
protesting against the raid on the Consulate, and bringing up similar
raids in Peking and Canton in years past. He called the Chinese
charge about the use of the Consulate for a meeting of the Third
International "a manifest, stupid invention, without rhyme or
reason". [1] He declared that the Chinese actions did not acquire
legality from the wholly unfounded and provocative explanations
being published in the Chinese press. He made veiled threats against
members of the Chinese diplomatic staff in the Soviet Union, stating
that rights of extra-territoriality, "with which international law
clothes them" would no longer be conceded to them. Nowhere did
he refer directly to the seizure of the telephone system.

The stage was now set for the next moves, and to be sure they
would be sudden and dramatic.

It is surprising how universal the opinion seemed to have been
among foreign diplomats that Russia would or could do nothing,
and that China would be allowed to ride with a high hand. Mr.
Hanson, the American Consul at Harbin, mentioned in a dispatch
to the Minister, MacMurray, that the Chinese had threatened to
apply the same measures against the Soviet consular officials and
citizens in Manchuria as those which had been taken at one time
by the Canton Government, unless the Soviets lived up to certain
conditions. "As local Russians know what vindictive measures the
nationalist officials in the south took against Soviet consular officers
and citizens, this outburst . . . caused considerable uneasiness among
the Russian community". [2] And again, after having mentioned the two
treaties of 1924, the one with the Peking Government and the other

---

[1]   F.R.U.S., 1929, II, p. 194.
[2]   *Op cit.*, p. 187.

with Chang Tso-lin, the latter of which cut down the concession period by twenty years, Mr. Hanson says that the local Chinese will interpret the agreements to suit their own interests, and that "the Soviet side will be too powerless to resist the Chinese officials in this respect". [1] Again Hanson reports on January 9, that the Chinese have just taken over the city telephone system on direct orders from Mukden and that the Russians fear that the Chinese will now proceed to take over the whole railway, "which is really the property of the Russian people..." [2] "Soviet Russia cannot take a strong action against Manchuria because of fear of complications on the Polish border and of Japan, and the Chinese authorities know this and are acting accordingly". [3] Hanson here reveals certain of his own attitudes and sympathies which are rather unusual in consular reports.

Russia at the outset apparently preferred to deal directly with Chang Hsüeh-liang rather than treat the dispute as one between Russia and China. But in response to Melnikoff's proposal for a new treaty. Chang curtly refused to negotiate, stating that he had no power to make a settlement on his own, as he also was a member of a party. Meyers, the Consul-General at Mukden, said in a report to MacMurray that Chang astounded everyone present, Chinese and Russian alike, by the cool and efficient manner in which he handled the conference. His grasp of the situation was such that despite all its legal and technical complications it was not once necessary for him to refer to his technical and legal advisers for advice or information. [4] He told Melnikoff that he personally knew Chan Ko-chen and was ready to back him in everything he had done. In an interesting aside he stated that he hoped that Melnikoff would stay at Mukden for a few days and see how universal were the opinions which he, Chang, had expressed, among members of the Manchurian Government.

One interesting opinion expressed in a consular report was the surmise: "Perhaps, there exists some sort of an understanding between the Soviet and Japanese officials in this respect (Japanese

---

[1] *Op. cit.*, p. 188.
[2] *Loc. cit.*
[3] *Op. cit.*, p. 189.
[4] *Op. cit.*, pp. 190—191.

action to forestall China's seizure of the C.E.R., thereby creating
a dangerous precedent) or, at least, the Soviet side might have
some knowledge of the attitude of the Japanese railway officials
towards this question". [1]

Another side issue of interest today, in view of Russia's new
strategy with regard to the White Russians in China, was the
revelation of a secret clause in the Mukden agreement whereby
Chang Tso-lin had promised not to employ White Russians on
the C.E.R. Young Chang was not aware of this and, in answer to
a charge of having broken the treaty by the employment of White
Russians, answered that there was no breach of treaty on the part
of the Chinese. Melnikoff seemed to be referring to the recent
appointment of Boris V. Ostroumoff, a White Russian, general
manager of the C.E.R. in 1924, as an adviser to the Communications
Commission at Mukden. On being informed of the secret clause,
Chang Hsüeh-liang threatened to publish it if the Russians pressed
the point. "He added that while the Chinese for humanitarian
reasons are giving these Russians a chance to earn a livelihood the
Soviet Government prevents them from returning to their homes
and only desires to persecute them..." [2]

In a report to Stimson on June 17, MacMurray mentioned the
fact that the Russian possession of the American consular seals was
a crime under Chinese law. He said that the Harbin police were
aware of the facts, but that it was questionable whether or not they
would prosecute unless pressed to do so by the American Consul
and stated that Hanson had requested telegraphic instructions. [3]
On June 25, Stimson wired MacMurray stating that the State
Department would make no request for the seals, nor did they wish
to push the matter. [4]

On July 10, Hanson informed MacMurray that the Chinese had
seized the telegraph system of the C.E.R. and closed Soviet trade
organizations in North Manchuria, making numerous arrests of
Soviet citizens. He stated that the arrests numbered sixty and
added: "It would appear that there will be little Soviet opposition

---

[1]   F.R.U.S., 1929, II, pp. 187—188.
[2]   Op. cit., p. 191.
[3]   Op. cit., p. 196.
[4]   Op. cit., p. 197.

and no strike of railway employees". [1] He stated that there was a carefully concerted takeover by Chinese agents at Harbin of the railway's central telegraph station at Pristen, the business town, and all along the railway. This had evidently been very carefully planned beforehand. He took an even more serious view of the arrests which included Knazieff, chief of the General Affairs section of the railway administration, and Markoff, assistant chief of the traffic department and head of the professional union of railway employees. The Chinese had also closed the offices of Gostorg (Government Trading Trust), Neftsyndicate (Government Oil Trust), Sovtorgflot (Soviet Trading Fleet) and other Soviet Government trade organizations. [2]

The Chinese justified these acts on the grounds that representatives of these organizations had been caught in the recent raid on the Harbin Consulate, "where evidence had been discovered that they and their organizations had been engaged in communistic propaganda dangerous to the Chinese Government". [3]

The English-speaking officials of the railway were given "leave of absence" and Fan Chi-kuan, a Russian-educated Chinese, was appointed General Manager, replacing Emshanoff, the Soviet General Manager. He stated that these orders emanated from the Nanking Government. Again Hanson reports: "The Soviet authorities are angry, but helpless, and it is not believed that they will make more than verbal objections". [4] It is interesting to observe Hanson's obvious sympathy for Russia and the consistency with which he misjudged the situation.

The situation in China was considered so inflammable in July 1929, that Stimson asked MacMurray on the 18th to continue at his post, despite the fact that all arrangements had been completed for him to sail home. In the cable asking him to remain, Stimson mentioned the fact that on that day he had held conversations with the British, French and Japanese Ambassadors, and particularly with the Chinese Minister, Dr. C. C. Wu, in which he had pointed out the grave responsibilities devolving upon the signatories and

---

[1] Op. cit., pp. 198—9.
[2] Op. cit., p. 199.
[3] Loc. cit.
[4] Loc. cit.

adherents to the multilateral peace pacts. Each of those mentioned agreed to cable his government supporting Mr. Stimson.

In his conversation with Dr. Wu Stimson pointed out the special responsibility which rested on the Chinese Government. From all reports available it was felt that the actions of the Chinese Government appeared to have broken the Sino-Soviet agreement of 1924. At least it seemed that her actions were interpretable as an attack on Russia. [1]

As the crisis heightened from hour to hour there was grave speculation as to the whereabouts of Chang Hsüeh-liang and the Chinese Foreign Minister, Dr. C. T. Wang, the former absent from Mukden, the latter absent from Nanking. One theory was that Chang Tso-hsiang and Wan Fu-lin — the generals sent in command of troops to the Manchu-Russian border as a result of the meeting between Chiang K'ai-shek, Chang Hsüeh-liang and C. T. Wang in Peking on June 3, 1929 — had taken advantage of the absence of Chang to oust him. But those who held the theory that this was done in connivance with Chiang K'ai-shek were unable to explain the absence of Dr. Wang from Nanking. [2]

---

[1] Op. cit., p. 210.
[2] Op. cit., p. 211.

CHAPTER VI

DEVELOPMENT OF THE CRISIS

By the middle of July, 1929, the tension in Manchuria had reached such a point that the Harbin consular body was reported have been considering mediation for a peaceful settlement. [1] But Stimson wired MacMurray telling him that, regardless of the precedents for such participation by the American Consul, the Department did not deem it expedient for him to participate in this case unless he was specially instructed to do so.

On July 13th, the long-awaited action by Russia came in the form of what amounted to a threat of war. Russia gave China a seventy-two hours ultimatum to accept the three following demands:[2]

(1) A conference to be held for the settlement of all questions concerning the Chinese Eastern Railway;

(2) The Chinese authorities to cancel at once all unilateral acts committed in respect of the Chinese Eastern Railway;

(3) All arrested Soviet citizens to be freed immediately, and the Chinese authorities to cease immediately all persecutions of Soviet citizens and all encroachments upon their rights and upon the rights of Soviet institutions.

The Note declared that:

"The Union government invites the Mukden government and the National Government of the Chinese Republic to weigh well the serious consequences that rejection of this proposal of the U.S.S.R. will have.

"The Union government states that it will await the answer of the Chinese Government to the above exposed proposal for three days, and gives warning that, in the event of non-receipt of a satisfactory answer, it will be obliged to resort to other means of defence of the lawful rights of the U.S.S.R." [3]

---

[1] F.R.U.S., 1929, II, p. 200.
[2] *Op. cit.*, pp. 201—6.
[3] *Op. cit.*, p. 206.

CHRISTOPHER, Conflict in the Far East   6

In this Note Karakhan claimed that the Chinese had flagrantly violated the treaty of May 31st, 1924, between the Peking Government and the Soviet Government and also that of September 20th, 1924, between the U.S.S.R. and the Manchurian administration of Chang Tso-Lin. He pointed out that according to Article I of the Peking agreement and Article I, Clause 6 of the Mukden agreement all measures concerning the railway must be examined by the Board of Directors numbering ten persons and concurred in by six of these ten. Further, the agreement stipulated that the Chairman, a Chinese citizen, and the Vice-Chairman, a Soviet citizen, should together conduct the business of the board and should both sign all documents for any actions to be legal; hence the unilateral action of the Chinese was unquestionably illegal. The Note further emphasized that the management of the railway rested with the General Manager, a Soviet citizen, and two Assistant General Managers, one of whom must be a Soviet citizen and the other Chinese; these persons were to be nominated by the Board and must be approved by their respective governments; therefore the removal of the Soviet Manager and his replacement by a Chinese, even though only temporary, was illegal. [1]

Unquestionably the Chinese action violated both these agreements and was legally indefensible. The Chinese had violated their treaty undertakings. From the legal point of view the fact that Russia was cleverly using these agreements as cover, behind which they might work to destroy the Chinese government and what little sovereignty China did possess, was no excuse for China's action. It had been a most unwise move on the part of Chang Hsüeh-liang and those who advised him. Apart from its illegality, it was not a realistic action, and caused great loss of face to all concerned in China, and especially to Chang Hsüeh-liang, who was the ostensible leader in the policy. It was also to reveal the ineffectiveness of the Chinese military forces in Manchuria, their gross inefficiency and lack of real training, discipline and equipment.

China could not possibly have chosen a more inopportune time for this offensive against Russia. The western powers led by America and Great Britain had finally decided that the just claims

---

[1] *Op. cit.*, p. 202.

of China must be met. They had already recognised autonomy, as it were, by default. They were on the point of taking up again in a serious manner the questions of extraterritoriality and all the concomitant problems. By forcing the issue with Russia, when she had no hope of military success if Russia chose to challenge her actions, China put the Americans and the British, who recognised the justice of China's cause, in a most embarrassing position. Had China been able to make good her stand, as Japan had done in the Sino-Japanese or the Russo-Japanese wars, it would have strengthened her hand, but the mixture of provocation and helplessness only alienated her friends.

It is necessary to recognise the fact that at this time Russia also needed an external cause to rally her people behind the Communist government, which, although in power, was not popular. She also needed to show the world by proving her strength, that she was a force to be reckoned with. It was imperative, however, that she should not be the *aggressor,* and here China put a perfect instrument into her hand.

As soon as Russia showed that she would contest China's actions, or force her to back down, it was a foregone conclusion what the outcome would be. But instead of playing a waiting game, which had been China's most successful policy in the nineteenth century, she went even further in defiance and on July 15th, consolidated the C.E.R. Land Department into her own land administration.

On July 17th, MacMurray informed the Secretary of State that (1) Mr. Mahlon E. Perkins, Counsellor of Legation, had been informed in strict confidence that Karakhan had told a person not named in these documents, in an interview in Moscow, that Russia was determined to force the issue with China. MacMurray also reported that (2) he had information that the Chairmen of the three Manchurian provincial governments, at a meeting at Mukden on June 3rd, had decided to take action with regard to the railway, and had subsequently exchanged telegrams with Nanking, whereupon Chang Hsüeh-liang went to Peking to confer with Chiang Kai-shek and Dr. C. T. Wang. (3) The Chinese government was seriously perturbed at foreign comment published in the newspapers in China and abroad and the same feeling existed in Mukden. Some of the Chinese leaders considered Russia to be powerless, but others were not so optimistic and feared that Russia would occupy Sinkiang and also sever railway communications between Siberia and Manchuria. [1]

Despite all this, China continued to discharge Russian railway employees and apparently intended to ignore the ultimatum, even as late as July 17th. In fact, on that date, the same day when the ultimatum was published in Harbin by the Japanese press, the Chinese authorities closed and took over the railway administration's four libraries at Harbin. On the same day, Chiang Kai-shek called a meeting of the Council of State to consider the Soviet note, recalling Dr. C. T. Wang from Peking to Nanking.

On July 18th, the local press in Peking published the outline of an answer to Russia's ultimatum. It said, in effect, that since the signing of the Sino-Russian treaty in 1924, the Chinese government had attempted to deal with Russia in mutual sincerity. But it had had called to its attention since that time many cases in which Russia had incited the Chinese people to rise against their government in an effort to undermine the Chinese social and political order. To preserve internal peace China had been forced to take action. The recent raid on the Soviet Consulate in Harbin had been carried out to forestall serious consequences, but, having taken the decision to make this raid, the authorities had taken every precaution to limit its scope.

With regard to the seizure of the railway, the reply stated that the Russian manager and other important Russian officials had never carried out the terms of the agreement of 1924, that they had committed so many violations that it had been impossible for the Chinese officials to carry out their duties under the pact. Moreover, China accused Russia of using the railway institutions to carry on propaganda forbidden by the agreements. These facts showed that the responsibility for the violation thereof rested on the Soviet Government.

The reply continued, that according to reports from the Chinese Consulates in Russia more than a thousand Chinese had been arrested and imprisoned there, and many others were being subjected to all sorts of restrictions. The Chinese government had

---

[1] *Op. cit.,* p. 207.

always been generous in its treatment of Russians and Russian commercial organisations and the recent action of the Manchurian authorities had only been taken to stop revolutionary propaganda and to preserve the peace in the Three Eastern Provinces.

China set forth the following two demands:

"(1) That all the Chinese arrived (sic.) in Russia should be returned with the exception of those whom the Chinese Legation (*Embassy?*) or Chinese Consulates want to remain on account of pending case against them;

(2) that the Soviet Government should accord all the necessary guarantees and facilities to Chinese merchants and merchandise originating in Russia and should not prosecute them. If the Soviet Government can do these things, the Chinese Government will set free all the Russians recently arrested in Harbin". [1]

The reply concluded by hoping that the Soviet Government would awaken to its mistakes and rectify its previous improper actions, that it would respect the law and the sovereignty of China and that it would refrain from making any proposals contrary to the facts of the case; on the Chinese side the Minister to Finland, then in Shanghai, would stop in Moscow on his way to Finland and talk over all the outstanding questions, particularly the C.E.R., with the Commissariat for Foreign Affairs for the purpose of reaching an amicable settlement. [2]

The foregoing account of China's reply is condensed from a lengthy report issued under Nanking dateline by Kuo Wen News and published in Peking on July 18th, 1929; it was quoted by MacMurray in his despatch to Stimson.

It is almost inconceivable that a responsible government should have drafted and sent to another state such a reply to an ultimatum, particularly in view of the fact that Dr. Wang and several others in the government were eminent statesmen. It recalls one of the old Chinese mandates to the tributaries, which ended with the words: "Tremble and obey". The reply would have been ironically humourous, had it not been so tragic.

---

[1] *Op. cit.,* p. 209.

[2] *Op. cit.,* pp. 209—10.

No wonder MacMurray winds up a report to Stimson by saying: "Such foreign press comment in China as has come to the attention of the Legation ... apparently regards the present issue as a test whether China may or may not be held to any of her contractual obligations". [1]

On July 19th, Soviet Russia severed diplomatic relations with China, announcing its decision:

> (1) To recall all Soviet diplomatic, consulate (*consular*) and commercial representatives from the territory of China.
> (2) To recall all persons appointed by the Government of the U.S.S.R. on the Chinese Eastern Railway from the territory of China.
> (3) To suspend all railway communications between China and the U.S.S.R.
> (4) To order (*invite?*) the diplomatic and consular representatives of the Chinese Republic in the U.S.S.R. to leave immediateley the territory of the U.S.S.R.

"At the same time", it was stated, "the Government of the U.S.S.R. declares that it reserves all rights arising from the Peking and Mukden agreements of 1924". [2]

In a report to Stimson, MacMurray said that from a confidential source, Perkins had learned that Russia suspected a third power as having been behind China in the action she took in Manchuria. [3] He suggested, parenthetically, that this meant Japan.

On July 19th, the Chargé d'Affaires in Japan, Neville, informed Stimson that the Vice-Minister of Foreign Affairs had said that Japan would not interfere in the dispute between China and Russia in regard to the C.E.R. and that the Japanese did not think, for the moment, that it would lead to war. He added that the Minister of Foreign Affairs said he did not expect the question to be taken up at the Japanese Cabinet meeting that day and that no Japanese action was contemplated for the present. [4]

The Secretary of the German Legation informed the American

---

[1] F.R.U.S., 1929, II, p. 211.
[2] *Op. cit.*, p. 214.
[3] *Op. cit.*, p. 207.
[4] *Op. cit.*, p. 212.

Legation on the 19th, that the Soviet Union had requested Germany to take over protection of Soviet interests in Peking while relations with China were suspended. [1] On the same day Stimson sent MacMurray an account of his conversation with Dr. Wu, held on July 18th. [2] Stimson said he had pointed out to Wu that the dispute was justiciable, if one took the press reports of both China and Russia as a point of departure. In these reports China had claimed that the origin of the trouble was the violation by Russia of her treaty obligation not to use the C.E.R. for propaganda, while Russia had claimed that it was China's unwarranted seizure of Russia's railway property in China. The Secretary said that he would like to know how the Chinese Government felt about the matter.

Dr. Wu stated that he understood America's deep concern in the matter, due in part to the fact that she was a signatory of the Kellogg—Briand pact. He informed the Secretary that the principal cause for China's actions arose from the discovery among the papers seized in the raid on the Russian consulate at Harbin of evidence which proved that the Russians were using the railway as a focus for Communist propaganda against China. He recalled to the Secretary the incident at Canton in December 1927, when Communists, under the leadership of Russian agents, had seized the city and instituted a reign of terror. The Secretary pointed out to him that there was a vast difference between a country trying to protect itself against individuals within its borders and taking direct action against a sovereign nation. He also told the Chinese Minister that one of the great difficulties was that China had acted too quickly in seizing the railway, and that in public opinion the seizure was regarded, whether rightly or wrongly, as an attempt to take possession of property belonging to Russia, and not as an attempt on China's part to protect herself against propaganda attacks. In response to a request from Wu for suggestions, Stimson inferred that, if China were to leave the matter to the arbitration of neutral nations, it would make it clear that her intentions were peaceful and provide evidence of the truth of her claim that she had

---

[1] *Op. cit.*, pp. 214—215.
[2] *Op. cit.*, pp. 215—17.

not meant to attack Russian property rights, but was only protecting herself against the acts of subversive propagandists. In answer to the question whether America would offer her good offices for negotiation the Secretary replied that this could never be done except at the request of both parties and that he thought Russia would not make such a request. He informed Wu that in his interviews with the Ambassadors of Japan, Italy, France and Great Britain all had agreed that no signatory of the Kellogg Pact could be indifferent to war between Russia and China, and that, although both countries were too weak to make war, this was no guarantee that war would not occur, even though it seemed unlikely. They had further agreed that the matter was highly justiciable and could easily be solved by arbitration, which should be brought about. Stimson added that they had decided to send cables along these general lines to their governments.

The French Ambassador informed Stimson that Briand, in a cable received by the French Embassy that morning, had forwarded his thanks to Mr. Stimson for the steps which he had taken in the Russo-Chinese dispute, and that he heartily concurred with Mr. Stimson's attitude. [1]

On the same day the Italian ambassador called at the State Department and asked whether or not in the opinion of Mr. Johnson, Assistant Secretary of State, China would force a war against Russia. Mr. Johnson replied "No". The Ambassador said that their information from the Italian Embassy in Moscow did not cover the latest developments in China. But he, however, was persuaded that Russia was in no condition to carry on war, from the point of view either of military organisation or material. The Italian reports indicated that, while there was for the moment a wheat reserve in Siberia, it was not large enough to cover the shortage in Russia as a whole, to say nothing of supplying a great military campaign. [2]

By July 20th, [3] according to diplomatic reports, the White Russians of the maritime customs had left Suifenho where Soviet aeroplanes were making frequent flights to break the morale of the populace.

---

[1] *Op. cit.,* p. 218.
[2] *Op. cit.,* pp. 218—19.
[3] *Op. cit.,* p. 219.

They also evacuated Lahasusu, where four Soviet warships had guns trained on the customs house and its vicinity and where there were also "flying Soviet airplanes much in evidence". He stated that he was reliably informed that the Soviet Consul-General had been instructed to leave Harbin immediately, that the Dal-bank was transferring its funds to New York and that the German Consul-General was to take charge of local Soviet interests.

In commenting on the report of a trip made to Manchuria by the American naval attaché in June, MacMurray observed to Stimson: ". . . it would appear that the question of some action being taken by the Manchurian authorities with regard to the Chinese Eastern Railway had been under consideration for some time." Evidently some advisers had advocated "confiscation of the railway", while others suggested "assumption of control with all the liabilities and assets". Those who advocated assumption of control argued that "the obligations which China is said to have under article V of the nine-power treaty ... and under resolution 12 of the Washington Conference regarding the Chinese Eastern Railway and the obligations 'in the nature of a trust' which China may be deemed to have in view of the terms of resolution 13 of the Washington Conference regarding the Chinese Eastern Railway", justified seizure. "Although the foregoing provisions were drawn op with a view to holding China responsible for 'discrimination', the view is now maintained by the advisers of the Mukden Government that China cannot now carry out her engagements in these particulars without assumption of full control of the railway", [1] and there was much to be said for that argument.

"It is further argued" that since, under the Peking agreement Article II stipulates that " 'the railway is a purely commercial enterprise' " and under Article 6 that " 'the Governments of the two contracting parties further pledge themselves not to engage in propaganda against the political and social systems of either contracting party' ", China was entirely "justified in taking over the railway" since "the provisions of these articles have been repeatedly broken by the Soviet Government"; certainly, "the railway, its funds and employees were being used for political purposes".

---

[1] *Op. cit.*, p. 220.

Further, they were being used to undermine the government of China. [1]

It may be argued that China was now finding justification for an act which she had unwisely committed and for which she had originally felt no justification necessary. Without attempting to condone her acts, however, it can be admitted in view of what is now generally known of Russia's methods of operation, as a result of the Canadian espionage trial and the disclosures of Kravchenko and others who write in exile, from experience, that China had a stronger case then anyone, and especially she herself, realised. There is no question that Russia did use the railway for propaganda and intrigue in violation of her solemn agreements, and that she worked for many years in China "boring from within". China had a right to protect herself. But she went about it in the wrong manner. The high-minded reasons for her actions set forth when the crisis became acute were not the only ones operative. Nationalist feelings and domestic political purposes, as well as financial and economic motives, played their part in the seizure of the C.E.R.

These considerations complicate the analysis of the case. As things stood at the time of seizure, China was unquestionably guilty of violating the 1924 agreements. Also, unquestionably, Russia was guilty of violating the same agreements, and had been for a long time. It may be argued that after Russia had broken the agreement it ceased to be binding on China. This is no doubt true, but the matter does not end there, nor is it as simple as that. Because of the importance of relations between sovereign nations there must be some acceptable method of giving notice to other nations of an intention to abrogate a contract, setting forth the reasons for doing so, unless one has such a strong army and navy and is, in general, in such a strong position as to make international opinion relatively unimportant as far as any suasion or coercion is concerned. A power may indeed feel itself strong enough to defy world opinion with impunity and think that the spoils or gains are great enough to justify such a course. But even such an invincible power will realise, if its affairs are wisely conducted, that reactions are cumulative and give rise to groupings and coalitions of injured and interested

---

[1] *Loc. cit.*

parties which may later prove highly embarassing to it. Hence, even a Great Power is constrained to take notice of international opinion to some extent, only defying it occassionally, and then on a matter of sufficiently great importance to justify the risk.

Much less can a weak state like China ignore the proprieties of international relations.

China did not take any precautions to build up her case in advance. She merely acted and presented the world with what she hoped would be a *fait accompli*. The irony of the case is that China had more justification on her side, had she followed the usual conventions, than any foreign observers at that time were willing to allow.

As the crisis developed, China placed herself in the wrong before world opinion, despite the fact that American sentiment as pointed out by Dorothy Borg was slavishly pro-Chinese, and also despite the fact that not only America, but the whole world, was strongly anti-Russian at that time. China expected general support, but found herself condemned in the liberal press of the world, led by the *Manchester Guardian*. Having been both arrogant and unwise in her actions, China was very infantile in her reaction to world opinion and Chinese diplomats scampered about whimpering and disavowing the plain implications of what had been done, seeking good offices, mediation and arbitration to extricate their country from its predicament.

In reading documents concerning China at this time, or for that matter of any period, one is constantly struck by the mixture of great arrogance with actual weakness. China assumes in herself a superiority, which she never questions, and is deeply shocked at anyone who does question it. China seems always to have scorned conventional international usages except, belatedly, when she invoked them for protection after she had fallen into such dire difficulties that it was nearly impossible for her to extricate herself intact. Little had changed in the basic Chinese attitude since the time of Lord Amherst's embassy, of which Dr. MacNair relates:

"Lord Amherst, whose boats bore the customary flags inscribed 'tribute Bearer' had to submit to one constant and continuous wrangle during his voyage from the coast to Peking, on the subject of the kotow, the mark of respect prescribed to the imperial throne. In this matter the ambassador had divergent instructions: his government had authorised him to consider it as a matter of expediancy, and to comply with the demand, if thereby he could secure the object of his mission; the directors of the company, however, advised him to make no concession, in point of ceremony or reception, which might diminish the national prestige. Lord Amherst maintained a consistent attitude and refused all concession on this one point. Arriving at Tungchow on August 28, the embassy was hurried on through the day and night over the rough roads to the palace at Yuenmingyuen, where it arrived at five o'clock in the morning of the twenty-ninth. The ambassador found, awaiting his arrival, a great number of princes and officials in full court dress, insistent, even to the extent of some hauling and pushing, on taking him to an immediate audience. He refused to proceed farther, however, alleging his state of extreme fatigue, his want of suitable apparel, and, especially, the absence of his credentials. The insult offered had been gross, and every member of the embassy accepted readily the decision of the Chinese authorities that they were to start at once on their return journey." [1]

One may well ask what all this has to do with the Sino-Russian dispute of 1929. The answer is simply that, if China could have carried off the business with a high hand as successfully as she did in dealing with the Amherst mission, there would not have had to be any world-wide attempt to mediate and to save China. When the Chinese can carry things with a high hand, no one can be more supercilious or arrogant, and in relation to Russia they had believed that they had the advantage of power on their side. Now they had started a fire in international relations and all the neighbours were busily trying to find a way to put it out before it spread beyond control. China had started it just as irresponsibly as a child and was now, like a child, leaving it for others to extinguish.

On July 19th, 1929, it seemed that it would be very difficult to prevent war. Stimson had the ambassadors from most of the important countries in constant touch with him. All agreed that neither country was in any position to go to war, but that, if either thought for one moment that she could carry it off, there would be war immediately. Further, all agreed that an incident might arise, a

---

[1] Morse–MacNair, *op. cit.,* pp. 46—7.

spark which would start a conflagration, and that some third power must arbitrate before it was too late. But who, and how could it be arranged? That was the big question worrying everybody. By this time China realised what a serious thing she had done and was thoroughly scared, but it was not easy for her then to draw back.

An interesting point can now be settled which has never been clear, about the seizure of the C.E.R. It has usually been held that it was an irresponsible act of Chang Hsüeh-liang, for the reasons given above. On July 21st, 1929, however, MacMurray forwarded to Stimson the following from Nanking:

> "Information has reached me indirectly from Kuomintang headquarters that decision to seize Chinese Eastern Railway was made in Peking at conference attended by Chiang Kai-shih, [1] Chang Hsueh-liang and C. T. Wang and that telegrams were immediately thereafter despatched to General Chang Ching-hui and Lu Yung-huan ordering execution of such decision. Same source states that in reaching decision those responsible envisaged possible failure of efforts to settle resulting controversy by negotiations." [2]

Here we see that the move in Manchuria was the considered action of the Chinese Government. The most important motive, MacMurray thought, was the alluring idea of using a coup against Russia as a precedent for depriving all Western powers of treaty rights in China. In a report to the Secretary of State he says that, whatever may have been Russia's responsibility for tutoring China in repudiation of obligations, or her fault or provocation in China, it is clear that China did force the issue "by what unquestionably is intended as an act of confiscation of the Chinese Eastern Railway. General Chiang Kai-shek and other Nationalist Government officials, furthermore, have linked this Russian phase of 'rights recovery' with the general problem of getting rid altogether of the unequal treaties". [3] MacMurray also made it clear in the same report that he feared China, in her conceit and ignorance concerning her true military position, which the people thought to be great, and carried away by her diplomatic triumph in whittling

---

[1] Chiang Kai-shek.
[2] F.R.U.S., 1929, II, p. 221.
[3] *Op. cit.,* p. 227.

away the existing treaty system, to overplay her hand so as to "create a situation which will prevent either side from withdrawing without hostilities." [1]

MacMurray warned Stimson that the political tendencies of contemporary Chinese thought would drive China to self-destruction unless it could be forcibly impressed upon her that her course was fatal. ". . . the seriousness of disregarding the rights of others as shown by them, not only in respect of Russia but of other countries also," must be driven home and China forced to realise that this would alienate the sympathy she had built up in the past few years. He also strongly urged the Secretary to make it clear in advance that America was unwilling for the Chinese to deprive her of her extraterritoriality rights. [2]

> It would be most opportune, therefore, for us now to submit our reply on the lines hitherto recommended by me to the Chinese note on this subject. Extraterritoriality and the Chinese Eastern Railway being inter-related, the delay by the United States and other governments in replying as to the former tends to encourage the Chinese authorities in a dangerously truculent attitude toward Russia in the latter, while any tactical success the Chinese might have in dealing with Russia would encourage their forcing upon us the extraterritoriality issue. [3]

On July 23rd, 1929, the Chinese Minister sent to the State Department a copy of a "manifesto of Chinese Government". [4] In this manifesto all the old points were recapitulated; China accused Russia of subversive activities in China, and of using the C.E.R. as a centre for infiltration and dissemination of propaganda and as a base of operations for the overthrow of the Chinese government. The manifesto claimed that conclusive documentary evidence of this had been found in the search of the Harbin Consulate. The local authorities had asked the government to take action to safeguard peace and order, and to remove the source of trouble. The actions which had been taken were essential, and the Chinese people and government, "with their tradition of peace,

---

[1] *Loc. cit.*
[2] *Op. cit.,* p. 228.
[3] *Loc. cit.*
[4] *Loc. cit.*

would never overreach themselves even though under compelling circumstances". [1] Russia had failed to realise its mistakes, but had sent a note contravening the facts and demanding a reply within a specified time; China, in accordance with its traditional policy of forebearance, "sent an appropriate reply based on the facts of the case, hoping that the Soviet Government would come to a self-realization" [1] and that thus the two countries might find a solution through negotiation. But Russia had severed diplomatic relations, recalled all her nationals from the C.E.R., and suspended railway communication between China and Russia. After throwing the entire blame for the incident on the Russians, the manifesto expressed the hope that the other powers and their peoples would take note of China's purity of intention, of her devotion to world peace, and of her exposure of the Russian plots and intrigues. [1]

The American Legation in Latvia forwarded a translation of a statement printed in the Moscow newspaper *Izvestia* on July 23rd, in which it was announced that France had taken upon herself the mediation of the dispute between Russia and China. This proposal was said to have been made in Paris by Briand on July 19th, to the diplomatic representative of the U.S.S.R. in France. Russia, through Comrade Karakhan, had had regretfully to reject the offer, since the "Chinese authorities (refuse) to restore the legal basis, by them violated, which is the necessary prerequisite for an agreement, pursuant to the note of the Soviet Government of July 13". The question of further complications was not dependent upon Russia, which was a peaceful nation. "There is no ground for doubting that the U.S.S.R. has been and remains the mainstay of the peace of the world". [2]

The Consul at Geneva informed the Secretary of State that, from conversations with responsible members of the League of Nations Secretariat, he did not believe that the League would take official action in regard to the Sino-Russian crisis unless forced to do so by the imminence of war. He said they placed their hopes on unofficial mediation by individual members of the League and added that the situation was then regarded as encouraging. [3]

---

[1] *Op. cit.,* p. 229.
[2] *Op. cit.,* pp. 231—2.
[3] *Op. cit.,* p. 232.

MacMurray forwarded a message from the Consul in Nanking to Stimson, informing him that the Chinese Foreign Minister was trying to settle the C.E.R. controversy through Chinese and Russian diplomatic officials and that in the meantime, on account of intense feeling and demonstrations in Russia, he had ordered all Chinese diplomatic and consular officials in Russia to leave the country. [1]

In a report to MacMurray the Military Attaché, [2] then on a trip to Mukden, observed that there was an "absence of military preparations" which "together with official assertions of determined passive attitude here convince me local government has no intention of accepting possible Russian challenge." He gathered from responsible Japanese that they believed "Russia contemplates nothing more than demonstration on frontier." Officials informed him that all negotiations were then in the hands of Nanking. He also noted a tendency "to admit that final steps in Harbin were precipitate" and placing of "responsibility for unauthorized action on President Lu Jung-huan". [3]

How seriously Stimson regarded the Sino-Russian situation may be gathered from glancing at the cables and reports from various countries on different aspects of mediation and good offices. On July 24th, 1929, the Italian Ambassador reported to Stimson that Mussolini appreciated his efforts, and was in accord with what he was doing. [4]

In a conversation with Sun Fo, [5] Minister of Railways, Mac-Murray told him [6] that discussions leading to direct negotiations were in progress between Russian and Chinese diplomats in Berlin; that the Chinese Chargé d'Affaires in Moscow was still at his post; that the Minister Designate to Finland and Russia was on his way to take up negotiations; and that a telegram had been received from General Chiang Tso-pin, Minister in Berlin, that Russia was opposed to having any third party involved in the dispute, but would welcome direct discussion. Sun Fo admitted that China also

---

[1] *Op. cit.,* p. 233.
[2] *Loc. cit.* and p. 237.
[3] *Op. cit.,* p. 237.
[4] *Loc. cit.*
[5] Son of Sun Yat-sen.
[6] F.R.U.S., 1929, II, pp. 244—5.

preferred this. He said that the Chinese action had been prompted by the fact that the Soviets had placed in highly paid positions in the railway administration propagandists who actually received much less than the nominal salaries, the balance going to propaganda funds, and that these propagandists had actually been building up subversive secret organisations among the Chinese. When questioned by MacMurray as to why they had not proceeded against the individuals responsible instead of against all the Russians, he said that this had been the intention of the Nanking government, but that the Manchurian authorities had, in their zeal, taken action more drastic than that envisaged by Nanking. He said there was no intention of depriving Russia of her legal rights. In reply to the inquiry whether or not China was willing to recognise the joint interest of Russia in the C.E.R. on the basis of the 1924 agreements and to restore the *status quo ante,* if Russia agreed in her turn to honour the clause forbidding propaganda, he replied that China would settle on these terms, subject to some more effective measure to prevent future recurrence of Russia's offences.

In response to a request for advice, MacMurray suggested to Sun Fo that China should disavow any intention of confiscating Russia's property, adding that it was most unfortunate that the action, which had professedly been taken to suppress Soviet propaganda, had been so drastic and so badly bungled as to create in American public opinion the belief, that China did not respect her obligations, since she was confiscating what belonged to a foreign Power.

MacMurray was not at all impressed with the sincerity of Sun's statement; quite the contrary. In a supplement, sent with the above cable, MacMurray gives his analysis of the situation which is cogent and interesting in view of the negotiations of the preceding two years on tariffs and those which were coming up shortly on extraterritoriality.

> It appears to be amply evident, from all the Chinese official and press references at the time to the matter, that in ousting the Russian staff it was the intention of the Chinese authorities to obtain possession and control of property and revenues of the Chinese Eastern Railway. The subsequent statements made by the Minister for Foreign Affairs and by the Minister of Rail-

ways that dismissing Soviet nationals was a means merely to suppress hostile propaganda, with no intention of prejudicing Russian legal rights in said railway, appear clearly to be a result of the realisation that maintaining publicly the position taken is not possible without discrediting the Chinese Government in the world's general opinion. Nevertheless, it remains to be seen if the Chinese Government, in direct negotiations with Russia, will yield any substantial part of its actual possession and control at present. [1]

At this point one becomes aware that what was bothering all the powers interested in China was the fact that she had confiscated foreign property. American public opinion had been very strongly pro-Chinese up to this point, even to the extent of practically condoning the numerous outrages against individual foreigners committed by Chinese nationalists during recent years. Yet now we find Secretary Stimson and Minister MacMurray playing an astute brand of politics almost unknown to American diplomacy, and nowhere is the head of the missionary raised in America. Why? In the period from 1925 to 1928 the missionaries had had vast influence in forming American opinion on Chinese affairs, as shown by Miss Borg. [2] Looking back today, it is incredible that the missionaries should have had such a great and such a questionable influence on American foreign policy in China. But now, in 1929, we see a change in the situation. None of the Great Powers was then inclined to favour Russia, and least of all America, who would not recognise her diplomatically for several years yet. At the same time we find all the powers in accord with the lead taken by America in forcing China to back down to Russia and restore the railway. One can explain the change partly at least by the transition from Coolidge and Kellogg to Hoover and Stimson. Both Coolidge and Kellogg were deeply religious by nature, and would have had a tendency to back the missionaries, if it did not cost them anything, especially if backing the missionaries proved popular, as well. Kellogg acted directly contrary to MacMurray's advice in the tariff negotiations with China and issued official statements which might be termed irresponsible from a diplomatic

---

[1] F.R.U.S., 1929, II, p. 246.
[2] Dorothy Borg, op. cit., pp. 68—82 et passim.

point of view, encouraging the Chinese in renewed demands while the propagandists fanned up the flames of anti-foreignism. Hoover and Stimson, on the other hand, were big business men; both were eminently practical and had a more realistic grasp of foreign affairs and diplomacy than their predecessors. Stimson, at least, was much less subject to pressure from any quarter than most of his predecessors. MacMurray, as mentioned, was greatly in favour of the new policy followed by Stimson, and had in fact laid down this policy in advice to Kellogg. It seems that it was generally recognised in 1929, that the missionaries had pulled far more than their weight in determining diplomatic policy in China in the past, and particularly in the past few years. There was general agreement among all concerned that this had not made for a wise policy, and the missionaries themselves were glad to drop into the background.

Meanwhile news filtering through from Russia indicated dissensions in high places on the policy to be pursued. On July 25th, Coleman, Minister in Latvia, reported that there was division in the Central Committee. At a meeting of this committee Radzutak had said that China, with the aid of England and Japan, had been preparing for war; the Politbureau had given the Soviet Government instructions to send China an ultimatum, and if the answer were not satisfactory, to recover the railway by force. The War Commissar said that the Chinese peasants would rise up against the Chinese government, since Russian tactics were defensive. Kalinin suggested a peaceful solution through external pressure on China. Smirnov, Smidovitch and Brukhanov all spoke along peaceful lines and said that war would upset the grain-stocking campaign and the internal situation in the Soviet Union, but Mikoyan said that the government could arrange for grain supplies to the army and to industrial centres, despite war. [1] Piatnitski saw a chance for a revolutionary uprising, overthrowing the Nationalist government; he declared that such an uprising was being prepared in south China, and that a war in the Far East was an excellent chance for revolution, especially as Russia was not the aggressor. [2] Resolutions were passed to take "needful measures to combat Chinese rapacity",

---

[1] F.R.U.S., 1929, II, p. 240.
[2] *Loc. cit.*

or organise protest demonstrations and to mobilise all organs in Siberia.

"Stalin" states the dispatch "is reported to be extremely annoyed by the speeches made by Smirnov, Smidovitch and Brukhanov, and the latter may be dismissed from the Political Bureau."

On July 25th, Johnson, Assistant Secretary of State, noted in a memorandum that the Japanese Ambassador had just been in and confirmed the report from Paris of Russia's refusal to accept French arbitration, but had said that it was emphasised by the Russian Ambassador in Tokyo, to Baron Shidehara, that Russia would not fight unless challenged by the Chinese. [1]

On July 25th, Stimson received an *aide mémoire* from the French Ambassador, [2] stating that the French Ambassador in Moscow thought the Russian refusal to accept mediation was due to increasing difficulties of internal policy. He said that the leaders, hoping to promote world revolution, were planning a huge demonstration for August 1st, pretending that Russia was acting in defence of the working classes against a war by imperialistic powers and hence could not admit the latters' peaceful intentions by accepting arbitration from one of them. He reported that the French Minister in China thought the Chinese would probably accept the *status quo ante* as a basis for discussion. In conversation, the French Ambassador told Stimson that he thought the present attitude of China in regard to the *status quo* was due to the effect of Stimson's talk with Wu.

On the same day Stimson read a memorandum [3] to the ambassadors of Britain, France, Italy and Japan, and the German Chargé d'Affaires, and gave a copy to each of them, requesting them to forward it to their respective governments. In the document he suggested that, if any one nation or individual suggested meditation, it might raise unfounded suspicion and suggested that they follow the same procedure as that used for Paraguay and Bolivia in the Chaco dispute, i.e., a full and honest inquiry into the facts of the case. He wanted the other countries, if they agreed,

---

[1] *Loc. cit.*
[2] *Op. cit.*, p. 241.
[3] See infra, p. 211.

to associate themselves with him in suggesting such a plan to China and Russia. [1]

The following day Wu informed Stimson that the Soviet Ambassador in Berlin had got in touch with the Chinese Minister and sounded him out on the question of meeting for negotiations. The Chinese Government had instructed the Berlin Legation to accept the offer. Stimson told Wu he was glad to see in the press that day C. T. Wang's statement disavowing any intention to seize the C.E.R., and declaring respect for private property and investment in China. [2]

It is clear that by this time the fear that China might injure vested interests in China had caused a shift in American opinion against her. It is rather ironical that it should have been a conflict with Russia, the arch-enemy of capitalism, which precipated this anti-Chinese feeling in the West. One would have thought that China would have been hailed as a great force of democracy for having "struck a blow against the Bolshevik peril". But the tide was now running fast against the pro-Chinese sentimentality of two years ago. The missionaries had led a movement which culminated under Kellogg in almost complete capitulation to every Chinese whim in the tariff agreement. The Chinese had attacked and mundered many foreigners in the interior and yet the missionary press and influence was so great at the time that this was completely overlooked. Congress outdid itself in advancing the "new deal to China", and hardly anywhere was a solitary voice raised against the Chinese nationalist outrages and the peremptory demands for treaty revision. For once not even the Hearst and McCormick press objected, where normally their jingoism would have sent them off into frenzies of rage at the abnegation of American rights. Not one voice was raised in Congress. Only the Shanghai Chamber of Commerce, a splinter missionary group, the *North China Daily News,* a British paper, and MacMurray, Minister to China, had had the courage to speak up and call a spade a spade. [3]

Suddenly the entire picture had changed. There was now a realistic and practical Secretary of State in Office who could

[1] F.R.U.S., 1929, I, pp. 242—4.

[2] *Op. cit.,* pp. 247—8.

[3] Borg, Dorothy, *op. cit.,* p. 259.

distinguish between religious emotionalism and his duty as cus-
todian of American interests. It is not possible to account for the
sudden change of attitude by any loss of face or prestige on the
part of the missionary pressure groups. This had not occurred. The
transformation can only be laid to a realistic policy on the part of
the State Department, for a change, and the growing alarm of
business men, who saw no sign of Chinese nationalist appetite being
sated with concessions.

The situation deteriorated rapidly and there was great international concern. On July 26th, the German Chargé, Leitner, came
to the Secretary of State and asked three questions concerning the
situation: [1]

> (1)   Whether or not Stimson had asked France to act as
> his agent in approaching Russia about arbitration with China,
> or whether France had acted on her own.

Stimson replied that France was not acting as his agent but was
co-operating and that he had called Claudel's attitude to the matter.

> (2)   Whether it was true that the United States had
> directly approached China only and not Russia also.

The answer was yes.

> (3)   Leitner said that Russia had led German officials to
> think that France had not conveyed any message to Russia,
> and asked Stimson for the details, whether it had been con-
> veyed in Paris or in Moscow.

Stimson explained. He also told Leitner that he had heard from
the American embassy in Germany that Russia was trying to convey
the idea to American newspaper men that there was trouble between
France and America. Such reports were being systematically fostered
from the Russian embassy in Germany. Stimson flatly denied this to
Leitner. He also told him that Wu had that day notified him
officially that the Russians had approached the Chinese Minister
in Berlin, asking if China would negotiate directly, that the Chinese
Minister had replied that she would, but had had no further word
from Russia on the matter.

The concern was not limited to breakdown of negotiations but

---

[1]   F.R.U.S., 1929, II, p. 248.

to Russian aggression and to the disparate military potential of the two protagonists. The American Naval Attaché, then at Harbin, sent a report on the relative strength of the two armies on the border, [1] the Chinese army poorly equipped in everything, averaging only fifty rounds of ammunition per man, while the Russians were a modern outfit, equipment not modern, but much better than the Chinese. Russia had about 50,000 troops, with another division on its way from Vladivostok, and was using airplanes.

Major John Magruder, Military Attaché in China, also made a most interesting and farsighted report, showing a keen analysis of the affair and what lay back of it. He pointed out the unethical motive of each country. From all the evidence at his disposal, he could not "avoid the conclusion, despite present official announcements, that the Chinese objective in their abrupt actions of July 10 and 11, was the complete recovery of the Chinese Eastern Railway and that only an unfavorable expression of world opinion and a menacing Soviet attitude forced an official renunciation of this objective and its replacement by demands for strict adherence to the Agreements of 1924." He said that it was inconceivable that the drastic steps taken at Harbin were taken by any Chinese official upon his own initiative. The Manchurian officials had for some time favoured seizure, the only difference of opinion being in methods of procedure. The foreign advisers, Donald and Ostroumoff, strongly favoured seizure and advocated it, but wanted it done in such a way that it would come within the framework of international law, and could be defended before world opinion. It was certain that Donald strongly advised against the methods pursued, but, now that it was done, tended to promote the official version that the Harbin authorities had acted on their own initiative. He added that the various attempts by Russia that year to negotiate on the outstanding difficulties had been rebuffed by the Chinese. He said that Nanking was closely informed about C.E.R. matters, at least since June, through Kao Chi-yi and that "this important official" was in Nanking at the time of the coup. Indications of deliberate policy were the significant meeting held in Peking between Chiang Kai-shek, Chang Hsüeh-liang and C. T. Wang

---

[1] Op. cit., p. 249.

on July 10, their hasty dispersal, the climax reached next day as a result of the Chinese actions at Harbin, and the very significant disappearence of Chang and Wang who remained under cover until after the affair had developed too far to stop it. This absence was only "an attempt to establish an alibi for some specific purpose." "The official declaration of the Mukden Government of July 22, 1929, was submitted to Nanking for approval prior to its release. The first official statements contained no censure of the Harbin officials." Magruder considered that the disruption of peace in the Far East had been made inevitable by Russia's insistence upon using a joint commercial enterprise to propagate her political ideas, and by China's determination to seize this joint enterprise, taking complete control and possession with scant regard to agreements, international practices and the responsibilities involved, through her "blundering or devious governmental mechanism." [1]

It was apparent to Stimson by this time that unless he took the lead in settling the dispute between the two powers, there would be open war, and he knew that, if this occurred, it might be impossible to limit it to the two countries and the area then concerned. He had already taken the initiative in circularizing the other Great Powers to sound them out about mediation or arbitration in the conflict and at first it had seemed as though his efforts were about to bear fruit. Both Russia and China had made declarations of peaceful intentions. All the governments approached had been hopeful, although Japan had, at the outset, been suspicious. All those countries and many others had a duty under the Briand-Kellogg Pact for the Renunciation of War to bring about a peaceful solution of the conflict. There seemed to be some justification for the optimistic attitude adopted by Stimson in a telegram to Schurman, Ambassador to Germany, on July 26, in which he said:

"It is especially gratifying to the other friendly Powers participating in the General Pact for the Renunciation of War that Russia and China have thus decided upon a course of action consistent with the principles underlying the Pact." [2]

On August 1, the First Secretary of the French Embassy notified

---

[1] Op. cit., pp. 251—2.
[2] Op cit., p. 250.

the State Department that he had just received a telegram from M. Briand stating that in Briand's opinion Stimson's suggestion was in every way in accordance with the Kellogg pact and that its basis was strong. He added that if China and Russia could not, between themselves, reach an accord, Stimson's note could be forwarded in accordance with the Kellogg pact, assuming that such transmission would be made with the approval of the principal powers interested in preserving peace in the Far East. [1]

In a conversation with Stimson on July 31, the French Ambassador handed the latter a report received from Paris which said that Karakhan had informed the French Ambassador in Moscow that there was not, and would not be, any negotiation with China until the latter restored the *status quo ante* of the C.E.R. The report also showed that the French Minister in Peking had assurances that the Minister of Communications had prepared regulations for the management of the C.E.R., but that if pressure were accentuated by Russia the regulations would be modified so that they would be more favourable to Russia. [2]

On July 30, [3] the Japanese Ambassador called on the Secretary of State and informed him that the Japanese Government greatly appreciated the effort which he had made to restore peace between Russia and China, and that Japan was willing to co-operate with the United States and other interested powers. He stated that it only remained for his Government to consider whether the Secretary's suggested plan offered the greatest hope of success. He pointed out that, if a proposal made by a third power or group of powers were rejected by either side, the nations would find themselves in a peculiarly embarrassing position. He stated that all information available in Tokyo indicated that the two disputant countries were anxious to compose their differences peacefully, and that neither side would welcome any initiative of a third power or group of powers. The Ambassador added that he presumed that none of the third powers were willing to follow up their suggestions with "material or effective pressure" to secure their acceptance, and

---

[1] *Op. cit.*, p. 264.
[2] *Op. cit.*, p. 262.
[3] *Op. cit.*, pp. 259—61.

the Japanese Government feared the repercussions of such an approach inside China and Russia. He concluded by saying that "recent reports ... are more reassuring, and the actual situation does not seem to call for any immediate action on the part of the Powers." Stimson in reply said that he had made it very clear that the "suggestion was not in the nature of a mediation ... but was intended as a suggestion of what was to be a voluntary action by China and Russia", and added:

> "... if the negotiations between Russia and China continued to go on I should take no further steps, but should reserve such action for any emergency which might occur on their failure to go on."

The Japanese Ambassador also informed Stimson that Tsai [1] was returning to meet Melnikov again and that the Japanese thought that this was the beginning of negotiations, but that nothing seemed to have come of the proposed conference in Berlin. [2] About this time, too, there broke out in the world press a rash of denials on the part of Russia that there were, or were about to be, any negotiations between the Russian Embassy and the Chinese Minister in Berlin. [3] There were many conflicting interests which might be held in uneasy equilibrium as long as the *status quo* was maintained, but which would be endangered if it were upset. Japan had too vital an interest and too much at stake in Manchuria to permit Russia, and especially a Communist Russia, to gain the ascendancy. On the other hand, Japan could not afford to have a strong and unified China with whom to have to deal as an equal. As long as China was weak and disunited, and torn by internal dissension, Japan could do much as she desired, and her hold upon Manchuria depended upon this.

France had a very large financial investment in the C.E.R. which she had written off as a total loss, but which she might recover if circumstances were propitious. On the other hand, France had to weigh the potentials against each other. Did she stand to gain more by trying to regain the railway investment at the risk of open

---

[1]   Chinese Commissioner of Foreign Affairs.
[2]   F.R.U.S., 1929, II, pp. 259—61.
[3]   *Op. cit.*, p. 262.

hostilities, which would almost certainly spread, and might well become another world-wide conflict, or did she stand to gain more in China, as it was, even in 1929, where treaty rights were still honoured, even though increasingly, in the breach?

There was no question where the interest of America and Great Britain lay. They had everything to gain by retaining the *status quo* in China, and everything to lose by permitting any other power to become disproportionately strong.

On July 26th, MacMurray notified Stimson [1] that C. T. Wang had stated that China was willing and prepared to start immediate negotiations with Russia to settle the issues involved. But the attitude of Russia was still in doubt. On July 29th, the French Ambassador informed Stimson that Russia had refused to accept Japan's good offices in settling the dispute, but that the Chinese Minister to Japan had informed the French Chargé d'Affaires that "direct and officious (sic) conversations between Russians and Chinese" had already started. [2] The Russian Ambassador had denied this. Furthermore the Soviet Commissariat for Foreign Affairs in a press release had denied that negotiations were in progress and stated that Russia was insisting upon fulfilment of the demands of July 13th, 1929, as a preliminary to any negotiations.

On July 29th, [3] Chang Hsüeh-liang sent a telegram to Karakhan, Acting Commissar for Foreign Affairs, proposing that:

(1) Each side should appoint representatives for a conference on the questions at issue with regard to the C.E.R.

(2) The prevailing situation on the C.E.R. be considered provisional, subject to regulation after the conference, on the basis of the Peking and Mukden agreements.

(3) All citizens of the U.S.S.R. arrested by China should be released and deported to Russia and all Chinese citizens arrested in Russia should also be released.

This communication resulted from an official discussion between Melnikov and Tsai, after which the latter went to Mukden to report to Chang.

MacMurray reported to the Secretary of State that on the

---

[1] *Op. cit.,* p. 250.

[2] *Op. cit.,* p. 257.

[3] *Op. cit.,* p. 258.

30th, [1] the first Sino-Soviet talks had been held at Manchuli, with Melnikov representing Russia and Tsai representing China, adding that it was understood that the time and place for a formal conference was the main point of discussion.

The following day [2] MacMurray cabled Stimson that American Press correspondents at Manchuli reported that Li and Tsai had met Soviet representatives at the frontier on the preceding day and agreed to appoint delegates to negotiate on the C.E.R. dispute. Tsai was quoted as stating that the Russian ultimatum was withdrawn automatically, that delegates would probably be named within the week and would meet at Harbin, and that Moscow had ordered a cessation of Soviet military demonstrations along the border.

However, just at the moment when it seemed that things might be settled peaceably, the situation took a turn for the worse. Karakhan sent a message to Chang Hsüeh-liang [3] repeating all the previous Soviet patter and adding new charges of bad faith. According to Karakhan's version of events, Melnikov had first received Tsai at the latter's request and Tsai had declared that he had just come from Mukden and had been authorised by the Mukden government to make the following proposals:

"(1) The arrested Soviet laborers and employees are to be released.

(2) The government of the U.S.S.R. is to appoint the director of the Chinese Eastern Railway, and his assistant.

(3) A conference of representatives of both governments is to be called, which is to settle the conflict on the Chinese Eastern Railway as speedily as possible.

(4) The Soviet government may make the statement that it does not recognize the order of things prevailing after the conflict, and that it does not prejudice the impending negotiations, and

(5) If the Soviet Government agrees to these proposals, Mr. Chang Hsüeh-liang will apply for the consent of the Nanking Government to these proposals."

---

[1] *Op. cit.*, p. 264.
[2] *Op. cit.*, p. 265.
[3] *Op. cit.*, pp. 265—7.

Karakhan went on to say that Melnikov had declined to discuss the matter, pointing out that he was not authorised to do so, but that at Mr. Tsai's insistence, he had forwarded the proposals to Moscow, and that Russia, "guided by its pacific policy, and not wishing to leave unused even this possibility of settling the conflict by means of an agreement", had sent the following reply:

"(a)   After the high-handed actions on the part of the Chinese authorities on the Chinese Eastern Railway, the Union government is unable to treat with confidence the proposals emanating from the Mukden Government through the medium of the Commissioner of Foreign Affairs, Mr. Tsai.

(b)   In the event, however, that the Nanking Government or the Mukden Government should officially make to the government of the U.S.S.R. the proposals submitted as emanating from Mr. Chang Hsüeh-liang, to wit:

1. Release of the arrested Soviet laborers and employees;

2. Appointment, by the government of the U.S.S.R. of the director of the Chinese Eastern Railway, and of his assistant;

3. Calling of conference with a view to settling the conflict on the Chinese Eastern Railway with the least delay;

and if, in addition to this, item 4 of the proposal of the Mukden Government will be altered in the following way:

Both sides agree that the situation which has formed itself on the Chinese Eastern Railway after the conflict is bound to be altered in conformity with the Peking and Mukden agreements of 1924,

the Union government will adopt a favorable attitude to these proposals."

Karakhan pointed out that this message was delivered to Tsai by Melnikov on July 25, and that on July 30th, Tsai arrived at Manchuli and asked for a meeting with Melnikov, to hand him a new note from Mukden, which he did on August 1. But, according to Karakhan, the terms of the Chinese reply were different from those offered at the outset by Tsai on Chang's behalf in two important respects: (1) the new note failed to include appointment of the General Manager of the C.E.R. and his Assistant by the U.S.S.R.; (2) Instead of the proposal made by Russia that the *status ante quo* be restored, in conformity with the Peking and Mukden agreements, China now proposed legalisation of the prevailing state of affairs. After accusing the Mukden Government of bad faith and of frustrating the possibility of settling the conflict by agreement, Karakhan closes on an ominous note:

> "This creates a situation pregnant with new and serious complications, the whole responsibility for which wholly and fully rests with the Mukden and Nanking Government(s)." [1]

On August 5, [2] MacMurray notified Stimson that negotiations at Manchuli were continuing, but said that he had no authentic information about them. The Japanese Chargé had informed him that an agreement had been reached to withdraw troops from the frontier and to resume operation of the trains from China to Russia.

MacMurray also reported that Karakhan, in an interview with the Japanese Ambassador in Moscow on July 30, had informed him that the Chinese Minister in Berlin had approached the Soviet representative with an offer to negotiate, but that this had been rejected, since, if the Chinese were sincere, they could telegraph Moscow direct, hence there was no need for intervention or mediation by third Powers.

This is one of the most revealing documents in the mass of papers on the Sino-Russian conflict. It shows clearly what any one following the course of events thus far must long have known, namely, that Russia feared above all things third-power intervention, and was willing to do almost anything to avoid it. She realised that, if third Powers once started intervening, they would not likely stop at the question of the C.E.R. Quite obviously she had not forgotten the Polar Bear Expedition, and under no circumstances would she have a recurrence of it, if she could avoid it.

On August 1, 1929, the State Department received from Mac-Murray a digest of an article printed in the *North China Standard* at Peking purporting to be a press interview with Sun Fo, Minister of Railways, in which he set forth "China's irreducible minimum" in negotiations with Russia. After stating that Russia dared not go to war with China because of her international isolation and internal difficulties, and saying that the indications pointed to an early

---

[1] F.R.U.S., 1929, II, p. 267.
[2] *Op. cit.*, p. 272.

opening of direct negotiations, he went on to say that while the form which the negotiations would take had not been determined, he foresaw three possible outcomes: 1. Complete restoration of the ownership and operation of the line to China, 2. Joint ownership but right of administration restored to China, 3. No change in the state of affairs existing before China recently took over control.

He said that, if the first possibility were not realised at the time, it should be the ultimate goal, and that the second as a temporary solution was the greatest possible concession China would consider, adding that past experience had shown that joint control could not be satisfactory to the Chinese people. He expressed his hope that the Chinese people would stand solidly back of their government in the present difficulty and concluded by saying that the Chinese Government was opposed to the joint methods of the other powers because they feared that it would end in international control of the railway. [1]

One sees here a typical example of Chinese diplomacy, putting up a colossal bluff and assuming or hoping that it will not be called. Sun Fo was whistling in the dark. The internal disequilibrium of China at the time is well shown by just such uncorrelated statements by Ministers who were presumably speaking with the authority of the Government behind them. Many of the statements made were totally irresponsible, although those making them were in responsible positions. One must remember that at the very time Sun Fo was talking in this way, the Chinese Ministers in Washington and Berlin were supplicating for intercession, Wang, the Foreign Minister, was giving out conflicting statements, and Chang Hsüeh-Liang was doing everything in his power to make a settlement of the outstanding issues with Russia, with or without the blessing of the Nanking Government.

---

[1] *Op. cit.*, p. 263.

CHAPTER VII

RUSSIAN INVASION OF CHINA

On August 8th, [1] MacMurray notified Stimson that General Boldyreff had been appointed Commander of the Soviet Army of occupation and Beykker, former director of the railway, Chief of Staff in China. From this it can be seen that Russia was early prepared to take military action and evidently at this time had decided upon invasion.

The first real Russian military action appears to have taken place on August 17th, though even before that time there had been reports of local raids and there had certainly been demonstrations with Soviet aircraft flying over Chinese territory and guns firing across the border. But the actual invasion which went on from August 17th, [2] to the middle of December, penetrating deeply into Manchuria, followed the deadlock in negotiations caused by Karakhan's rejection of Chang Hsüeh-liang's proposals for settlement at the beginning of August. Tsai and Li, the delegates sent to Manchuria Station, returned to Harbin on August 15th, having failed to make contact with any Soviet representatives, and Hanson, the Consul at Harbin, in a report to MacMurray dated August 16th, [3] stated:

> "The situation at present is deadlocked. General Chang Tso Hsiang of Kirin, the outstanding leader in Manchuria, does not want war. Neither, really, does the Soviet side, but its intimidating actions on the frontier might precipitate graver troubles at any time." [4]

Hanson, however, as events showed, was too optimistic in supposing that the Russians did not really want war. If they did not want real hard fighting, they, at any rate, were willing to do as much as was necessary to put to flight the low grade Chinese troops

---

[1] F.R.U.S., 1929, II, p. 274.

[2] Op. cit., p. 285.

[3] Op. cit., pp. 278—284.

[4] Op. cit., p. 283.

who defended the Manchurian frontier and thus force Mukden to accept the terms laid down by Moscow. The Chinese had an absurdly high estimate of their own fighting capacity, but the Russians had taken their measures and knew that it would be a walkover.

On August 18th, MacMurray forwarded to Stimson a wire from the Consul at Mukden: "August 17th, noon. Have learned confidentially that a telegram has been received by the government this morning that Soviet troops started bombarding Manchuria Station 3 o'clock this morning." The Consul sent another message the same day announcing the receipt by the Manchurian Government of an official telegram stating that 10,000 Soviet troops with "30 field pieces and machine guns crossed the border and attacked between Manchuli and Chalainor". [1] Fifty Chinese soldiers had been killed on the same afternoon when a clash occurred between Chinese and Soviet troops near Manchuria Station, [2] the Soviets using heavy artillery and aircraft at both places... On the 19th, Dr. Wang announced that the Foreign Ministry had not thus far received official reports of the Russian invasion, but added: "We are determined to resist to the limit of our ability if these raids continue for unless we are in the grip of the Communists or are conquered by them we must fight our invaders, and" he said, "China remains firm". [3] He said that the Russian associate managers of the C.E.R. could not be reinstated prior to negotiations between China and Russia and that "China's only course is for the entire nation to unite and resist Red imperialism or perish in the grip of Communism". [4]

On August 19th, [5] China notified the signatories of the Treaty for the Renunciation of War that, if Soviet aggression resulted in war through China's determination to defend her own interests and national rights, the responsibility for violation of world peace would lie with Russia, with whom China was willing to discuss and settle

---

[1] *Op. cit.*, p. 285.
[2] *Loc. cit.*
[3] *Op. cit.*, pp. 285—6.
[4] *Op. cit.*, p. 286.
[5] *Op. cit.*, pp. 288—92.

the difficulties at any time. On the 20th, [1] Wu called Stimson's attention to Russia's attacks upon China and stated that Chinese troops had been ordered to limit their actions to self-defence. He stated that he had been instructed by his Government to bring to the notice of the American Government the Russian violation of Chinese territory resulting in Chinese casualties. He cited a report from Chang Hsüeh-liang dated August 19th, which stated that "the Russians, having designs on Delainor in order to cut the Chinese (Eastern) Railway between Manchuli and Hailar, had made an attack ... upon Delainor ... On the morning of the 17th at the Delainor mines Russian forces opened artillery attack which was still going on at the date of the report". Wu stated that he had communicated directly with Chang who had told him that there were repeated Russian incursions across the line, but that "he was keeping his troops in control pursuant to instructions from Nanking". [2]

On the 18th, [3] the Chinese forces were on the point of evacuating from Taheiho and "raiding parties, presumably Soviet, are crossing the Amur and pillaging on Chinese side". As the Russians started crossing the Amur, the fighting spread. On the night of the 17th, [4] there was fighting at Tungning, "which was evacuated next morning upon the arrival of 1,400 Russian cavalry and infantry with artillery and machine guns. Russians were through this morning upon appearance Chinese reinforcements. Telegraphic and radio communication with Suifenho interrupted last night". It was reported that Russian troops had withdrawn from Chalainor. It seemed that they were raiding Chinese territory and seizing foodstuffs rather than attempting occupation of territory. [5]

It is obvious that Russia was feeling her way, by these incursions into Chinese territory, to learn what the actual resistance would be and whether or not it would be wise for her to undertake a large-scale operation. So far, there had been mere pinpricks, thrusts and withdrawals, but, make no mistake about it, this was as much war

---

[1] Op. cit., pp. 293—4.
[2] Loc. cit.
[3] Op. cit., p. 294.
[4] Op. cit., p. 295.
[5] Loc. cit.

as Japan's later invasion of Manchuria would be. The difference
between the Russian and Japanese invasions was one of degree
rather than of kind.

On August 20th, [1] it was reported from Pogranichnaya that
regular Soviet troops had occupied Tungning. The Chinese Commissioner at Taheiho telegraphed Consuls complaining of the Russian incursion into Chinese territory, which was, he pointed out,
a violation of international law. Russia, on her side, evidently
realized that her aggression in China was causing world-wide
discussion, for on the 21st, she came out with a statement accusing
China of attacking Soviet citizens and of invading Russian territory. [2] It claimed that the Russians had, at first, refrained from
taking counter-measures as a result of these "raids" and "attacks
on Soviet territory", which "have gained in frequency causing many
killed and wounded on the Soviet side". The statement added that
"the various crossings of the border by the Red Army were the
results of raids on Soviet territory made by Russian White Guards
and Chinese detachments". Russia demanded that China disarm
the White Guards and stop attacks by Chinese forces; "otherwise
the guilt of further complications caused by new raids will be
entirely on the Nanking and Mukden Governments". [3]

As Russia persistently claimed that her military action was only
undertaken in self-defence, and repeated this defence later in her
uncompromising reply to the American note of December 3rd, 1929,
on the obligations of the Kellogg Pact, it must be asked whether
there was any substance to these charges. There has, in fact, never
been any evidence of serious incursion either of Chinese or of White
Russian forces into Soviet territory during this period. This does
not exclude the possibility that there may have been one or two
raids by small bands, for much of northern Manchuria was wild
country and control over outlying areas was very loose. Among
the Russian exiles in Manchuria there were always some who would
take any chance to be avenged on the hated Bolsheviks. But there
was certainly no organized invasion of Soviet territory similar to

---

[1] *Op. cit.*, p. 296.
[2] *Loc. cit.*
[3] *Loc. cit.*

that which the Russians now started, and the Chinese had no possible motive for doing anything of the kind; even if they had intended to confiscate the Russian interest in the C.E.R., the C.E.R. was in their own territory and there was no need to invade Siberia to take over a railway in China. The Russians, on the other hand, had the purpose of forcing the Chinese to accept their terms in settlement of the C.E.R. controversy and their invasion of Man- churia was clearly designed for this end. When China submitted to the Russian terms, the Russian troops were withdrawn and nothing more was heard about the alleged attacks on Siberia. These charges were no more than excuses to cover a deliberate aggression, and it was, indeed, a fundamental weakness of the Kellogg Pact that it left it open for any aggressive power to say that it was not "using war as an instrument of national policy", but merely defending itself against attack — as Japan also claimed in 1931. Without some provision for deciding who is the aggressor, a promise not to be aggressive has no value, for any thug can say "He hit me first". The Kellogg Pact made no provision for identifying the aggressor, and when China proposed a neutral commission for fixing the responsibility for the frontier incidents, Russia naturally rejected the proposal.

On the 22nd, [1] it was reported that the Soviet troops had seized and burned half the town of Tungning. A general attack for the purpose of cutting the railway was feared. This would prevent evacuation of Chinese civilians and cause a panic. Soviet aircraft had appeared over the Muling coalmines. It could now be said that Russia had extended her military operations. It seemed that she was attempting to cause a shutdown of the mines, hence preventing delivery of coal to the railways and interrupting service, in order to disrupt business and intimidate the people to the point where they would bring pressure upon the government to settle with Russia.

The Japanese Chargé d'Affaires, Horinouchi, informed Mac- Murray that Karakhan had stated on the 16th, [2] in a discussion with the Japanese Ambassador at Moscow, "that the Soviet Govern- ment had no intention of invading Chinese territory and that it was for the present simply watching developments". It seemed according

---

[1] F.R.U.S., 1929, II, 298.

[2] Op. cit., p. 299.

to this Japanese version, that both Russia and China were seeking a way out of the impasse. The Chinese Minister at Berlin had had a conference with an official of the German Foreign Office, looking for an arrangement for informal negotiations. These had been refused by Russia, who feared the misinterpretation of such, as evidence of the willingness on its part to hold unconditional negotiations without a return to the *status quo ante*.

On the 20th, [1] the Chinese Minister at Washington reported to Stimson that Soviet troops had bombarded Dalainor apparently with the purpose of cutting railway communications between Man-chuli and Hailar. Nanking had given instructions that a calm attitude should be maintained and that defensive measures only should be taken. The Chinese Minister informed him that China was determined that the new general manager of the C.E.R. should not be Russian.

But Russia was now prodding China by military aggression into remembering that Russia still demanded settlement on her own terms. On September 3rd, American correspondents reported from Manchuria Station that Soviet troops had again invaded Chinese territory and shelled Chinese outposts. [2] On the 8th, Soviet aircraft were reported to have bombarded the railway station at Suifenho. The correspondents felt that the situation in Manchuria was grave. [3] They reported destruction by bombing of railway tracks and cars and the wounding of Chinese soldiers. Later unconfirmed reports said that the entire railway station had been destroyed. On the 9th, this fact was confirmed. [4] On the 11th, Wang an-nounced that the "renewal of Soviet attacks on Chinese border towns..." would show that "China had made adequate preparation and that, if Russia were set on provoking conflict, the Chinese army would not hesitate to defend the country against Red aggression". He added that "by renewing its campaign of blood and intimidation the Soviet government had shown the world that its (word) could not be trusted". [5]

---

[1] *Op. cit.*, p. 293.
[2] *Op. cit.*, p. 313.
[3] *Op. cit.*, p. 315.
[4] *Op. cit.*, p. 316.
[5] *Op. cit.*, p. 318.

Each time Russia made an aggressive military move she began by announcing to the world that Soviet territory had been attacked by the Chinese. Upon this new outbreak of Soviet aggression Russia handed the German Ambassador in Moscow a statement requesting him to transmit it to Mukden and Nanking. This statement claimed that there had "been nineteen new cases of attack on Soviet territory ... for which (the Soviet Government) lays full responsibility on the Nanking and Mukden governments". Soviet troops had been forced "in self-defence to take firm retaliatory action to protect the frontier and the peaceful population". In an ominous warning to China the message concludes: "painful consequences may take place in case of new provocative attacks by Chinese troops and Russian White Guards". [1]

On the 1st and 2nd of October, [2] there was a new Soviet attack on Manchuria Station. Soviet planes bombed the town, but after a short fight the Russians withdrew. On the 4th, Hanson, [3] Consul at Harbin, made a long report on the conflict around Manchuria Station. After reciting the facts of the Russian attacks he added: "It is possible that the Soviet side, which wishes Manchuria to suffer economically, saw that Chinese merchants were returning to Manchuria station to resume business and desired by military demonstration to drive them away again". At any rate there was another exodus of merchants. Hanson concluded: "It also may be that these Soviet troops have become restless on account of dissatisfaction and lack of action, so that their officers thought it might be advantageous, as far as morale was concerned, to let them attack the Chinese positions". On October 8th, 1929, [4] Hanson wired Mac-Murray: "Reliably informed Soviet regulars or partisans recently killed unarmed male inhabitants White Cossack villages .. Heilungkiang Province, reasons unknown, possibly provocation to cause White indignation against the Red". On the 16th, [5] it was reported that Lahasusu was captured by Soviet forces following heavy fighting in which artillery and aerial bombardment were

---

[1] *Loc. cit.*
[2] *Op. cit.*, p. 323.
[3] *Op. cit.*, p. 324.
[4] *Op. cit.*, p. 325.
[5] *Op. cit.*, p. 327.

used, together with naval units. On the 28th, [1] the Vice-Consul at Harbin verified the fighting at Lahasusu through a foreign captain of a ship on the Amur who was present at the bombardment; in fact his own ship was shelled. This was a major engagement with heavy losses on both sides. In a memorandum Lilliestrom, Vice-Consul at Harbin, recorded:

The sea captain, who has just returned from Lahasusu, dropped in this morning. He was in the midst of the Soviet shelling, and 46 Chinese soldiers were killed on his steamer. He gave me the following story.

On October 12th, at 5.30 in the morning, heavy artillery fire was started from the Soviet flotilla against the Chinese fleet and land positions at Lahasusu. The signal for firing was given by the Soviet gunboat *Liebknecht*. At 6.10 in the morning the Chinese gunboats *Chantai* and *Chanan* were sunk. At 6.20 a fire broke out on the Chinese gunboat *Chianping*, which sank at 6.40. At 7.05 the big former German, now Chinese, gunboat *Lichi* was abandoned by its crew and taken in tow by the Russians. It was subsequently brought to Habarovsk. Seven barges, formerly belonging to the Chinese Eastern Railway, were also captured by the Soviet forces, as well as army transport steamer No. 18. These were also taken to Habarovsk. The Soviet gunboats participating in the attack were: *Liebknecht, Kalmuk, Batrak, Arachanin* and *Lenin*. On the *Kalmuk* was killed the Chief of the Amur River Fleet, as well as 16 men. The Soviet side lost no gunboats, steamers or barges, nor any airplanes.

On October 13th at 8.45 in the morning the Chinese troops stationed at and near Lahasusu retreated in complete disorder to Fuchin, 45 versts distant. Soviet infantry and cavalry detachments pursued the retreating Chinese troops and killed great numbers with shrapnel fired from light artillery pieces. The Chinese troops completely robbed all the stores in Fuchin, and through their actions there were casualties among the civilian population of that town.

The Soviet detachments were brought to the Chinese shore in eight barges towed by the S.S. *Krasny* (Krasnoie?) *Vimpel* and landed seven versts from Lahasusu on the Amur bank.

On October 14th and 15th the above barges were loaded with military stores, including 6 $3\frac{1}{2}''$ and 1 $6''$ guns, 4 machine guns and 346 riffles, Russian model, left behind by

---

[1] *Op. cit.*, pp. 337—8.

the Chinese troops. The Soviets also captured two barges loaded with ammunition and dynamite. From the mill at Lahasusu were taken 74,000 poods of wheat flour belonging to the winter reserve supplies of the Chinese forces, On (sic) the barges were also loaded large quantities of potatoes, cabbage, etcetera, stored by the military. The Chinese coolies engaged for this work were paid 6 chervonetz roubles per day. These coolies and the rest of the civilian population were not harmed by the Soviet troops.

On October 16th and 17th the above work of loading stores was continued. On the 16th a meeting was held, and those Chinese who so desired were invited to join the red army and proceed to Habarovsk. My informant did not know whether or not any volunteers came forward. On the same day at 5 P.M. the *Krasnoie Vimpel* took on board 172 hastily made board coffins with dead Soviet soldiers. At five o'clock in the evening of October 17th the red troops left Lahasusu, and only two Soviet gunboats were left at the mouth of the Sungari $3\frac{1}{2}$ verst from Lahasusu.

The Soviet casualties were 275 men killed or wounded, while the Chinese casualties were 964 killed or wounded, including 148 sailors from the gunboats and 225 marines killed.

On October 19th several Soviet airplanes appeared over Fuchin, and sunk with bombs the Chinese gunboat *Lisui.* By orders of Admiral Shen there were sunk at a place called Shalbatai, 5 versts below Fuchin, army transport steamer *Lochin* and three barges, in order to prevent the Soviet fleet from sailing up the Sungari River.

At the present time 16 steamers are held at Fuchin by order of Admiral Shen. On these steamers are Chinese land troops, which, in case Fuchin is taken by the Soviets, will be immediately transported on to Harbin. The number of the Chinese troops in that neighborhood is approximately 3,000.

On November 1st, [1] the Consul at Harbin notified MacMurray that Soviet aircraft had bombed Fuchin which was now rumoured to be in Soviet hands. Communications between Fuchin and La-hasusu were cut. He reported that Soviet gunboats were lurking in the vicinity. He concluded that a freight train had been blown up early that morning. On the 4th, [2] the Consul reported that Fuchin had been in the hands of the Russians for some days but had been

---

[1] F.R.U.S., 1929, II, p. 342.
[2] *Loc. cit.*

recaptured by the Chinese. The fighting and the naval action had
been serious; "this raid and loss of practically entire Chinese gunboat fleet" had caused panic and depression.

On November 18th, [1] heavy fighting was again reported beyond
Manchuria Station by the Consul at Harbin. He said that "Soviet
planes bombed, November 16, railway line between Tsagan, 61
kilometres from Manchuria Station, and Chalainor". Communications were broken. There was no longer any railway traffic
in that section further than Hailar. "Unconfirmed reports state
heavy fighting last two days Manchuria Station which practically
destroyed and that Chalainor coal mines ruined." "On 19th, [2] a
large number Soviet planes reached Mutanchiang, 191 kilometres
from Pogranichnaya." It was reported that they had destroyed
the Chinese depot there, where fourteen planes were stored. On
the 19th, the Consul reported again heavy air raids on Chalainor,
Tsagan and railway lines "of which 30 kilometres destroyed between
Chalainor and Hailar and at Mutanchiang, confirm. "On 17th [3]
passenger train fired upon, held up, and robbed near Tsagan by
Red irregulars". On the 20th, [4] the Consul at Mukden reported that
"twenty seven Soviet aircraft are reported to have dropped more
than 300 bombs which did much damage; fighting still continues,
with Chinese forces reported to be generally holding their positions".
On the 21st, Wu held a long discussion with Johnson on the above
reports. He was really making indirect enquiries as to what international action should be taken against Russia for her aggression.
He mentioned the League Covenant and the Kellogg Pact. On the
same day the Russians captured Manchuli and Chalainor.

On the 22nd, [5] there was a further report of damage caused by
Soviet aerial bombardment in the same districts. The Chalainor
mines and electric plant machinery had been destroyed "resulting
in the flooding of mines and drowning of hundreds employees who
had taken refuge underground". It seemed that this was now an
all-out drive by Russia. The Consul reported annihilation of

---

[1] *Op. cit.*, p. 344.
[2] *Loc. cit.*
[3] *Loc. cit.*
[4] *Op. cit.*, pp. 344—5.
[5] *Op. cit.*, p. 346.

four echelons of Chinese forces by Soviet aerial bombing. Communications were cut and many towns had fallen into Russian
hands. The Russians were trying to destroy coal mines and utilities.
The Argun River was now frozen, making it possible for the Russians to attack as they pleased; "later reports indicate that Chinese
inhabitants have withdrawn from Manchuria Station to the empty
shores of Lake Chalainor pursued by Red forces and that entire
district between Manchuria Station and Horhonte is in Red hands".
On November 26th, [1] Kelley, Chief of the Division of Eastern
European Affairs, drew up a memorandum in which he stated that
the Soviet forces east of Lake Baikal were organised into a " 'special
Far Eastern army' and consist of two army corps (3 rifle divisions,
1 cavalry brigade, 30—35 airplanes each) with a total strength
of about 113.000 men. Before the seizure of the ... railway the
troops in this region numbered about 34,000." He reported that
there had been also 7,000 OGPU troops and added the information
that the commander of this army was General Vassily Blucher who,
under the name of Galens, was military adviser to the Chinese
nationalists at the time that Borodin was political adviser".

On November 30th, [2] the Consul at Harbin reported that Soviet
planes had bombed Buketu, but that the panic among the Chinese
had apparently not been as great or disastrous as that at Hailar.
It seems that this was Russia's last aggressive action before China's
capitulation. China was rapidly succumbing and the affair was
virtually all over except for the signing—on Russia's terms. China
had indeed been asking for trouble by her own obstreperous and
irresponsible action, but the fact remained that she had been forced
to her knees by open warfare in defiance of the recently signed
Kellogg Pact by one of its signatories and with the acquiescence,
if not approval, of the other signatories.

---

[1]   Op. cit., p. 352.
[2]   Op. cit., p. 365.

CHAPTER VIII

STIMSON CONVOKES THE KELLOGG PACT

As we have already seen, it was realised by responsible statesmen of all nations as early as July that, unless action were taken,
the Sino-Russian conflict would eventuate in war. It was realised
that because of the combustible situation and the many conflicting
interests, an armed struggle probably could not be localised and
might easily result in another world war. For those who had any
doubt that there was a danger of war, Karakhan's ultimatum of July
13th, should have been a warning. Superficially, indeed, the demands
were not unreasonable, and Russia did not immediately take
action on the expiry of the ultimatum. But the next important
development was Karakhan's statement that Russia intended to
force the issue and the subsequent moving of troops by both sides
towards the border. As we have seen, China saw fit to ignore the
Soviet ultimatum and continued to take over the C.E.R. administration. The situation was made worse by the note, in which
China shifted the entire onus for the seizure on to Russian shoulders
by the charges and accusations which she made.

Stimson had taken the lead in attempting to settle the dispute in
conversations with the British, Japanese and French Ambassadors
and the Chinese Minister. He had pointed out the threat to world
peace and the responsibility of all nations signatory or adherent to
the Treaty for the Renunciation of War (the Kellogg Pact) to do
all in their power to preserve peace. He had, in effect, proposed
that one of the signatory powers holding diplomatic relations with
both Russia and China (of which America was not one) approach
the two nations with a view to getting them to settle their differences
by arbitration. He pointed out that the problem was highly justice-
able and that there was no need to proceed to a solution by force
of arms. In his discussion with Wu he had observed that Chinese
action in the case of the C.E.R. was being interpreted abroad as
an attack on private property. Stimson had considered the matter

serious enough to request MacMurray to delay his annual leave
and as an indication of the concern with which statesmen in other
countries viewed this situation we may cite Briand's cables to
Stimson approving the steps which he had taken in the matter.

Stimson's next move was to call in Wu and try to persuade him,
as we have already seen, of the wisdom of issuing a statement
showing China's willingness "to lay its case before the public
opinion of the world and submit to impartial arbitration or mediation". [1] Stimson emphasised to him in this conversation that
America, traditionally a friend of China, "was anxious not to see
her alienating public opinion on this question" and pointed out to
him "that public opinion had now been alienated both by the appearance which had been given that she had deliberately sought to
seize this railroad and by the truculent statements which were being
given out by her public officials". Stimson implied that he considered
these statements indicated "a non-peaceful attitude and that the
seizure had been deliberate, was justifiable and was a step towards
other seizures". [2]

It soon became clear from the response of Britain and France
that they were favourable towards the action which Stimson urged.
Conversations with the French and British Ambassadors on the
20th and 21st, completely verified their sympathies with the plan.
In line with this plan, France had made an offer of meditation to
both countries on July 19th, but Karakhan, on July 23rd, while
expressing Russia's appreciation, had declared the offer to be
without basis since China refused to restore the *status quo ante*. [3]
The following day Briand sent for Armour, American Chargé in
Paris, and told him that he had just seen both the Soviet and Chinese Ministers. He stated that "the Chinese Minister had expressed
his country's willingness to arbitrate and to abide by its obligations
under the peace pact", [4] but he added that the Soviet Ambassador,
who seemed to be uninformed concerning his country's views on the
matter, "had expressed the opinion that the Soviet Government

---

[1] F.R.U.S., 1929, II, p. 223.
[2] *Loc. cit.*
[3] *Op. cit.*, pp. 231—2.
[4] *Op. cit.*, p. 239.

could not consider arbitration until the Chinese had restored matters to the *status quo ante*". Briand remarked to Armour that this
would actually amount to a complete surrender on the part of
China, leaving nothing to arbitrate, and added that he had "impressed upon the Soviet Ambassador the ever-present danger of an
explosion unless something were done immediately to relieve the
present tension". The steady progress towards war was being
continued by the passing of resolutions at the meeting of the Com-
nunist Party's Central Committee on July 17th, requiring the Soviet
Government to take military action against China.

By now it was a foregone conclusion that Russia was giving
China the alternative of war or settling for the *status quo ante* on
the C.E.R. In fact the Russian Ambassador in Tokyo had told
Shidehara that the reason for his country's refusal to accept the
French proposal for mediation was the fact that the return to the
status quo ante was not provided for in this proposal.

It must be remembered that at this time Russia was in the throes
of the greatest crisis she had faced since the Revolution. The country
was being held together largely by the secret police and by wholesale deportations and shifting of populations. This was the period
of the liquidation of the Kulaks, the sturdy and independant peasant
owners who were the backbone of Russia. It was a period of horror
in Russia, accompanied by widespread famine. The Soviet Government needed a diversion. It was imperative, if possible, to distract
the attention of the populace away from the blunders and failures
of the Communists and centre it upon some foreign enemy, so as to
whip up a nationalist sentiment. Without this the regime was in
great danger, for even a secret police army cannot for long hold
down 180,000,000 people, suffering as the Russians were at this
time, however patient and long-suffering and inured to hardship
and privation. In these circumstances, it can be understood that
nothing short of absolute surrender on the part of China would
satisfy Russia, because in this case war would be a blessing in
disguise to her. She had nothing to lose and everything to gain.

These facts were borne out in the *aide mémoire* cited above,
which was handed to Stimson by the French Ambassador on July
25th. The Ambassador at the time expressed his belief that China's
tractability in agreeing to accept "the return of the status quo"

mentioned in the foregoing dispatch was due to Stimson's actions and "to the effect of (his) talk with Minister Wu". These remarks referred to the French document, which reported:

> "The Chinese Minister of Foreign Affairs made a new declaration on July 23rd, stating that the Chinese Government had not seized the railway, had no intention to do so, and that the rights of the Russians were still intact.
>
> The French Minister in China thinks that the Government of Nanking would probably accept the return to the *status quo* prior to a general discussion of the question".

The Ambassador's closing remark, "It is impossible for you to appreciate the extent of the influence which your country wields in these matters", was ironical in the extreme, because, as a matter of fact, "the extent of the influence" was being *wielded* to force China to knuckle under to Russia, to back the stronger against the weaker power.

It might be said that in pressing China to yield unconditionally, an example was being set for aggressors, of which advantage would very shortly be taken by three other nations, after they had learned in the present case that force might be employed with impunity. Here we have jumped another high hurdle on the road leading to the Second World War and to Pearl Harbour. But at that time pacifism was in fashion, and people still believed in international honour. America, although she had refused to join the League of Nations, had in the past few years become an adherent of the idea of international co-operation for the prevention of war, provided that she could pursue an independent course and reserve for herself *freedom of action*. This policy was now being put to the test.

Stimson's next move was the drafting of a plan for conciliation which he hoped to carry out in possible joint action with other interested powers. As we have seen, he read an *aide mémoire* to the British, French, Italian and Japanese Ambassadors and the German Chargé, and handed each a copy, adding: "I venture to present these suggestions for your consideration, since I am sure that the nations which you represent, all earnestly desirous of peace, will wish to be prepared to take any helpful initiative should this

prove necessary in the maintenance of peace between China and
Russia". [1] The following is the text of the proposal:

> Pending the investigation mentioned below both countries
> agree to commit no act of hostility against the other country
> or its nationals and to prevent their armed forces from crossing
> the boundaries of their respective countries.
>
> Pending such investigation the regular operation of the
> Chinese Eastern Railway will be restored and carried on, the
> interests of both Russia and China in said railway being
> guarded by the appointment as President and General Manager
> with full powers, of a prominent national of some neutral
> country approved by both China and Russia, and by the
> recognition and continuance in their respective positions as
> directors under the agreement of May 31st, 1924, of the five
> Russian and the five Chinese appointees.
>
> Pending such investigation the obligations upon both China
> and Russia of the treaty of 1924, including particularly the
> obligation of the mutual covenants contained in said treaty —
> "not to permit in their respective territories the existence and/or
> activities of any organisations or groups whose aim is to
> struggle by acts of violence against the governments of either
> contracting party" and "not to engage in propaganda against
> the political and social systems of either contracting party"
> will continue in full force and effect.
>
> The grievances and claims of both countries shall be in-
> vestigated by an impartial commission of conciliation, the
> membership of which shall be agreed upon by Russia and
> China and which shall have full power to investigate all the
> facts concerning such grievances and claims and to render to
> both countries and make public its conclusions both as to the
> facts and as to any suggested remedies for the future. [2]

It seems almost incredible today that statesmen could have
believed that this naive and honest offer would have been accepted.
Stimson was assuming that the litigants wanted a fair and honest
settlement. By July 25th, it seemed that the case might have been
settled honourably and by mutual agreement. Sun Fo announced [3]
that "discussions with a view to arranging for direct negotiations
are already in progress between the diplomatic representatives of

---

[1] *Op. cit.*, p. 243.
[2] *Op. cit.*, pp. 243—4.
[3] *Op. cit.*, pp. 244—5.

China and Russia at Berlin".[1] Sun further admitted "that the Chinese Government is prepared to recognize without prejudice joint interest of Russia in the Chinese Eastern Railway as a commercial enterprise in accordance with the treaties of 1924 and would therefore be prepared to restore Russia to the *status quo ante* with respect to the railway if assured of Russia's observance on its part of the provisions of those treaties against propaganda". He limited this, however, by stating that it was subject to "the condition that some more effectual safeguard against the recurrence of Soviet propaganda would have to be arranged".

Russia, however, was aiming at complete diplomatic victory and was avoiding negotiation until her terms were conceded in advance. When it seemed that the two countries were about to get together, except for some minor point, about which China indicated a reservation, there would be a statement issued either from Moscow or by a Soviet Ambassador in one of the major Capitals that negotiations had been broken off, when later China announced that they had been resumed, Russia would absolutely deny this fact. Or if China seemed to be getting a little too hopeful that outside pressure might be applied to Russia, for China's benefit, or if she showed a spark of independence and intention of negotiating with Russia on a basis of equality, Russia would then launch a heavy military attack on the frontier. For instance, on the 27th, the Chinese Minister at Tokyo announced that direct and official discussions had been re-opened, but the Soviet Ambassador denied this, though continuing also to deny that there would be military action taken by Russia, on the condition that there were no molestation by China of Soviet citizens. He insisted "not only upon the re-establishment of the status quo, but upon the granting of guarantees for the future". The official news agency or press bureau at Moscow "states that the Soviets are in no communication with the Chinese in any capital, and sticks to the rupture until fulfilment of conditions of the Soviet note of July 13th". Here we see Russia's strategy, and, as remarked by Briand, "this would virtually mean having the Chinese give in to the Soviet demands", leaving nothing to arbitrate.

At this point Chang Hsüeh-liang proposed to Karakhan that each

---

[1] F.R.U.S., 1929, II, p. 244.

country appoint a representative to a conference to clear up not only the misunderstanding about the C.E.R., but all matters at issue between the two countries. Here it seems that Chang was honestly trying to make a settlement, for whatever reason. Had Russia been sincere in her efforts, or had she been willing to negotiate instead of dictate, the issue could have been honourably settled. At any rate Karakhan had here a direct and open proposal from Chang to settle all outstanding issues — but these would include cessation of Communist infiltration, efforts to undermine the government, and use of the C.E.R. and of diplomatic establishments, for these purposes. This was too much to ask of Russia. Karakhan answered (see infra, pp. 108–110) that Chang had deceived him, had changed his proposal from that on which negotiations had been opened, had in effect been stalling for time and wanted to go back on his previous undertakings. Karakhan made it amply evident that Russia had no idea of compromising, that China would be forced to accept Russia's type of "negotiations" with a predetermined solution. Here Karakhan was by subterfuge refusing real negotiations while throwing the onus for their breakdown on to the shoulders of Chang. It is the pattern which Russia was to follow in the future. No one except Russia could ever, under any circumstances, be right. Karakhan was righteously indignant at the hideous dishonesty of Chang, at the enormity of his expecting negotiation which might give China justice or help save a little face and allow China to withdraw from the desperate position in which she had placed herself through her own stupidity.

In the meantime negotiations had in fact continued between Russia and China. Reports came from many quarters that the Chinese had gone to meet the Russians at Manchuli. Even while the men were in actual conference, the Soviet press and embassies were officially denying that there was any negotiation in progress, or that there was likely to be before China accepted Russia's demands. Karakhan had outlined the course of negotiations in his reply to Chang, from which we know that Tsai and Melnikov had taken certain steps leading up to a conference. Before Karakhan delivered his last note to Chang he had already despatched an answer which two Manchurian officials had gone to the border to receive. The Consul at Harbin in imparting this information added:

"Reported that Chinese authorities have published secret note to Soviet authorities yielding much and that Soviet and Chinese troops have drawn back a considerable distance into their respective territories". [1] On August 5th, it was reported that negotiations were continuing at Manchuli, but that there was no official information about the results. [2] On the 7th, however, there was an official communiqué from Nanking that the conference had reached a deadlock and that China would refuse to reinstate Soviet Assistant Managers prior to opening of formal negotiations. [3]

At this time the Chinese Minister in Berlin asked the German Foreign Office to help China find a face-saving device to get out of the situation. The German official to whom he made the request said that as Germany represented the interests of both countries, he could not give the advice asked, but would make the Russians acquainted with the information. Nothing came of this approach and Russia now announced that she would only negotiate locally, with the Manchurian authorities. In this, Karakhan was obviously trying to drive a wedge between the Manchurian and Nanking Governments. He fully realized the differences which existed between them and he intended to widen the breach and take advantage of it. He was applying diplomatically Nelson's famous naval strategy, "splitting the line". On the 15th, Karakhan issued a statement declaring that the Chinese were misappropriating the C.E.R. locomotives and rolling stock, that they had ruined the railway, and that he was issuing a warning to Foreign Powers not to mix into the affair, as he would not "recognise a single deal" made concerning the railway. He was evidently getting worried that there might soon be international interference to settle the matter fairly. He must have been greatly aggravated at the obstinacy of the Chinese in insisting on negotiation instead of giving in at once, as he was determined that they should do, but he feared that time might be getting short, therefore it was necessary to intensify the "softening-up" treatment; hence the military campaign which was now launched, beginning with the Russian attack on August 17th.

---

[1]   *Op. cit.*, p. 262.
[2]   *Op. cit.*, p. 272.
[3]   *Op. cit.*, p. 273.

At this point China issued a statement to the signatories of the Kellogg Pact, setting forth the conditions leading up to the present conflict, and stating China's readiness at any time to arbitrate with Russia. [1] On the 20th, it was learned that the League was considering some action in the Sino-Russian dispute. This was certainly not calculated to make Karakhan happy, and it was only to be expected that he would counter with some apparently generous, but meaningless, gesture. He did indeed try to confuse China by raising false hopes. Wang announced to MacMurray that Russia had offered to make a deal with China whereby she could gradually redeem Russia's share in the C.E.R., provided China would immediately agree to the appointment of a Soviet Manager. He stated that China had at once replied in the affirmative. This was a pretty bold move on Karakhan's part, in view of what we know today. But it was fairly safe to make such an offer for the future as a device for getting China to give way on the immediate issue. No more was to be heard of this proposal for ending Russian control of the C.E.R. But the Japanese Ambassador told Stimson a few days later that China had agreed to the appointment of a Soviet manager and a return to the *status quo ante,* as long as that did not mean reinstatement of the same manager and assistant manager. Debuchi said the talks were progressing steadily.

More or less as a means of keeping two strings to the bow of settlement, Stimson invited the British Ambassador to call on him on the 26th, to discuss the dispute. They worked the thing out historically and arrived at the conclusions: "(1) That China had been guilty of an initial wrong in her action toward the railroad; (2) she had been also wrong in afterwards refusing to make amends and restore the *status quo*; but neither of these actions would justify an act of war upon China, particularly after she had solemnly sworn, in the Kellogg Pact, to settle such controversies only by pacific means". They agreed that, if Russia should "go to war and invade Manchuria", particularly if China offered to restore the *status quo*, "Russia would be so clearly in the wrong that it would probably be easy to *eventually* [2] rally public opinion of other

---

[1]   *Op. cit.,* pp. 288 *seq.*
[2]   Italics mine.

nations of the world to put an embargo on trade with her and thus check her military operations". This last part of their discussion seems, today, so puerile and naive that it is difficult to believe that two of the most important statesmen of their days could have held such views. They were, it is true, the official views of the demo-cracies of the era, but the fallacy of the whole premise is transparent today. In the first place, what did they think Russia's incursions, bombings and bombardments constituted if not going to war and invading Manchuria? As for Russia's being "clearly in the wrong", it is difficult to understand what more Russia would have had to do — it could only be a matter of more extensive wrongs, but by international law the wrongs had already been committed by Russia. The idea of having to let Russia be "so clearly in the wrong" that *eventually* public opinion could be rallied to stop trade, and hence her military aggression, is so futile as to be maddening. Did they think being wrong was a rope which would automatically hang Russia after a graduated amount of violation?

Eventually it would be too late to save Manchuria, as the same sort of diplomatic psychology and tactics were shortly to prove in another case in the same country. The idea that Russia could be stopped by an embargo is ridiculous. Her foreign trade was prac-tically nonexistent, and certainly Russia's tender conscience would not be chafed by adverse opinion. Russia was lucky to be dealing which such men. One cannot avoid the analogy of a good poker player getting into the game with a very poor player who calls and raises on every card. That was exactly the psychology which prevailed then. Such unrealistic behavior made possible Hitler's rise, the invasion of Ethiopia and the rape of the Orient. We are dealing in detail later in this study with the latter, in which there was the same exploitation of futile hopefulness. The "Umbrella psychology" of the conversation in Washington in 1929 would have its after-math over Pearl Harbour in December 1941, and still further at some date beyond 1949, when realism on our part will force us to call Russia's bluff and use the atomic bomb.

The Japanese Chargé in China confirmed, in a conversation with MacMurray, the general yielding of China to Russian pressure. He had learned officially, but confidentially, that the Chinese were prepared to give way on several points. He did not know whether the negotiations would proceed in Berlin or in China, but he knew definitely that Nanking had wired Chang to take a more con-ciliatory attitude to the Russians in Manchuria.

The Chinese Chargé in Washington, Yung Kwai, was advised by Johnson in a conversation on August 28th, that his country should accept Russia's offer to settle on the basis of appointing a new Soviet manager and assistant manager of the railway. This principle was embodied in a *Note verbale* handed by the Chinese Minister in Berlin to the German Ministry of Foreign Affairs on August 27th, for transmission to Moscow. [1] The settlement proposed by China was already an acceptance of what were thought to be Russia's conditions, but Russia countered with the proviso that Russia would reappoint the former manager. Russia modified the document submitted by China for acceptance, and it is interesting to compare the two texts.

Text of the joint declaration proposed by China [2]

(1)   Both sides declare that all disputes between the two sides they will settle in conformity with the agreement of 1924, and more particularly they will settle the conditions of buying out the Chinese Eastern Railway in conformity with article 9 of the Peking agreement.

Both sides will immediately and duly appoint plenipotentiary representatives to attend a conference which is to settle all the questions under dispute, mentioned in the previous paragraph.

(2)   Both sides hold that the situation on the Chinese Eastern Railway, come about after the conflict, should be changed in conformity with the Peking agreement and the Mukden agreement of 1924, it being understood that all such changes shall be resolved upon by the conference to be called according to the previous article.

(3)   The Soviet government will recommend a new Director and a new Vice Director for the Chinese Eastern Railway, who will be appointed by the Board of Administration of the said Railway.

---

[1]   F.R.U.S., 1929, II, p. 307.
[2]   *Op. cit.*, p. 309.

The Soviet government will instruct the railway employees of Soviet nationality on the Chinese Eastern Railway to the effect that they are strictly to observe the provisions laid down in article 6 of the agreement of 1924.

(4)   Both sides will immediately release all persons arrested in connection with this incident, or after May 1, 1929.

On August 29 [1] Comrade M. M. Litvinov, Acting Commissar of Foreign Affairs, received von Dirksen, German Envoy in Moscow, and informed him that the Soviet Government was "prepared to accept the proposal of the Chinese Government to sign a joint declaration worded as follows". What in fact follows is not China's proposed text, but a Russian version, in which clause 3 reads:

(3)   The Soviet government will recommend a *Director* and a Vice Director for the Chinese Eastern Railway, who will be *immediately* appointed by the Board of Administration of the said railway.

The Soviet government will instruct the railway employees on the Chinese Eastern Railway, who are citizens of the U.S.S.R., *and the Chinese Government will instruct its local authorities and their organs,* to the effect that they are strictly to observe the provisions laid down in article 6 of the agreement of 1924.

As a seeming concession Litvinov agreed to present to the Soviet Government for consideration the possibility of appointing a new manager and assistant-manager if China would replace the present Chairman of the Board of Directors.

The Nanking Foreign Office denied knowledge of any settlement, but admitted that negotiations were progressing satisfactorily. The Foreign Minister stated that the question of replacing the Chairman had never arisen but that, if it should, China would find the condition unacceptable. This denial by Wang was followed two days later by a despatch to Stimson from Schurman, in which he said that there was no confirmation at the German Foreign Office of the fact that the Nanking Government found the Soviet reply unacceptable, and added that the German Foreign Office felt that the road to a definite settlement had been opened. It is interesting to note that between each of these diplomatic exchanges and notices

---

[1]   *Op. cit.,* pp. 310—11.

the Russians were steadily applying military force, as related in the last chapter. They were giving China no chance to forget that she must settle on Russia's terms—ultimately.

On September 6th, Wang made a statement in Nanking that the appointment of a Soviet railway manager "should not be gazetted until after the formal conference opens. Agreement on this point remains to be reached". He stated "that the Sino-Russian agreements confer too great a power on the Soviet general manager and make the Chinese president of the railway a mere figurehead. This state of affairs should be remedied". [1] Two days later a wire was received from Chiang Tso-pin that "the Soviet Government has withdrawn its demand for the appointment of new manager and assistant manager of the C.E.R. as a preliminary to the opening of formal negotiations between the Soviet and Chinese", and MacMurray told Stimson that "official circles in Nanking believe that it is only a question of time before an agreement with regard to procedure for settlement of the C.E.R. dispute is reached". [2]

During these negotiations Russia was engaged in a wholesale military operation against China. It was just at this time that she destroyed the railway station at Suifenho. It was also at this time that Wang made his speech about the Chinese army not hesitating to defend their country against Russian aggression and that Moscow accused the Nanking and Mukden governments of provocative attacks upon Russia.

On September 11th, [3] during one of the heaviest and most persistent military attacks made by Russia upon China, China delivered, through the German Foreign Office, a *note verbale* to the German Ambassador in Moscow, for delivery to the Soviet Government.

1. The National Government of China has declared repeatedly its readiness to enter into negotiations with the Soviet Government in order to reach a just and fair settlement of the recent dispute. The National Government is therefore appreciative of the attitude of the Soviet Government in expressing its readiness to sign the joint declaration when agreed upon by both parties and agrees completely that the proposed

1 *Op. cit.,* p. 315.
2 *Op. cit.,* p. 316.
3 *Op. cit.,* pp. 316—7.

conference should be opened as soon as possible in order that the representatives of both countries may effect a final solution of all the questions outstanding between the two countries.

2. The National Government has no objection to the proposal of the Soviet Government to insert the word 'immediate(ly)' before the word 'ratifications of (recommend)' in article 3 of the proposed joint declaration but regrets that it cannot see its way to agreeing to the suggestions of making the appointment of a new manager and an assistant manager as a prerequisite for the signing of the said declaration, or for the opening of the congress because such a procedure would be contrary to the general principle laid down by article 2 of the draft declaration which has already been accepted by the Soviet Government.

3. With regard to the other amendments proposed by the Soviet Government the National Government is of the opinion that they may very well be left to be considered by the forthcoming conference and that should the conference decide in favor of the proposed amendments of (the) National Government will not oppose to their being adopted.

4. The National Government proposes that the conference be held in Berlin instead of Moscow as suggested by the Soviet Government and also hopes that the signature of the agreed joint declaration shall likewise take place in Berlin by the representatives of both parties.

An official in the German Foreign Office explained to Schurman that the note was in fact "a refusal of all the preliminary conditions of Russia". He described it as a "typically Chinese reply" and said that it would "exasperate Moscow greatly" [1] and do nothing to facilitate a settlement. He remarked that, had the Foreign Office been asked its advice, it would have counselled China not to deliver the note. He remarked that China's procrastination in answering had greatly exasperated the Russians, whose principal purpose in their aggressions and reprisals had been to hasten China's reply. He felt that this answer was evasive in the extreme and showed that Nanking was much less concerned with the settlement than was Mukden.

Here we see verification and recognition of the fact on the part of at least one Power that Russia was actually using war as an instrument of policy. We see also another glaring example of

---

[1] *Op. cit.*, p. 317.

China's diplomatic imprudence — unless indeed one argues that she was using this method to gain time for the Powers to come to her rescue, but even so the risk was great. She had already seen that Russia was ruthless, and that each time she had attempted to thwart her, Russia had retaliated with a military campaign. Each time China threw away an opportunity to settle, the more harsh were the terms demanded by Russia upon the reopening of negotiations and the more China lost face.

China evidently realised that she had made a grievous error immediately after the dispatch of this note and followed it quickly with an alternative proposal for article 3 of the *note verbale* quoted above, which read: "The Soviet Government shall nominate an Assistant Manager of the Chinese Eastern Railway Company who will immediately be appointed by the Board of Administration of the said road, and who, jointly with the Chinese Assistant Manager, will manage the railway pending negotiations between the two governments".

This amendment was delivered by the German Ambassador in Moscow two days after the date of delivery of the original *note verbale*.

As might have been expected, Karakhan immediately rejected China's *note verbale* on the grounds that, as it declined the principal conditions "preparatory to the signing of the declaration and the conduct of negotiations, the question as to the place of the negotiations becomes deprived of its object, and the responsibility for the development of the conflict devolves fully upon the Nanking Government".

Certainly the last sentence of Russia's reply leaves no doubt as to Russia's intentions nor the means by which she would carry them out. If China was diplomatically irresponsible, Russia was an international outlaw. It was not possible to negotiate, to differ or to bargain with her; it was a question of accepting whatever terms Russia saw fit to give, or being attacked by land, sea and air. Russia had no mercy and gave no terms. She gave (and still gives) a peremptory summons and demanded (and still demands) prompt compliance.

On September 17th, Johnson discussed with Yung Kwai the crisis which had arisen between Russia and China. [1] Johnson told Yung that he understood that relations had been broken off because China refused "to accept the appointment of a new Russian manager and a new Russian assistant manager prior to the actual convening of a conference". Yung said he thought that what China had refused "was the reinstatement of the old Russian manager and the old assistant manager". Johnson argued that this was not the case and that the Russians no longer requested reinstatement, but the appointment of new officials which was "quite in accord with the 1924 agreement and that China's refusal to accept these men indicated that they were not quite reasonable in their attitude and that this attitude created a bad impression here". Johnson pointed out to him that it would be smart to acquiesce in the new appointments, since by "so doing they would really have won a victory as they would thereby have established their right to rid themselves of appointees not agreeable to them".

Johnson said that, since China was already in possession of the railway, which according to the treaty should be in joint possession, and that, since Russia could only regain physical possession by military aggression, China was in the stronger position of the two and should be willing to make some concessions, but that, if she did not, she would be blamed by the world "if matters should go on to a situation where there would be open conflict". Johnson asked him to transmit to his government America's concern in the matter and the views which he had just expressed to Yung. In this interview Johnson came very near to saying that Russia was entitled to use force if she could not secure her property rights otherwise.

A week later Wang and Chiang approved a new "draft" reply to the Soviet Government in which China proposed "that to facilitate the opening of formal negotiations Soviet Russia may appoint an assistant manager" of the C.E.R. "who will function until such time as the appointment of a general manager is decided upon at the formal conference". The note added that the "agreement(s) of 1924 are valid pending conclusion of the new agreement". [2]

On October 14th, the German Foreign Office proposed to both the Chinese and Soviet governments the reciprocal cessation of

---

[1] F.R.U.S., 1929, II, pp. 321—2.
[2] Op. cit., p. 323.

arrests and the release of each other's nationals, which Russia promptly refused. The German Minister to China, who gave MacMurray this information, also told him "that the recently proposed joint Sino-Russian declaration", which each claimed to be originated by the other, "was ... initiated through the German representative in Moscow by the Chinese". This proposal was that one of the "present assistant managers" of the railway "be allowed temporarily to act as manager". The Russians refused, demanding that a "Russian manager be appointed immediately, as provided by the 1924 treaties", whereupon China withdrew the proposal. He stated that, as far as he knew, the representatives of the two countries in Berlin were not in contact with each other "despite reports in China". [1]

Several days later it was learned upon good authority that Chiang Kai-shek had urged Chang Hsüeh-liang "to undertake negotiations with the Soviets" in regard to the C.E.R. dispute. It was learned through inside information that "the local government has already taken steps with a view to bringing about the opening of negotiations with the Soviets". [2] On October 25th, the Chinese Government issued a manifesto on the Sino-Soviet conflict setting forth the efforts of the National Government to reach an amicable solution and declared that, if war resulted "from the Soviet Government's incessant provocation", the responsibility for violating peace would rest with Russia. [3]

A week after the issue of the manifesto Chiang again authorised Chang Hsüeh-liang to make a direct settlement with the Russians, since it was impossible to do anything more through Berlin. He gave Chang a free hand to settle without interference from Nanking, and it seemed that an agreement would shortly be reached for holding a new conference. [4]

After Chang had been given a free hand he wired Karakhan that his "attitude towards the problem has not changed from that originally expressed by him". He stated that "if Russia sincerely wishes to negotiate with Mukden", he was as "sincerely ready to

---

[1]   Op. cit., pp. 326—327.
[2]   Op. cit., p. 331.
[3]   Op. cit., pp. 333—6.
[4]   Op. cit., p. 338.

negotiate with Russia on the basis of the 1924 agreement between Mukden and Russia". Chang told Karakhan that he was certain "you understand why an amicable settlement has so far not been effected". Chang stated that he had not "received directly or indirectly the terms which you state were sent to the Mukden authorities on August 29" and requested him to "kindly wire ... as soon as possible an exact copy of the terms given to the German Ambassador". [1]

The American Consul at Mukden reported to MacMurray on November 15th, that a reply had not been received more than a week later and that consequently a new request was despatched to Karakhan. The Consul said that it was not now expected that a reply would be received. It was felt that Karakhan would wait and see the outcome of the struggle between the Kuomintang and the Kuominchun forces in China before reopening conversations and that he "possibly intends in the meantime to invade and occupy Chinese territory".

There were very good grounds for the fear expressed by the American Consul at Mukden. Certainly Karakhan took advantage of the situation in every possible manner. He gave Chang the "silent treatment", while in the meantime softening up the Chinese by the most extended and prolonged military campaign of the war, in which a number of Chinese towns were occupied and great damage was done, especially by bombing raids. We can see here the beginning of a policy which is becoming familiar to us today. Russia was developing a new type of warfare and a new military-political technique. Since the foreign powers did nothing but moralise, it was a foregone conclusion that China would shortly have to settle on Russia's terms.

After Karakhan had let Chang stew for a month and after the Soviet armed forces had thoroughly terrorised Manchuria, he suddenly and quite unexpectedly announced from Moscow that China had accepted Russia's terms for settlement. [2] It was not known to anyone that negotiations were going on, and it is not

---

[1] *Op. cit.*, p. 343.
[2] *Op. cit.*, p. 356.

known officially even yet exactly how he forced Chang to capitulate so completely.

On November 28th, Acting Commissar of Foreign Affairs, Litvinov, acknowledged receipt of Chang's telegram and sent him the following wire: [1]

> We have received your telegram of the 26th instant declaring your full acceptance of the preliminary conditions as communicated in writing on the 22nd instant through Mr. Tsai Yun-sheng, the Diplomatic Commissar at Harbin.
>
> These conditions were as follows:
>
> 1. The official consent of the Chinese side for the restoration of the situation which existed on the Chinese Eastern Railway prior to the conflict on the basis of the Peking—Mukden agreements of 1924.
>
> 2. The immediate reinstatement of the manager and the assistant manager of the railway recommended by the Soviet side in accordance with the Peking—Mukden agreements of 1924.
>
> 3. The immediate release of all Soviet citizens arrested in connection with the conflict.
>
> In accordance with point 2 of the above-mentioned conditions, the Soviet Government recommends the reinstatement of Mr. Emshanov as manager and Mr. Eismont as assistant manager of the railroad, and expects your immediate official confirmation thereof.
>
> As regards points 1 and 3 which have been also accepted by you, the Soviet Government proposes as soon as point 2 has been fulfilled that you send your representative to Habarovsk with official written credentials; and for its part the Soviet Government appoints Mr. Simanovsky, the Soviet agent of the People's Commissariat of Foreign Affairs at Habarovsk, for the discussing of the technical questions connected with the carrying out of these points as well as for the settlement of questions concerning the time (and) the place of the Soviet-Chinese conference.

In all negotiations with Russia the other party has to agree to whatever the Russians say or there are no negotiations. This is typified by the statement "and expects your immediate official confirmation thereof". This is icy. It implies more bombers over Chin-

---

[1] Op. cit., p. 362.

ese towns if confirmation is delayed. This is not negotiation; it is
duress. Could China have refused? She had baulked every time so
far, but it was not Chiang Kai-shek's followers who were being
killed and terrorised: it was Chang Hsüeh-liang who was bearing
the brunt and he knew that if he tried to hold out for better terms
Russia would begin the *blitzkrieg* over again. He had no alternative
to surrender. He got no help from foreign powers, quite the contrary, they were putting pressure on China to give in, as is shown
in an interview between Stimson and Wu on November 21st,
recorded in a memorandum by Johnson: [1]

> The Chinese Minister called upon the Secretary today and
> in conversation stated that the Russians made a further attack
> upon the Chinese frontier at Manchuli and at Dailainor. He
> said that they had counted as many as 27 aeroplanes in the
> raid and that nearly 30,000 Russian troops and a large number
> of tanks had invaded Chinese soil. He said that China intended
> to lay the matter before the League as there was an article in
> the League Covenant under which they could do this. The
> Secretary asked whether Russia was a member of the League
> and the Minister said that he thought not, but a provision of
> the Covenant provided for that. The Chinese Minister asked
> whether as sponsors for the Kellogg Treaty the United States
> intended to do anything about it. The Secretary replied that
> he thought the United States had done everything it could do
> in the matter; that we had called to the attention of the Chin-
> ese and the Russians their obligations under the Kellogg Pact
> and both had announced their pacific intentions. He reminded
> the Chinese Minister that in conversation with him he had
> suggested to him the advisability of setting up a commission
> voluntarily by the Russians and the Chinese without dictation
> from the other Powers for the purpose of investigating the
> facts and for the reestablishment of the *status quo*. The Se-
> cretary stated also that he felt that the Chinese were in their
> present predicament because they had very unwisely, it seemed
> to him, refused to accept the settlement proposed by the Rus-
> sians, insisting upon the only difference between the two,
> apparently over the question as to whether the new Russian
> manager should be appointed before or after the discussions or
> investigations began. And now the Russians were refusing to
> negotiate and apparently were exerting pressure while waiting
> upon the course of events in China.

---

[1] F.R.U.S., 1929, II, p. 345.

Stimson here does not challenge Wu's assertion that 30,000 Russian troops are carrying out offensive operations on Chinese territory, but all he can say is that the Chinese ought to settle on Russian terms. His reference to a Russo-Chinese commission "for the purpose of investigating the facts" must be regarded as hypocritical, for he must have known from the reports reaching him that Russia was not willing to have any investigation of the facts, either as regards the Soviet political activities in Manchuria which China had made the pretext for taking over the railway or as regards the alleged raids on Siberia which Russia had made the pretext for her military invasion of Manchuria. Stimson's point that the difference between the Russian and Chinese positions was so small as to be unimportant is made against China, who is charged with unreasonable obstinacy, yet it really aggravates the guilt of Russia, who was not merely "insisting" on getting her way in such a minor matter, but was killing thousands of Chinese soldiers and civilians because of it. Finally, it is clear that what Stimson's advice amounts to, is that China had better submit at once, because she will have to in the end anyway.

On November 28th, Tsai Yun-sheng returned to Mukden from Vladivostok bringing the Soviet terms for the holding of a conference, reinstatement of the Soviet manager and the immediate release of prisoners. After a meeting of high officials at the Young Marshal's villa at which the subject was thoroughly discussed, it was decided to accept these terms, provided that parts 1 and 3 "be first referred to a joint committee to arrange procedure". On the same day "a telegram was sent to Moscow accepting in principle Soviet terms". The reservation noted above was made in the case of points 1 and 3.

On the same day that Marshal Chang Hsüeh-liang's telegram was delivered to Moscow, the German Ambassador delivered to the Russian Government [1] the following telegram from Nanking: [2]

(1)   The National Government of China, being a signatory of the Pact of Paris, refrained, even after the break with the

[1]   Op. cit., p. 370.
[2]   Op. cit., pp. 360—1.

Russian Government, from engaging in provocative or aggressive actions against Russia, though Chinese citizens were being treated badly in Russia.

(2) The Russian Government at the same time sent armed forces to the Sino-Russian frontier, and they attacked Chinese garrisons and entered Chinese territory, which resulted in loss to life and property. Chinese forces neither returned these attacks nor entered Russian territory.

(3) The National Government of China is surprised by the Russian declaration ... that either Chinese troops alone or together with Russian White Guards had attacked Russian troops and had raided the Russian frontier.

(4) Taking into account the Russian Government's stubborn insistence that the Chinese began hostilities on the frontier, the National Government of China, while solemnly denying the accusation, proposes the formation of a mixed commission in order to investigate and to establish the responsibility for the serious situation. The mixed commission would consist of both Chinese and Russian representatives, with a citizen of a neutral country as its Chairman.

(5) For the purpose of meeting the anxious wishes expressed by the Russian Government in its note dated September 25 to establish peace on the frontier, the National Government of China proposes the withdrawal of armed forces of both countries from the frontier to a depth of 30 miles.

(6) Should the foregoing proposal be accepted by Russia, the National Government of China, as a signatory to the Pact of Paris, is prepared to submit the entire dispute to a neutral, impartial resort for adjustment.

The Russian Government acknowledged receipt of this telegram, saying that since they had "already received an official communication from Marshal Chang Hsiao-liang (sic.)" in which he stated "his acceptance of the preliminary conditions necessary for the speediest settlement of the conflict by direct negotiations", the proposals of the Nanking Government stated above "which are (likely to) only protract the conflict, are therefore of no avail".

The Nanking Government chose this particular time to deny the report from Moscow that the Young Marshal had agreed "to the restoration of the status which prevailed on the Chinese Eastern Railway before the Chinese took the line over last July or that he had agreed to the reinstatement of the Soviet general and assistant-manager." It was stated that the Manchurian and the Nanking authorities were in complete agreement concerning the Russian situation, and that "Marshal Chang has never indicated such intentions in his recent wires to the Government". The statement was called another piece of Soviet propaganda.

Dr. C. T. Wang confirmed the above denial which was published by the Kuo Wen News Agency, Nanking, November 29. On December 1st, Chargé Perkins wired the State Department concerning the "conflicting reports as to the acceptance by Mukden of Soviet terms" and the continued aggression of Soviet forces since November 26th, saying that the situation indicated:

> (1) The likelihood of the correctness of the report that Soviet terms have not as yet been fully accepted by Mukden, or;
>
> (2) An apprehension on the part of Soviet Government lest, if pressure be at all relaxed, Mukden may, at the instance of Nanking or from hope of foreign mediation, repudiate terms which, if correctly reported, constitute an abject surrender by Mukden and a dangerous loss of prestige by Nanking. [1]

We have here in Perkins' despatch an absolute acknowledgment that Russia and China are both fully cognisant of the fact that China was being forced to settle under duress, as well as an acknowledgment that America is both aware and seemingly in favour of it. The internal evidence contained in the cable is incontrovertible.

It is easy to understand why Russia so brusquely rejected the proposal of the Nanking Government for third party judgment. As it was, in the settlement with the Young Marshal, Russia was getting everything and making no concession. The problem was being settled on Russia's terms bi-laterally, whereas, as Russia well knew, if the Powers had not been so selfish and so concerned with their short-term interests, the case might have been brought up for arbitration and many embarrassing points opened and aired. Russia was indeed in a vulnerable and untenable position, if international arbitration, which was implied and almost mandatory, should come about. If the Nanking Government's wire should be used as a basis of negotiation, Russia would not be able to ram her solution down

---

[1] *Op. cit.*, p. 374.

China's throat. It is difficult to understand how even a government as ill-organized and incompetent as that in power in Nanking could have failed to take more advantage of China's position as a co-signatory to three instrumentalities which offered her international protection. We shall see shortly what efforts were made by the powers to effect a solution under international pressure, but China, in spite of her defiant attitude towards Russia, did very little to avail herself of her legal rights.

In a discussion with the Chinese Minister to Washington on December 2nd, Johnson made a very interesting point when he said: "I pointed out to the Chinese Minister that this note, although dated November 14, apparently was not handed to the Russians until November 29. I asked him if he knew why that was. He said he did not". [1] In passing it is interesting to note that the delivery of Nanking's note coincided exactly with Moscow's announcement of the Young Marshal's acceptance of Moscow's full terms. One can only suspect that Germany was not acting as an honest broker and that the relations of secret semi-alliance existing between Germany and Russia at this time made the German Foreign Ministry anxious not to do anything to embarrass Moscow.

While the rumours and denials were flying thick and fast, about Chang's acceptance of Moscow's terms, the American Consul at Nanking wired Stimson that he had learned that Chang had been given a free hand to negotiate with Russia and was reporting to Nanking daily. [2]

The State Department learned through reliable channels on December 2nd, that Mukden had "replied to Moscow requesting the appointment of a new manager and assistant manager and proposing to remove certain high Chinese officials connected with the railway", and that "Tsai Yun-sheng and Li Shao-keng, and . . . Mukden representatives, have already left Pogranichnaya for Habarovsk". [3]

The following day Nanking again denied that the Mukden authorities "have committed themselves to an agreement with the Russian Government upon the basis of the Russian terms". Wang

---

[1] *Op. cit.*, p. 378.
[2] *Op. cit.*, p. 380.
[3] *Op. cit.*, p. 381.

said that there had been merely an "agreement to discuss points 1 and 2 in the forthcoming conference", since he expected no difficulty over point 3. He did admit, however, that Chang had "asked the Russian Government to nominate Russians for the position of general manager and assistant general manager for possible appointment by Chinese Government". [1]

This is an excellent example of Chinese diplomacy and "face". Chang says nomination for *possible* appointment, as though China had anything at all to do with it. A Westerner is constitutionally unable to understand the value of such "face". Anyone can understand the value of "face" when it deceives one or more parties to a transaction or to a social relationship, but when it fools no one except the principal, it may be an expensive bargain.

On December 3rd, Tsai and Li were reported to be "en route to Habarovsk" where they were expected to discuss the technical questions involved in Soviet terms 1 and 3 and in connection with point 2 to try to make a dicker "to persuade Soviet representatives to select new general and assistant managers" in return for which the Chinese President of the Board of Directors would be relieved of his post. Four hours later Perkins notified Stimson that there were "unconfirmed reports ... that Tsai and Li have recrossed frontier and are on their way to Mukden via Harbin". [2]

---

[1] *Op. cit.*, p. 384.
[2] *Op. cit.*, pp. 385—6.

CHAPTER IX

THE C.E.R. CRISIS: SETTLEMENT

On December 3rd, [1] Reuter, under a Moscow dateline, reported that the Russo-Chinese dispute over the Chinese Eastern Railway had been settled by a protocol at Nikolsk-Ussuriisk signed by Tsai for China and Simanovsky for Russia. The protocol provided for "the reorganization of the administrators of the railway in strict conformity" with the 1924 agreements. It also provided for the dismissal of Lu Yung-huan, chairman of the Railway Board, and an agreement on the part of Russia "to recommend other candidates for the managership and assistant managership than Messrs. Emshanov and Eismont", who, however, might be given other positions on the railway.

On the following day the Tass Agency confirmed that the protocol had been signed at Nikolsk-Ussuriisk by Tsai and Simanovsky: [2]

> "On behalf of the Mukden Government, the Diplomatic Commissar, Mr. Tsai Yun-sheng, declares that the chairman of the Board of Directors of the Chinese Eastern Railway, Mr. Lu Jung-huan, has been (*is to be*?) dismissed from the post of chairman of the board.
>
> On behalf of the Government of the U.S.S.R., the Agent of the Foreign Commissariat (at) Habarovsk, Mr. Simanovsky, declares that when the chairman of the Board of Directors of the Chinese Eastern Railway, Mr. Lu Jung-huan, will be (*has been*?) dismissed from the post, the Soviet Government, in accordance with declaration of the Acting Commissar of Foreign Affairs, Mr. Litvinov, handed the German Ambassador at Moscow on August 29th, will be ready to recommend new candidates for the post of manager and assistant manager of the Chinese Eastern Railway, instead of Messrs. Emshanov

---

[1] F.R.U.S., 1929, II, p. 387.
[2] *Op. cit.*, p. 392.

and Eismont. But in the (*this*) case, the Soviet Government reserves the right to appoint Messrs. Emshanov and Eismont to other posts on the Chinese Eastern Railway, whereupon Mr. Tsai Yun-sheng, in personal conversation with Mr. Simanovsky, expressed his consent.

The Deputy (*Diplomatic*) Commissar, Mr. Tsai Yun-sheng, of the Mukden Government declared that the latter, desiring by all means to contribute towards the settlement of the conflict between China and the U.S.S.R. and to remove all causes for further complications, will strictly conform with the Mukden and Peking agreement(s) of 1924, in whole as well as in each part.

The Agent of the Foreign Commissariat (at) Habarovsk, Mr. Simanovsky, on behalf of the Soviet Government, accepted with satisfaction the declaration of Commissar Tsai Yun-sheng that the Mukden Government will fulfill the agreements of 1924 and declared on his part that the Government of the U.S.S.R., which has always stood on the basis of the agreement(s) existing between China and the U.S.S.R., will, of course, strictly fulfill them in whole as well as in each part.

The above declarations in the first and second clauses of this protocol are considered as accepted by both parties". [1]

The announcement from Moscow that a settlement had been reached was soon confirmed by the Consul at Mukden, [2] from a secret source. He substantially confirmed each point. There was a point of difference, however. Chang Hsüeh-liang sent a wire to Moscow informing the Russians that the "Chinese could not concede Soviet demand appointment Emshanoff, Eismont".

Perkins was notified the same day, from Harbin, [3] that judging from the quick return of Tsai and Li, it seemed that the Russians had told them that negotiations were over, that Russia would accept no new terms, and that China had to settle immediately. It was implied that, if Mukden did not settle immediately, bombers would next visit Tsitsihar. This would create a panic among the Chinese troops turning them into a rabble, creating great danger, particularly at Chalainor and Manchuria Station, where things were now quiet again.

---

[1] *Op. cit.*, pp. 392—3.
[2] *Op. cit.*, p. 394.
[3] *Op. cit.*, p. 396.

The discussions continued, despite rumours to the contrary, con-cerning the appointment of Emshanov and Eismont. [1] The Young Marshal was eventually forced to capitulate on this point also and agreed to their appointment to new posts. "A reply to Litvinoff's telegram of November 27th in this sense was sent today. Apparently no message was sent last night . . . . Mukden has now agreed to the conditions of Soviet for starting negotiations". This cable was sent on December 5th.

On December 4th, Moscow *Izvestia* published a communiqué issued by the Soviet Foreign Commissariat confirming the previous announcement of the settlement and quoting a pious declaration by Simanovsky that "on his part . . . the Government of the U.S.S.R. which has always adhered to the agreements existing between China and the U.S.S.R. will of course observe the strictly in general as well as in particular". [2]

In the same issue of *Izvestia* a vitriolic attack was made upon America for having attempted mediation to settle the Sino-Soviet dispute. This matter will be dealt with in detail shortly.

On the afternoon of December 7th, [3] three press despatches were issued. The first one was from Tass Agency and contained the texts of the telegrams exchanged between Chang and Litvinov agreeing on the conditions for a formal conference. The second was from Reuter under a Mukden dateline. It announced the resignation of Lu Yung-huan, president of the C.E.R. The third one was issued by Reuter under a Nanking dateline and announced that Nanking had officially approved the Sino-Soviet protocol, and had appointed Tsai "as plenipotentiary delegate for the formal Sino-Soviet negotiations".

By this time the recently appointed railway officials were com-pletely demoralised and thoroughly dejected. [4] They realised that they had been deserted by their Government and left in an untenable position. The feeling was general that Chang's sole desire was now to settle the Sino-Soviet conflict at any price, that he was "willing to grant any Soviet demands in order to restore normal conditions

---

[1] *Op. cit.*, p. 397.
[2] *Op. cit.*, p. 402.
[3] *Op. cit.*, pp. 410—11.
[4] *Op. cit.*, p. 412.

in North Manchuria". [1] The White Russians were equally left in the lurch, and those of them who had not escaped in good time from the areas overrun by Soviet troops found that Bolshevism had overtaken them. It was reported by the Harbin Consul that the Soviet forces had instituted a reign of terror among the Russians "suspected by them of having carried on White propaganda principally at Manchuria Station and Chalainor". [2] That region was being patrolled by Mongol and other Red military units and by the dread G.P.U. No questions were going to be asked about what the Soviet troops did during their brief occupation of part of a foreign country.

Russia knew that no more would be heard about her undeclared war on China after China had submitted, because, with submission, peace was restored — the "peace" which it was the purpose of the League Covenant and the Kellogg Pact to preserve. Once China had given in, there was no longer any need for the bombers to drop bombs, and it was as if they had never dropped any. This was to be the principle of appeasement in years to come; let everyone persuade the victim of aggression to submit to the aggressor and then there will be peace and politicians can boast about the success of their efforts to prevent war. Russia had known all along that she could get away with it.

Certain that America and the other Powers would take no more drastic action than talk, she realised that she could, with impunity, compel China to settle on Russian terms. China was initially wrong, not in seizing the railway but in the manner and in the methods used. She cannot be defended on a legal basis, but fundamentally Russia was more in the wrong than China, and much more vulnerable if an impartial investigation had come about. It is not being argued that two wrongs make one right, or that because Russia violated the treaties China had a right to do likewise. But China had moral right and international law on her side, had she proceeded in a legal and proper manner, however, it seems to have been incontrovertibly demonstrated that China's original intention was to seize the property, income, assets and business of the C.E.R. for material reasons. Certainly it cannot be denied that China would have done

---

[1] *Loc. cit.*
[2] *Op. cit.*, p. 418.

this had she been allowed to do so with impunity. On the other hand, Russia was in the wrong both in the original misuse of the railway administration for political purposes and in going to war to protect her material interests in China after having adhered to the Kellogg Pact. Russia was initially guilty of breach of contract, treaty and international law—of course, these things mean nothing to Russia when she does them; she only pretends to regard them when she can use them against another nation. As far as Russia is concerned, her cause is always a holy one and her attitude pragmatic; the ends justify the means. So the situation was that China was in physical possession of the railway and Russia was using war as an instrument of policy. By November the dispute had dragged on over five months, and America, who assumed leadership in getting the nations of the world to apply concerted moral pressure, was less concerned to bring pressure to bear upon Russia than to persuade China to settle on any terms. Instead of having the backing of international opinion as a victim of military aggression China felt herself, on account of her confiscation of foreign property, almost a pariah nation among the capitalist powers. It is certainly not pleasant to have to admit the truth of the statement, but it seems incontrovertible that China had been deserted by the other powers over a question which had a direct bearing upon the fate of property rights, private investments and vested interests in China. In short, because they would not allow her to establish a precedent for the unilateral nullification of treaty rights.

In the light of our present knowledge we can see that this policy was extremely short-sighted and took into consideration only the short-term interests. America preferred to let Russia, the great protagonist of the complete destruction of capitalism, win a victory over China, who, at the very worst, could only have abrogated the treaties but who, almost certainly would not in fact have done so. Russia, once allowed a major victory, would ultimately compromise at nothing short of absolute destruction of the capitalist world. She needed an initial victory. The Powers preferred to present her with this rather than allow China to set a precedent of which she could take advantage in the shortly forthcoming negotiations for treaty revision.

America, nevertheless, did make, at the last moment, an attempt to give an international lead for asserting the principles of the Kellogg Pact and it remains for us to follow the steps of Stimson's diplomacy in this move. The action was taken in two stages: the first a simultaneous American-French note to Russia and China (France being the original co-sponsor with America of the Kellogg — or Kellogg-Briand — Pact and also in diplomatic relations with Russia) and then an attempt to get as many other signatories as possible to follow suit. As the news of the signing of the Nikolsk-Ussuriisk protocol on December 3rd, intervened in the middle of the diplomatic exchanges of the second stage, it has never been possible to say just how much support the move would have had if the Russo-Chinese war had continued, but the responses which did come from various capitals indicated both on the one hand the general eagerness of the smaller nations to follow a moral lead for peace and, on the other, the impossibility of getting unanimous action, even on the purely diplomatic plane, because the fear of, or common interest with, Russia, on the part of certain nations.

It is not clear from the documents at what date Stimson first made up his mind to take a diplomatic action in support of the Kellogg Pact, but part of the stimulus seems to have come from Kellogg himself, who kept a paternal interest in the treaty which bore his name. On November 22nd, Dawes sent Stimson a message from London: [1]

> Frank B. Kellogg sends the following to the Secretary of State: He suggests whether the time has not come for the Secretary and the other governments to make the appeal, considered last July, or something like it, to China and Russia before the Manchurian border disorders drift too far.

On the 25th, the Japanese Ambassador saw Johnson, who tried to prepare the way for getting Japan into a joint declaration. [2]

> The Secretary said he wanted the Japanese to understand that he desired to keep them informed of his thoughts in this matter. He said that there was no question of special interests or such like questions involved in his own mind. It was a

---

[1] F.R.U.S., 1929, II, p. 346.
[2] *Op. cit.*, p. 349.

question of the disturbance of peace in the Far East and he thought the Japanese and ourselves were equally interested in seeing the peace preserved and his only proposition at the present moment, or at any moment was to find some way in which peace might be preserved.

The Secretary stated that he was thinking very seriously of what possible steps might be taken by the Powers party to the Kellogg Pact to bring about an amicable settlement of the troubles now besetting the Chinese and the Russians. He said he would be very glad if the Ambassador would communicate that fact to his Government and obtain for him any thoughts or suggestions the Japanese Foreign Minister might have.

The Secretary stated that he had not reached any conclusions in his own mind but he thought perhaps it might be necessary for him to make some kind of a public statement on the subject, calling the attention of the Chinese and Russians to their obligations under the Pact. He said he had not thought of consulting the other Powers on the matter but he wanted to let the Japanese know.

The Ambassador stated he would make inquiry and let the Secretary know what Baron Shidehara had to say. The Ambassador then departed.

The following day Stimson sent instructions to the American Ambassadors in London, Paris, Rome and Tokyo to approach the Ministers of Foreign Affairs in their respective capitals with an American proposal; the Ambassador in Berlin was similarly instructed on the 27th. The brief given by Stimson was to the effect that it was clear that "serious hostilities which approximate a condition of actual warfare" were proceeding between the armed forces of China and Russia. Both China and Russia had adhered to the Paris Pact renouncing war, and when the obligations thus assumed had been called to their attention in July, both countries had reaffirmed their adherence. The United States Government, however, was now so alarmed by "the serious extent to which both China and Russia have recently carried hostile acts" that it considered that the current development of the situation "should not be permitted without protest by those powers who sponsored the pact against its violation". The United States Government proposed to make a statement to be communicated to both the Russian and Chinese Governments as follows: [1]

---

[1] *Op. cit.*, p. 351.

The Government and people of the United States have observed with apprehensive concern the course of events in relations between China and Russia in the phase which has developed in reference to the situation in Northern Manchuria since July 10.

On July 18 this Government took steps, through conversations between the Secretary of State and the diplomatic representatives at Washington of five Powers, to see that the attention of the Chinese and the Russian Governments be called to the provisions of the Treaty for the Renunciation of War, to which both China and Russia were signatories. Both the Russian and Chinese governments then made formal and public assurances that neither would resort to war unless attacked. Since that time that Treaty has been ratified by no less than fifty-five Powers, including China and Russia.

The American Government desires again to call attention to the provisions of the Treaty for the Renunciation of War, particularly to Article II, which reads, 'The High Contracting Parties agree that the settlement or solution of all disputes or conflicts of whatever nature or of whatever origin they may be, which may arise, among them, shall never be sought except by pacific means;' and the American Government takes occasion to express its earnest hope that China and Russia will refrain from measures of hostility and will arrange in the near future to discuss between themselves the issues over which they are at present in controversy. The American Government feels that the respect with which China and Russia will hereafter be held in the good opinion of the world will necessarily in great measure depend upon the way in which they carry out these most sacred promises.

Each American Ambassador was to enquire whether the Government concerned would "be ready to make public a statement, along lines similar to those quoted above, but not necessarily in the same wording, on a date which will be fixed to coincide with this Government's issuance of such a statement on an early date to be decided upon and to communicate it at the same time textually to the Chinese and Russian Governments". A reply was requested by November 28th, and hope was expressed that each Government agreeing to make a declaration would try to bring in other nations adherent to the Paris Pact "so that the protest represents the widest possible signatory group and thereby the broadest possible world opinion". America had thus approached five other major Powers — Great

Britain, France, Italy, Germany and Japan. The request was for parallel statements and not a joint statement. This would leave room for differences of wording and also enable some powers to go ahead if others were unwilling. The British Foreign Secretary, however, told Dawes that he would have preferred a joint statement, though he was "entirely willing" to accept the "general sense" of the American statement. [1] From Paris Armour reported that M. Briand "agrees in principle with the proposed action and is ready to make public a statement, similar to the one you outlined". [2] From Rome the American Ambassador reported that "the Italian Minister for Foreign Affairs is in entire sympathy with the action you have suggested and assures me that his Government will join those of the United States and the other powers you mention in carrying it out"; he also, however, like the British Foreign Secretary, thought a joint note would be more effective. [3]

Responses from Britain, France and Italy were thus favourable, but obstruction came from Germany and Japan. The German Foreign Minister said that Germany was prepared to do "everything in its power, in accordance with the Paris Pact, to further peace in the Far East", but could not give any final decision until there was news of the result of Chang Hsüeh-liang's latest peace move. If America still proposed to go on with the matter "in spite of the change taking place in the situation during the last two days", the German Foreign Minister wanted to know whether the communication was to be made jointly or by each power separately, as "the German Government would find it inconvenient to act alone". [4]

The documents indicate that Germany was definitely on the Russian side in spite of acting as an intermediary in the dispute. It was, indeed, only because of the general pro-Russian orientation of German policy at this time that Russia consented to any channelling of negotiations with China through Berlin. Germany, which determined not to do anything to offend Russia, was anxious not to offend America either, and therefore tried to gain time by delaying.

Japan was even less willing to act as America wished, and in connection with the Sino-Russian dispute she had, of course, a key position among the powers. No joint statement could be impressive

---

[1] *Op. cit.*, p. 356.   [2] *Op. cit.*, p. 357.
[3] *Op. cit.*, p. 359.   [4] *Op. cit.*, pp. 359—360.

if it left out the Great Power nearest to the scene of conflict. Stimson's failure to persuade Japan in 1929 was ominous for his future failures from 1931 to 1933. Japan in fact, though hardly on good terms with Russia, shared with her a vested interest in the system of foreign railway rights in Manchuria and was secretly wanting to see China completely defeated on the C.E.R. issue. So Shidehara told Neville on November 27th, that "he doubted the practical benefit which would ensue from the issuing of a joint statement by the powers". He said that, as China had announced her intention of appealing to the powers, Russia would regard any public statement by them as "instigated" by China. However, he was willing to "tell both the Russians and the Chinese privately that the recent disturbances were attracting the attention of the world and producing a bad impression". He did not believe that "actual warfare" would result from what had been happening and he would hesitate to recommend any action which would "prejudice" direct Sino-Russian negotiations for a settlement. [1]

All this was typical of Shidehara, prophetic of what would be the Japanese line of argument when Japan herself was invading Manchuria. It would not be "actual warfare", just an "incident" or an "affair", and nothing ought to be done to "prejudice" direct negotiations with China, even though military aggression and the bombing of open towns might produce "a bad impression" abroad.

In view of the lack of co-operation from Germany and Japan a joint statement was out of the question, and Stimson decided to proceed in special co-operation with Briand as one of the two original sponsors of the Paris Pact. On November 30th he instructed Armour: [2]

> Having received replies from all of the Governments addressed, and finding the replies in general favorable in principle to my proposal that attention be called to the obligations assumed by the signatories of the Pact of Paris, but finding, further, a variety of opinions, suggestions and proposals as to method of proceeding, the American Government intends for its own part to communicate directly to the Chinese Government and to ask the French Government to transmit to the Russian Government substantially the statement con-

---

[1] *Op. cit.*, pp. 355—6.   [2] *Op. cit.*, pp. 366—7.

tained in paragraph 6 of the Department's telegram under reference, and to make statement public on the morning of Monday, December 2.

I appreciate the promptness and cordiality with which the French Government gave its frank reply to my inquiry, and I hope that the French Government will see its way clear to addressing the Chinese and the Russian Governments in a sense similar to or identical with the communication which the American Government intends to make.

The alterations which will be made in the text as supplied in paragraph 6 of Department's telegram under reference will appear in the next to the last sentence after the semi-colon and will read after "refrain": "or desist from measures of hostility and will find it possible in the near future to come to an agreement between themselves upon a method for resolving by peaceful means the issues over which they are at present in controversy". What precedes and what follows will remain as previously submitted.

I request that you communicate the above immediately to the French Foreign Office.

The American Note was delivered in Moscow, together with a French note on similar lines, by the French Ambassador on December 2nd (and directly to China by the American Minister at the same time). The following reply was received three days later from the Soviet Government: [1]

(1)   The U.R.S.S. has practiced since the first day of its existence a policy of peace and, not following the example of the powers, it has not once had recourse to acts of war, unless one counts the necessary measures of defense calumniating (*called*) into action by a direct attack on the Union or by armed intervention of certain powers in its domestic affairs. It has constantly followed this policy of peace, and it has the intention to follow it, independently of the Treaty of Paris for the Recunciation of War.

(2)   The Government of Nanking, in the course of the last few years, turning aside from the methods which habitually serve (to) resolve, by diplomacy, the disputes which have arisen, has practiced towards the U.R.S.S. (a) policy of provocation which consists of violating the usual international regulations and treaties, although these treaties had not been

---

[1]   F.R.U.S., 1929, II, pp. 404—6.

imposed on China by armed force or other compulsory measures, but had been concluded on the basis of full equality and good will, and although the Soviet Union, as is known, had spontaneously abandoned in these treaties (the) extraterritorial rights, consular jurisdiction and other privileges, the suppression of which the Chinese Government has vainly endeavored up to the present to obtain from the other powers.

(3)   The culminating point of this policy has been the seizure of the Chinese Eastern Railway, without any warning and without previous notification of any claim, in violation of the existing agreements on the conjoint administration of the railway.

(4)   The Soviet Government considers that like conduct on the part of the Government of Nanking, if it had taken place vis-à-vis the United States of America, Great Britain or France, would have been considered by the Governments of these countries a sufficient pretext for invoking the reservations made when signing the Treaty of Paris for the Renunciation of War. The Soviet Government has declared, in its time, that it did not recognize these reservations and that it had no intention of invoking them.

(5)   The Nanking Government has not limited itself to the illegal seizure of the Chinese Eastern Railway, but has mobilized along the Soviet-Manchurian frontier an army, of which certain units in accord with the Russian counter-revolutionary bands which it contains have executed systematic attacks against the U.R.S.S. penetrating into Soviet territory, firing on units of the Red army and on the frontier villages, pillaging and violating the peaceful population and causing, by its acts, considerable loss of life and property. In spite of the repeated warnings given to the Nanking Government, by the intermediary of the German Government, these attacks have not ceased and (but?) they have rather multiplied and become more and more intense. These attacks have obliged the Soviet army of the Far East, in the interest of the defense and protection of the peaceful population of the frontier region, to take counter-measures. Thus the acts of the Red army have been caused by consideration(s) of legitimate defense, absolutely necessary, and do not constitute to any degree the violation of obligations, whatever they be, resulting from (the) Treaty of Paris; this cannot be said of the armed forces which are on Chinese territory and in Chinese ports and which belong to powers which have today addressed identical declarations to the Government of the Union.

(6)   The Government of the Union notes that the Gov-

ernment of the United States of America has forwarded its declaration at the moment when the Soviet and Mukden Governments had already come to an agreement on a series of terms and when direct *pourparlers* are taking place which open up the possibility of a rapid settlement of the Soviet-Chinese conflict.

By reason of this circumstance, the *démarche* in question cannot fail to be considered as a pressure, which nothing justifies, on the *pourparlers*, and consequently it can in no way be considered as a friendly act.

(7)   The Government of the Union notes in addition that the Treaty of Paris for the Renunciation of War does not envisage, either by an individual state or by a group of states, the putting into effect of this pact.

In any case, the Government of the Union has never stated that it agreed that the states (whichever they may be) in their own name, or by virtue of a mutual understanding between themselves, should arrogate to themselves such a right.

(8)   The Government of the Union declares that the Soviet-Manchurian conflict can only be settled by way of direct *pourparlers* between the Soviet Union and China on the basis of terms which are known to China and which are already accepted by the Government of Mukden, and it cannot admit the intervention of anybody in these *pourparlers* or in the conflict.

(9)   In conclusion the Government of the Union cannot fail to express its astonishment that the Government of the United States, which, by its own will, does not entertain any official relations with the Government of the Soviet Union, should find it possible to address to (the) latter advice and recommendations.

This masterpiece of hypocrisy and insolence has since remained presumably in the files of the State Department, but it seems to have been forgotten, for if it had been read by all those concerned in American international policy in 1944 and 1945, it is difficult to believe that the trustfulness shown towards Russia at Teheran, Yalta and Potsdam would have been possible.

We have now reached the end of the story of the C.E.R. crisis, for the news of the settlement came two days after the Franco-American statement and the collective action of the Paris Pact signatories was left with nothing to push against. Meanwhile, however, on December 1st, Stimson sent a circular telegram to

American diplomatic representatives in all countries signatory to the Pact, instructing them to communicate to each Government the American declaration about to be delivered to Russia and China and ask for support on the ground that "if the recent events in Manchuria are allowed to pass without notice or protest by any of these Governments the intelligent strength of the public opinion of the world in support of peace cannot but be impaired." Stimson's instructions concluded: [1]

> It is desired that in presenting the above communication you lay urgent stress upon the importance at this moment to the world movement toward peace that the Powers that have so un-reservedly joined in the Covenant of the Pact of Paris record themselves publicly and to the two Powers so unhappily embroiled as condemning a recourse to arms for the solution of this controversy and as believing that a solution should be reached by pacific means. You will conclude by expressing this Government's earnest hope that the Government to which you are accredited will find it possible as a party to the Pact of Paris to participate in this action by issuing on its part a statement along lines similar to that quoted above and at the same time communicating its views to the Governments of China and Russia. I am addressing communications in this sense to the Governments of all the countries party to the Pact, and I am informing the press with regard to the statement addressed by the American Government to China and to Russia and with regard to this circular communication.

Some of the Governments approached made declarations as suggested, others delayed and then avoided committing themselves on the ground that the crisis was now over, one or two definitely refused. Perhaps the most notable event of this last-minute diplomatic activity was Litvinov's action with regard to the note which Rumania, having no diplomatic relations with Russia, but following the American example, addressed to Russia through the French Ambassador in Moscow. When the latter said that it was his duty to present it, Litvinov took it and tore it up without reading it.

On January 2nd, 1930, Russia reassumed control of the C.E.R.,

---

[1] *Op. cit.*, p. 373.

CHRISTOPHER, Conflict in the Far East   11

when the new Russian Manager and Assistant Manager took charge of administration, and on the 3rd, they reappointed former Russian heads of departments who had been discharged by the Chinese. This completed China's defeat and made it doubly humiliating. She had lost a great deal more than "face".

For this abject surrender the Western Powers could thank themselves, since they had preferred it to a strong China fresh from a victory over Russia in the forthcoming treaty revision negotiations. Property rights must be protected at all costs, even in alliance with proletarian revolution.

It was wise, from the short-term view, in 1929. Was it wise from the long-term view? Looking from the vantage point of 1949, the answer is emphatically no.

American policy with Italy led to the conquest of Ethiopia, with Germany to the attack on Poland, with Japan to the bombs on Pearl Harbour. What did American policy in the C.E.R. dispute in 1929 lead to? At any rate to the Iron Curtain on the Elbe, the Adriatic and the Yellow Sea: the question 'how much more?' is before each of us today. It haunts us, goes to bed with us and gets up with us. Will the United States in future have the moral courage which they did not have in 1929? And if not, what will be the result? The use of the atomic bomb?

CHAPTER X

THE PROBLEM OF RELINQUISHING EXTRATERRITORIALITY

The question of the relinquishment of extraterritoriality was one which had to be faced by the Powers after China had succeeded in establishing the semblance of a strong, popular Government. The Powers could either take a firm, uncompromising stand or give careful and sympathetic attention to the possibility of revision. The latter did not mean, or should not mean, immediate abolition with no preparation on the part of the Powers or China. This would have been manifestly unfair and unfortunate to all concerned. It is not being argued that extraterritoriality was a just or desirable institution, though it was perhaps morally defensible in the circumstances under which it arose. There is no question that great abuses of the institution existed. Some of the Powers were much more to blame than others in this respect. But at the time it was conceded by or extracted by force from the Chinese there was, as we have seen, no alternative, considering the contrasts of Western and Chinese law and legal concepts. In course of time a certain operable framework had been built up which, if suddenly abolished without preparation and establishment of a modern legal system and means of enforcement by China, would have resulted in chaos. China would have suffered as much as the West by an abrupt change, and has in fact so suffered from the ending of foreign administration in Shanghai since 1945.

On May 3rd, 1929, [1] Stimson wired MacMurray that the Chinese Minister had left with him a note requesting " 'immediate and sympathetic consideration' to the desire of China 'to have the restrictions on her jurisdictional sovereignty removed at the earliest possible date' ". He stated that similar notes were being presented

---

[1] F.R.U.S., 1929, II, p. 561.

to a number of other states. Stimson asked MacMurray to verify this, and in reply [1] MacMurray stated that it was true, and that as a result the interested Ministers had met to discuss the matter. [2] At the meeting they had agreed in the belief that the sudden termination would lead to a progressive intensification of tension and ill-feeling between China and the Powers. They had decided that they should advise their Governments that replies should be "substantially identical" in stating that "any modification is deemed to be premature pending further demonstration by Chinese judicial institutions of their capacity to deal with cases which affect foreign interests". MacMurray said that the Chinese request was based upon a series of "assumptions which are contrary to facts" and that the seeming unity was really a truce, if not a stalemate, between various factions whose interests were "if indeed not irreconcilable, still unreconciled and the stability of the central governmental authority . . . precarious". He pointed out that the experience of the Powers which had lost the right did not augur well for present relinquishment by the other Powers and that there was no hope that foreigners would be given justice by the Chinese if relieved of all restrictions.

MacMurray and the other interested Ministers worked out a reply to the request for abolition of extrality which he forwarded to Stimson for his consideration: [3]

> The following is the text which the British, Dutch and French Ministers and myself have elaborated for submission to our respective Governments as a basis for substantially identical replies:
>
> 'I have the honor to acknowledge the receipt of the note under date of April 27th in which you expressed the hope that the Government of (blank) would take into immediate and sympathetic consideration the desire of the Chinese Government to be enabled to assume jurisdiction over nationals within the domain of China.
>
> Having carefully considered this request, my Government has instructed me to recall to Your Excellency that it was happy to participate in the resolution adopted on December 10,

---

[1] Loc. cit.

[2] Op. cit., pp. 562—3.

[3] Op. cit., pp. 563—4.

1921, by the Washington Conference on Limitation of Armament under which was established an international commission to inquire into the present practice of extraterritorial jurisdiction in China and into the laws and the judicial system and the method of judicial administration in China. Your Excellency will not fail to recall that that Commission which rendered its report under date of September 16, 1926, laid down a variety of recommendations upon reasonable compliance with which it considered that the several powers would be warranted in relinquishing their respective rights of extraterritoriality. In view of the findings of fact of the Commission and of its recommendations (in which as will be recalled the Chinese member unreservedly concurred) my Government cannot but feel that as a condition precedent to the relinquishment of American extraterritorial rights (in accordance with article 15 of the commercial treaty of October 8, 1903) it is now incumbent upon the Chinese Government to carry the reform of its laws and judicial system and of its administration of justice to the point indicated as necessary by that Commission. My Government feel that it would be less than frank if it were not to acknowledge that its subsequent observation of the workings of the Chinese courts, and particularly of the Provisional Court established in the International Settlement at Shanghai by agreement between the Chinese and foreign authorities, has not tended to inspire its confidence either in their administrative functioning or in the independence of Chinese judicial institutions from outside influences.

My Government further instructs me to assure you that until such time as the relinquishment of extraterritorial rights may become necessary it will continue to observe with attentive and sympathetic interest such further progresses as may be effected in these matters, and such demonstration as may be made by the Chinese Government of its capacity and willingness to do justice in cases affecting foreign persons and interests and that it will continue to hope for opportunities of helpful cooperation with the Chinese authorities with a view to hastening a situation in which it would feel warranted in agreeing to modifications of the present juridical status of American citizens in China.

Some time later MacMurray notified Stimson that the Japanese and Belgian Ministers had told him and several colleagues that they had learned confidentially that the Chinese planned to abolish extrality on January 1st, 1930. The Chinese Foreign Minister was the source of the information. The next move was a visit to Johnson by Millard, an American adviser to the Chinese Government, who told him that the Chinese must and would abolish extrality, and that they hoped to be able to ask the nations to do so on January 1st, 1930. He said that it was the smart thing to do because it would strengthen the present Government, which was a moderate one, and enable them to keep power, but that if the radicals could use as propaganda the fact that the present government had not got rid of it they might overthrow Chiang and establish a Government much less friendly to the Western Powers.

Stimson asked MacMurray his opinion of future prospects and the line America should take if the Chinese unilaterally were to denounce their extrality treaty with the U.S. MacMurray replied that firm and definitive action should be inaugurated by sending the draft note and standing firm with the other Powers. He felt that this would prevent premature or precipitate action on the part of the Chinese in cancelling the treaty.

On July 9th, [1] Stimson sent a wire in which he told MacMurray that he wanted more information and wanted him to telegraph his views immediately on several points. He wanted to know what obligations China had evaded, before he "discuss(ed) with the Chinese Minister the question of the Chinese presuming upon our good will and their evasion of obligations". But the really important point about the wire is the statement, which Stimson adopted and acted upon consistently throughout the extrality negotiations: "Your recommendation . . . is, as I understand it, that this country take the leadership in organizing . . . an anti-China international bloc. Of course, such a step would involve my substituting for the independent policy followed hitherto, a policy of international cooperation". He pointed out that this was a very momentous step, and that he wanted to know his opinion of the "obvious dangers which are involved" by the certain withdrawal of one or more Powers cooperating, "when its (their) national interests can be better served by some other policy" thus leaving the United States "isolated". It would, further-more, be very likely that this "reversal of policy would mean losing the country's support" which Coolidge had for his "independent China policy". He felt that the Government would only be justified in taking such a risk "in facing some supreme emergency". He

---

[1] *Op. cit.*, pp. 581—2.

wanted a detailed opinion on how the international cooperation would work, and pointed out that it depended on acting soon enough "to forestall the Chinese in initiating and publishing plans which would commit them so far that their withdrawal without loss of face would be impossible". This raised the question "whether the hour may perhaps have already passed when anything can be accomplished . . . as suggested".

In answer to this wire [1] MacMurray pointed out that "no obligation binds China if it is found to be irksome", as far as the "unequal treaties" are concerned. He showed that this view was held as axiomatic by all alike. He quoted the case of the illegal institution of the $2\frac{1}{2}$ % interim surtax, the Chinese promise and refusal to abolish likin, China's unilateral denunciation of the tariff prior to the agreed date of abolition, and the attempted use of the American treaty, through a "construction" of the text, in later negotiations with other nations, "which would largely have nullified the non-discriminatory treatment principle". He cited many other cases as well. The document must be read to realize just how serious the whole problem was and how well informed was the Minister. He held that his proposals did not imply a reversal of policy, and felt that it was definitely not too late for strong action to prevent "a forcing of the extraterritoriality issue".

After numerous conferences it was decided to follow the new policy of international co-operation. He had MacMurray, and later, Johnson, co-operate closely with the other Powers, and he developed and adopted to all intents and purposes a policy identical with that of Great Britain until the question was dropped after the invasion of Manchuria by Japan at the end of our period. After a long and arduous period of negotiations, during which, on several occasions, deadlocks were reached and talks temporarily abandoned, a mutually satisfactory plan was finally worked out.

On August 1st, Stimson drafted a reply [2] to the Chinese Government's request for abolition which in effect devise "a method for the gradual relinquishment of extraterritorial rights", either on a territorial basis or on a basis of kinds of jurisdiction or both,

---

[1] *Op. cit.*, pp. 585—90.
[2] *Op. cit.*, pp. 596—9.

provided this proceeded in accompaniment with progress and improvements on the part of the Chinese Government "in the enactment and effective enforcement of laws based on modern concepts of jurisprudence". Arrangements were made that the American, British, Dutch and French replies would all bear the same date and be delivered on the 10th of August. They would not be identical, but similar. Other powers were notified to enable them to take similar action. [1] Evidently the Chinese realized that they had to be satisfied with this, because, after the Chinese Minister had talked to Stimson [2] and expressed his disappointment, upon learning that it was all Stimson would do, the Chinese Government notified America on September 10th, that they wished to start negotiations immediately. [3] As a further indication of this fact, Sun Fo talked with the Consul at Canton and told him that the National Government had just considered abolition by mandate but decided "to negotiate with the powers for extraterritoriality cancellation over period of years". [4]

It was felt by Great Britain that it would be better to delay the delivery of the notes until November 1st, 1929, to give them more time to come to an agreement on the most mutually satisfactory terms in which the notes could be couched. It was decided by all the interested Powers to delay delivery of the note until November 1st. Stimson was concerned to start as soon as possible, since he felt this was the only way to prevent unilateral denunciation and abrogation by China. The notes were delivered on November 1st. They were so worded that they left no doubt about the intention of the Powers to prevent cancellation by the Chinese Government. They reiterated the conditions set forth in the note of 10th August, and said that, if China wished to negotiate on that basis, the Governments were anxious to begin negotiations at once. The Chinese Minister inquired when negotiations could begin and was told that they would begin as soon as Stimson, who was away, returned to Washington. On November 20th, C. T. Wang reiterated his determination to abolish extrality on January 1st, 1930.

---

[1] F.R.U.S., 1929, II, p. 599.
[2] *Op. cit.*, p. 600.
[3] *Op. cit.*, pp. 604—6.
[4] *Op. cit.*, p. 607.

Stimson assigned the Assistant Secretary to work out the details with the Chinese Minister. Since China had no suggestions, the Americans had to work out a plan in collaboration with the other Powers, primarily Great Britain. On the 21st, [1] the notice of abrogation [2] again appeared in the press in China, specifying that this did not mean abrogation of treaties but just of the clauses pertaining to extrality. At a meeting of the Ministers in China the British Minister told his colleagues that his Government had warned China against abrogation and had refused the Chinese request to hold the negotiations in London. At this point the British and Americans asked the Chinese Ministers in London and Washington to notify their Government to appoint delegates to work out the details.

On December 5th, Wu told Stimson that he was making no progress with the Assistant Secretary. On the 17th, he presented the Assistant Secretary a memorandum proposing that on January 1st, 1930, all Americans be subject to Chinese laws and courts, stating that special courts would be established in certain cities to handle cases in which Americans were involved, either in civil or criminal actions, with foreign legal advisers to observe proceedings. This fitted in with a notice from the British Minister in China, that the Chinese Government had decided to abrogate extrality rights on January 1st, and would establish at Canton, Hankow, Harbin, Shanghai and Tientsin, modern courts in which foreign advisers would be employed. [3] On the 21st, the Assistant Secretary of State told Wu that his proposal was unacceptable, and proposed establishment of a commission to examine Chinese laws and see if they were being effectively applied in the courts. Wu made a counter-proposal which was simply a restatement of China's abrogation of extrality on January 1st. [4] He called on Hornbeck on the 28th, and asked how the Department felt about the counter-proposal; he was told that it, also, was unacceptable, but Hornbeck suggested certain changes which, in effect, constituted a revised

---

[1] *Op. cit.*, p. 627.

[2] There had been a number of hints and threats of unilateral abolition. *Op. cit.*, pp. 575, 607, 617, 620, 626.

[3] *Op. cit.*, pp. 631—2.

[4] *Op. cit.*, pp. 651—2.

proposal, providing for relinquishment by stages. He then read Wu a statement in which it was pointed out that these rights were created by agreement and that America could not by law, and would not on principle, agree to "their abolition by any other process".

On December 28th, [1] the Chinese Government issued a mandate abolishing the right as from January 1st, and ordering the executive and judicial branches of the Government to prepare for its full execution. Perkins immediately ordered the Nanking Consulate not to acknowledge the mandate and told the officials that, pending instructions, they should maintain the same attitude as in the past and carry out their duties in the same manner. Wang, true to the oriental tradition, left a loophole for retreat by issuing another statement that the Chinese would welcome discussion before implementing the mandate. Stimson instructed Perkins that "the Department does not regard the declaration of the Chinese Government as having altered the legal *status quo*". [2] Wu asked Hornbeck to give American approval to the mandate, as he said that the British Government had done. Hornbeck told Wu that he did not believe that the Chinese Government intended to abrogate, but would be willing to negotiate, and Wu admitted that this was so. On the same day Stimson instructed Perkins to say, in reply to any inquiries, that America had entered into no agreement on the question and no encouragement had been given to the idea that America would assent to unilateral abrogation, but that discussions were continuing with the Chinese Minister and that they would continue as far as America was concerned.

On January 2nd, 1930, Wang Chung-hui, President of the Yüan, told Meyer, Consul at Nanking, that: "There are some phases of the question of extraterritoriality concerning which the Chinese Government is prepared to negotiate and there are others which it is not", stating that "It is not willing to negotiate with the powers on any question of principle". [3] He said that, if the Powers

---

[1] *Op. cit.*, p. 666. On the 6th, Wang told J. B. Powell, an American editor in Shanghai, that unless the Powers agreed to the abolition, China would unilaterally abolish it as from January 1st, 1930.

[2] *Op. cit.*, p. 671.

[3] F.R.U.S., 1930, Vol. II, pp. 353—4.

wanted to discuss details of the new mandate which had recently been issued and make suggestions, the suggestions would be welcome. On the same day Wu went to see Stimson and said he was dissatisfied with the proposals being presented by America. He suggested abolition in all places except Canton, Shanghai, Tientsin, Hankow, and Harbin; Americans to come under Chinese jurisdiction in all parts of China except in those places; an agreement that after a short time abolition would be final in all parts of China. Stimson, of course, refused.

On January 15th, Jenkins wired Washington that the impression was gaining ground in China that America was the only country opposing abolition of extrality. Cotton, Acting Secretary of State, replied that this was untrue, but that America was not prepared to see it end abruptly or in violation of treaty rights. He added that negotiations for a mutually acceptable solution were progressing satisfactorily at Washington. In reply to a question from the Japanese Ambassador as to how negotiations were going and what had been done and agreed to by America, Stimson replied that the "American Government is not as yet committed definitely to any particular plan, but is considering" in discussions between members of the Department and the Chinese Minister "various plans and possibilities".

Negotiations continued, a plan would be drawn up to which Wu would object and work would begin on a new one. Really the Department was marking time to see what would happen. As long as they could keep negotiating, whether or not they were getting anywhere, the Chinese Government could not throw the blame on America if they were suddenly to implement the mandate. The Americans were working together on a proposed draft of their own and were also discussing and revising one originally made by the British. They took the best points of the American and British drafts and tried to make a new one out of them. They differed on several important points. As a matter of fact the British and American Ministers had worked out in China what promised to be an acceptable agreement. After having referred it back to their Governments for comments and suggestions, they finally got to the point where they were ready to work on a final draft. They were keeping their Ministerial colleagues informed, and these, in turn, kept in touch with their respective Governments. Suddenly Stimson sent a message to Perkins which, even after having been decoded became clear only after many previous despatches had been gone through, clause by clause and paragraph by paragraph. Stimson instructed him not to reveal any more information or to refer any further inquiries to Washington, but to continue working alone with the British on the matter. His sending the message as he did must have had some special significance. In those simple times nations had not had to worry about such sinister things at "cracking codes". The message ended "Defer action until further instructed". This action seems to have been directed against the Japanese, because in a previous exchange the Japanese Chargé had asked for a draft. Stimson instructed Perkins: "Department suggests that unless it be embarrassing for you communication of copy of draft to Shigemitsu be by British Minister rather than by American Minister".

On May 15th, Wu went to the State Department and asked that negotiations be resumed. On May 16th, the British Councillor of Embassy sent Hornbeck the revised draft which the ministers in China had largely worked out and enclosed some amendments suggested by the British Foreign Office. This was sent to Johnson in China after it had been revised to include the new points for comment.

On August 5th, 1930, the State Department wired the British Foreign Office asking whether or not it was true that they were about to communicate proposals to the Chinese and whether or not they would be willing to agree that neither country should submit proposals without giving the order two weeks notice before so doing. The Ambassador told Stimson that the Chinese Government had already been told that the British Minister would spend some time at Nanking in September working on the question and carrying out discussions — political conditions permitting. [1] He also informed Stimson that the Foreign Office was in agreement with his suggestion about giving two weeks advance notice before submitting proposals to the Chinese Government.

Cotton wired Dawes on September 7th, that he did not consider it a propitious time to make a simultaneous presentation of pro-

---

[1] *Op. cit.*, p. 453.

posals, but that, if Britain did present hers, the Department would let the Chinese know that America had full knowledge of the matter, and that in October they would present their own proposal which was almost the same. He instructed him so to inform the Foreign Office, and the latter informed Dawes that previous commitments made it impossible for them to delay presentation. The Assistant Secretary of State for Foreign Affairs confidentially informed Dawes that "the recent conversations between the Governments, with the inference that other Governments were excluded, had caused in some quarters a certain resentment against his Government". On September 11th, 1930, the British draft was presented to the Chinese Minister for Foreign Affairs. On the 25th, the Chinese announced that it was unacceptable and that they would present counter-proposals. On October 28th, Hornbeck handed to Wu a copy of the American draft. Stimson wired Johnson that he did not expect that there would be an immediate discussion of the draft. On November 7th, Wang, in anticipation of the American draft, delivered an inflammatory address in which he stated that the most important thing in the world to China was the abolition of extrality and that only the complete backing of the people could assure it. On the 12th, Wu turned up to say that the draft was most unsatisfactory and that he considered it better for China to enter into no new proposal than to enter into this one. He made no counter-proposals.

On December 17th, [1] Stimson asked Johnson what he thought of the likelihood of unilateral abrogation. Johnson did not know, but said the Chinese had practically given an ultimatum to the French. In reply to a query as to what new moves the British intended to make, he replied that the British Minister was leaving until February and intended taking no new action until his return. On the 18th, the Assistant Secretary of State noted in a memorandum that in a discussion with Wu, the latter had said that he wanted an answer to his counter-proposals by the first day of the new year, and discussed unilateral action. [2] On the 19th, Wu told Stimson that the proposal was unsatisfactory, but that he hoped it

---

[1] *Op. cit.*, p. 494.
[2] *Op. cit.*, p. 496.

could be remedied by the end of February and that his Government believed that the matter could be satisfactorily solved without China's having to take a different course of action. On the 23rd, it was the view of all the Ministers in China that the Chinese Government would implement the mandate.

On the 31st, [1] Stimson told Dawes that he felt that the time was more propitious than it would be later for concluding new agreements.

Despite the threat to abolish extrality on the 1st January, 1930, 1st January, or end of February 1931, no such action was taken. China was very foolish to alienate the sympathy of America and of Great Britain by her constant threats. In any case she was not able to carry out any threats against another Power. She was not able to defend herself against Russia, after she had precipitated the war. She was about to prove herself helpless against the Japanese. She was not even able to set her own house in order. China had been engaged in a war with Russia, while Communists, bandits and local militarists had large parts of the country under their control — as far as Nanking was concerned — and these same two nations which she was now so vociferously threatening were in daily contact with Chinese officials in all parts of China protesting kidnappings, murders, and outrages against their citizens and seizure, looting and occupation of their property. How could they, no matter how reasonable they might be, nor how friendly to China, be expected to give up a treaty right under such circumstances?

Whether or not we like to admit it there is no blinking the fact that, from the documents available, America and Britain began to turn against China over the treaty question, over her nagging threats and total undependability, both nationally and internationally. If China had had a slight chance of using military force to get "justice" over the "unequal treaties", there is little question that the nations would have been more amenable to her requests and demands, that they would have been willing to yield more and to compromise, as they were soon to do with Japan. This may be a callous thing to admit, but it is true of human nature, regardless of other considerations. On the other hand, in all fairness it must

---

[1] *Op. cit.*, p. 504.

be added that, if China had ordered her own house properly or had made a serious and honest effort to do so, as Japan had done between 1865 and 1885, she would not have needed to threaten, for the powers would have been willing to concede and co-operate. Certainly one sympathises with China but one must not be blind to the facts.

Opinion among the well-informed in 1931 was agreed that the wise thing to do in China was to make concessions and make them willingly and gracefully. The alternative was military action on a large scale. Not war but a sort of guerilla activity, attacking and fading away, everywhere outside the large cities, a perpetual irritation with continuous attacks on isolated westerners, and an incurable and fatal spread of anti-foreignism, used as a political whip and a plank in every political platform.

This was well expressed by Sir Victor Wellesley, Deputy Under Secretary of the Foreign Office, to Atherton, American Chargé in London. He pointed out that as civil war gradually died down "the demand for the abolition of extraterritoriality would unite all factions" and unless foreigners made some gesture, or token concession, there would likely be an "antiforeign boycott by Chinese". He said it would be better for foreign governments to make concessions now than later, though fully realizing "that however much foreign governments offered to give way China would demand further concessions". He felt that a united front between Japan, England and America was a *sine qua non* and "a scheme for gradual abolition, giving away the shadow at first, to be followed later by part of the substance, must be worked out". He was thinking along the lines of territorial abolition, that is abolition excepting large cities, heavily populated by foreigners. He thought it better to give way on criminal jurisdiction than on civil, because "Chinese courts would be competent in criminal cases, while corruption in civil cases would completely destroy foreign investment in China". [1] Stimson felt the same way and was anxious to make some acceptable settlement which would be fair to China and at the same time protect legitimate personal and property rights of American citizens. He had in the past kept the negotiation going with Wu, as a sort

---

[1] F.R.U.S., 1931, Vol. III, pp. 716—7.

of glorified stall while the Department worked out just what was required and what was the minimum America must concede. He cannot be blamed for this. No matter how unfair may have been the treaties on which extrality was based, he was not responsible for them, but he was Secretary of State and bound to protect the interests of his people. China was being as selfish in trying to get rid of certain treaty rights (in relation to Stimson, not to ultimate justice) as he was in trying to preserve those same rights. He was working closely with Britain, but both were becoming more and more liberal and more in a mood to make concessions. In fact, they had jointly worked out a new and revised plan which seemed very fair.

On the 21st, Johnson wired Stimson setting forth the points he thought should be insisted upon, under all circumstances. The principal points were tax exemptions, personal status, protection of real property titles, and exclusion of the International Settlement at Shanghai. These were comments upon or suggestions for revision of the draft treaty worked out by America and Great Britain and rejected by the Chinese.

The State Department resumed negotiations early in February more in line with Britain's idea of gradual relinquishment over a much longer time than America had originally planned to do. On February 7th, Hornbeck handed to the Chinese Minister a statement attempting to reconcile the differences between the proposals and counterproposals, which had passed so freely in the past three months. At the same time he emphasized the importance to foreign governments of internal stability in China, and said that America would not assent to any arrangement failing to safeguard her citizens.

Because of the crippling, if not subversive tactics of Wang and the Minister at Washington, Stimson ordered discussions discontinued, and asked Johnson so to inform Sir Miles. He also told Johnson to let Wang know that it might help if he took a less truculent attitude in the approach to negotiations. He also told Johnson to tell Wang that America and Britain could not be played off against one another, and would not outbid one another in making concessions. Stimson said neither would "give their assent to a non-gradual, complete sweeping away of extraterritorial rights", and that the "problem is to substitute for the present system an arrangement regulating better than at present the contacts between foreigners in China and the Chinese people". He suggested that negotiations be returned to Nanking. Wang refused this point as soon as Johnson made it. Nevertheless Stimson advised Wang that he was instructing Johnson to take up the discussions with him there. Wang still refused unless America was willing to concede the three points on which the two nations were deadlocked:

> The surrender of criminal jurisdiction over American nationals in China in addition to the surrender of civil and police jurisdiction.

> The appointment of legal counsellors (who shall function without any rights as co-judges) by the Chinese Government without restriction of choice.

> The elimination of any reserved areas from the proposed scheme for the relinquishment of extraterritorial rights.

The Americans knew that Sir Miles and Wang were making little, if any progress in their talks, and the Americans were given a detailed account of the situation concerning the discussions. The British were getting rather dispirited by the lack of co-operation on the part of Wang. Stimson instructed Johnson to work closely with his British colleague and to do nothing without first discussing it with him. Wang again refused to reopen the discussions on a basis of their transfer to Nanking unless assured that the change would not alter China's adamant stand on the three points; he said he had never been willing to negotiate on a basis of gradual relinquishment.

When it seemed that the game was lost, the discussions between Wang and Sir Miles developed, by the end of March, to the point where there were only a few minor points to clear up. But as an indication of the seriousness with which Britain and America regarded possible action on the part of China in unilateral denunciation, the British ambassador discussed with Stimson, Castle, and Far Eastern experts the problem of what action to take in such an eventuality. It was agreed that, as soon as China felt strong enough she would take this action, and that war, seizure of the customs, stoppage of aid, etc., were no solutions; the only solution was to negotiate a treaty as soon as possible.

CHRISTOPHER, Conflict in the Far East   12

Things had progressed so far that by April 23rd, 1931, Wang said he believed the treaties might be signed within a few days, and asked Johnson to enquire as to place and date of signing the treaty, whether Washington would demand that it be signed there, or whether it might be signed in Nanking. Johnson replied that it could be signed simultaneously in both places. This was confirmed by Washington a few days later and Wang was notified. But things were moving too fast and too smoothly. Lampson found Wang's final offer unacceptable, and a few days later the People's Conference met and issued a mandate accompanied by regulations, putting an end to extraterritoriality on January 1st, 1932. Chiang Kai-shek, Ho Ying-chin and Chang Hsüeh-liang were present when the decision was taken. At this point Stimson instructed Johnson to keep in close touch with Lampson and if necessary make certain new concessions if he thought wise. On the 13th, a new manifesto was issued declaring that China did not recognize any unequal treaties previously signed between China and any other foreign power, and that she would now put into force the freedom and equality of China. Unfortunately China had not yet learned that reforms, equality and freedom cannot be decreed and hence come into existence merely by the decree. Stimson realized that the matter was serious and instructed Johnson to try to dissuade Wang from sending an official diplomatic notice of the manifesto to America, but that if he insisted, as a last resort to accept it without comment. He suggested that he and Lampson agree on the same action and carry it out.

On June 19th, Peck was notified by Wang of the resignation of Wu and informed that the Chinese would like to resume negotiations at Nanking. However, it was decided to let them proceed in Washington for the time. Wang became less recalcitrant and agreed to compromise on the question of Shanghai, among other points. It was decided by the Americans and British that, if the internal strife then going on between the Chinese were settled, it would be wise to drive through a treaty. By the middle of November it seemed that this was possible, because as soon as China became involved with Japan, anti-foreign incidents lessened throughout China and the officials became more amenable. However, it was reported by Peck that although he had "good intimations", and despite the fact that no definite machinery had been set up for implementation, steps were being taken in that direction and that there might be "unfortunate incidents after January 1st".

Johnson had a long and frank talk with Wellington Koo about the possibilities of implementation of the manifesto, and Koo, Acting Foreign Minister, said that the fact that America was ready to resume negotiations would greatly help in handling the question. The U.S. therefore notified China on the 19th, that she was ready to resume the discussions. There was great speculation and uneasiness about the action China might take to enforce the mandate and there was general resignation in Washington, London and in the Legations in China. But the worry came to an end on December 29th, because the Chinese issued another mandate postponing the effective date of the May 4th mandate.

After all, China had got through one war with Russia and was now deep in another with Japan in Manchuria. Japan was by the end of 1931 in practically complete control of Manchuria. It was rather ironical that America and England should be sitting shivering about the Chinese mandates for abrogating their treaty rights, while they were at the same time making an attempt, though less than half-hearted, to stop Japan on China's behalf from breaking all the treaties to which she was a signatory. China unfortunately has never been thankful for anything done for her, but a sense of expediency, if not of gratitude, led her to suspend her threats against America, Britain and France at the time when her appeal for help was before the League of Nations.

CHAPTER XI

MEASURES TAKEN BY THE UNITED STATES FOR THE PROTECTION OF AMERICAN LIVES IN CHINA

In reading the literature and the documents covering the period 1929—'33, or in discussing China with those who lived there during that period, one is struck by the seeming lawlessness and violence of the time. Actually, when one reviews the history of the era, one realizes that this is a superficial observation. It is true that there was much violence, but one should think of the period as one of anarchy. All semblance of organized central government was gone and a new one had not yet been established. There is cause for surprise at the infrequency of murder, kidnapping and banditry, rather than at the excesses.

Chiang Kai-shek, it must be remembered, rose to power under the aegis of Sun Yat-sen and the Russian Communist advisers who gave the Kuomintang at least the semblance of an efficient organisation, a good army, and a functioning administration. Above all, the Communists organized a deadly propaganda machine, which was even more responsible than was the army for the successes of the Kuomintang, because it undermined the morale of the anti-Nationalists and disheartened their troops. It must also be remembered that in the beginning Chiang was just as much a part of the Communist-directed movement as the most radical left-wing members of the Kuomintang. He used, and profited by, the effects of the propaganda and the tactics of the Communists to rise to power. He used the system of vilification, hatred and mob action against foreigners and all the other devices of the Communists as instruments of policy. Then there was a scramble for power.

There is justification for the embittered Kuomintang left-wing and the Communists in their charge that Chiang sold out to the bankers and merchants at Shanghai to get funds and support to enable to seize control. He not only seized control, but he has firmly held on to it — not real control, in an orderly sense of the word, not the sort of control which is positive and leads to national stability and democracy — but a personal, political and military ascendancy which has been continually exploited for the benefit of special interests.

When his fortunes were at a low ebb, he suddenly discovered the Soongs — or the Soongs discovered him — just as Americans discovered the Klondike, and with much the same results, but with one big difference. It is questionable whether or not the Klondike benefited much from the discovery. There is no such question where the Soongs are concerned.

Chiang rose to power, then, on the tide of rampant nationalism. He stayed in power on the subsidy of special interests, Chinese and foreign. But after the mutual discovery he did not drop the anti-foreign propaganda. He could not. It was his hold on the people, which made it possible for him to get financial backing from business interests who regarded him both as a menace to be bought off and also as a potentially strong ally against the Communists.

He rose to power on the propaganda platform of abrogation of the "unequal" treaties and special rights of foreigners in China. He started a fire he could not extinguish, had he so desired. He had little direct control over his minor subordinates, who, through appeals to nationalist sentiment, were stirring the masses in the interior even more than on the coast. It is natural that these simple people, who had for so long suffered every imaginable type of injustice at the hands of their former rulers — and lack of responsible rulers — should go to excesses. The situation was explosive. The radicals and super-nationalists did all they could to aggravate the situation. One of the principal reasons for this, after the Kuomintang was recognised as the *de facto*, and later as the *de jure* government of China, was the diversion of their attention from the government and its shortcomings.

The documents on the subject "Measures taken by the United States for the Protection of American Lives and Property in China" are legion. They fill a large part of several volumes issued by the State Department covering this period. A few typical cases will be chosen at random and one or two followed through, to indicate American diplomatic policy in this field under Stimson. It is obvious that only a few cases can be dealt with and the high points touched upon, within the limits of this study—on the other hand such a work would be incomplete if it did not touch upon this important phase of American policy in China.

On July 17th, the American Consul-General at Hankow, Lockhart, suggested to Stimson [1] that the Legation request the National Government of China to issue a number of proclamations signed by the appropriate officials, and bearing their seals, forbidding the occupancy of American property by Chinese troops. This was done as a result of the tremendous loss suffered by American institutions in China through seizure, occupation and looting by the soldiers. It was a very serious problem. Such acts were often done maliciously to show the contempt and resentment of the Chinese troops toward foreign rights, at the instigation of superior military and civil officials.

On August 6th, the same Consul sent a long despatch to Stimson [2] in which he pointed out that the previous despatches covering such cases of seizure and occupation in the three consular districts under his supervision during the past three years numbered 112. In most instances, and in all those of the past year, assurances had been given by high officials in Nanking. These had been violated consistently by the military authorities. He stated that there had been times when few of these cases had concerned missionary property, but that invariably these instances occurred when there were no military operations under way. He said that the most persistent representations of the Governments whose nationals were the owners had been absolutely ignored, with the exception of a few isolated cases. This continued even after Chiang Kai-shek's arrival at Hankow, and oral representations made to him by the Consuls concerned. It was only after troops were transferred to other areas that the properties were vacated. He pointed out that General T'ang Sheng-chi, with whom we are already acquainted, was the most notorious in this respect and that it was "his long established policy of occupying foreign mission property whenever and wherever it may be required". He ridiculed the Kuomintang's claim of control of

---

[1] F.R.U.S., 1929, II, pp. 465—6.
[2] Op. cit., pp. 466—70.

China, which "would be ludicrous if it were not so serious", [1] since it made the Nanking Government assume a responsibility, the performance of which it was patently unable to carry out. "There is but one conclusion that can be drawn from this situation, and that is that the National Government either does not possess sufficient authority to prevent its own troops from occupying such property or else the National Government, with its full knowledge and consent, encourages its military leaders to use the properties in whatever manner they may choose .... I thoroughly believe that the National Government ... possesses sufficient authority ... to cause every piece of American mission property to be vacated within five days time ... and prevent henceforth ... occupation ... by soldiers" [2] (sic). (There seems to be a discrepancy in Lockhart's statements here.) He thought that if the government wished to protect foreign property as it claimed to be in a position to do, it could do so if the officers were disciplined by the government as the same officers disciplined "so-called agitators and petty law breakers". He believed that he was right in saying that almost every case of such occupation "has been at the instance, or with the consent, of an officer of considerable rank". [3] He cited eighty-six such cases in recent months, and felt that there was no improvement.

On September 12th, MacMurray notified C. T. Wang, Chinese Foreign Minister, that military authorities on August 9th, had made an unauthorised boarding and search of an American ship, enclosing a statement of the captain. He requested Wang to "investigate the matter", to order "the punishment of the military authorities involved" and to take appropriate steps to "ensure cessation of such illegal activities in the future". [4]

On the 24th, the Government at Canton issued and circulated a despatch requesting that foreigners should not proceed to the interior without first consulting responsible Chinese officials. They were, at the time, engaged in attempting to save a number of missionaries captured by bandits some time previously in that area

---

[1] *Op. cit.*, p. 468.
[2] *Loc. cit.*
[3] *Op. cit.*, p. 469.
[4] *Op. cit.*, p. 472.

of south China. There were large bodies of disaffected troops roaming the countryside who refused to submit to the Canton authorities and who could not be controlled. All foreigners in the area outside the large cities were in danger from these irresponsible soldiers. Jenkins, the American Consul General at Canton, said the request was certainly reasonable under the circumstances, in that instance, but that it might be used as a precedent to refuse authorisation to proceed to the interior. Under the circumstances he requested an official attitude. [1]

MacMurray instructed him [2] that there was no objection to Americans consulting local authorities before proceeding to the interior, but that in replying to the Commissioner for Foreign Affairs, the Consul should state that it was for information only, that he wished to be kept informed of conditions in the interior, but that "the right of the Chinese authorities either to authorize or to forbid American citizens traveling to interior points of the country" could not be admitted.

On September 30th, due to the trouble brewing and the likelihood of the fleet having to go into action, the Commander of the Pacific Fleet issued a statement of policy [3] (1) reaffirming the policy of the U.S. Navy; (2) stating that the better the preparation the better able it would be to prevent war; (3) citing a certain naval regulation, specifying conduct and behaviour of men and officers; (4) urging cultivation of good will and encouragement of mutual respect; (5) "The policy of the United States with particular reference to China as enunciated by our Government from time to time is as follows:

    (a)   Open door policy.
    (b)   Aloofness from interference in the internal affairs of China.
    (c)   Maintenance of the territorial integrity of China.
    (d)   Traditional friendship for China."

(6) warning that the unusual conditions in China prevailing at the time places an unusually heavy responsibility on the Asiatic Fleet

---

[1] *Op. cit.*, pp. 472—3.
[2] *Op. cit.*, p. 480.
[3] *Op. cit.*, pp. 475—7.

to prevent occurrence of incidents which would require use of force to protect American interests. "The policy of units of the Fleet on duty in China will be:

(a) The protection of American lives.
(b) The protection of American property.
(c) The promotion of American interests.
(d) The cultivation of friendly relations with the Chinese."

Considering American policy, as we have seen it develop, it is obvious that things were, indeed, bad in China for America to have to make such a declaration and take such action. At the time there was serious question whether or not the Nationalist Government could hold out long enough to consolidate its hold on the country, have a chance to pacify the nation, and establish a regular administration. Perhaps never since the "Boxer" days had America been so concerned and so close to taking military or naval action. The Government at Nanking was still only a shadow government. There was a government at Canton in opposition to that at Nanking; a number of the provinces were really separate governments, the entire country was torn by dissension, corruption and discontent. Fanatical groups of left wingers, both Kuomintang and Communists, seized local areas, and instituted reigns of terror, holding drum-head courts and carrying out executions indiscriminately, land-owners, rich people, and prosperous peasants; taxing people beyond all reason (many people had receipts for taxes paid for years in advance — each new conqueror demanded the same or more); impressing labour, soldiers and "girls", and confiscating all kinds of possessions. Where the "left" did not have control, the "right" went to as great, and often greater, lengths. There was no centre, no middle-of-the-road liberal group, no surcease for the people. The Americans had good reason to be worried. They were beginning to realise that the situation might explode and that then only a miracle could prevent foreign interests from going down in ruin together with China.

On October 1st, Lockhart notified MacMurray that there had been 7 foreigners killed in his consular district, including 3 Americans. He told MacMurray that he was warning all returning missionaries of the dangers in the interior and trying to dissuade

them from returning at this time. As an indication of the prevailing
spirit he quoted a slogan posted on a missionary compound:

> "It is the aim of the revolution to drive out the foreign devil;
> drive out the foreign devil and recover liberty and power;
> strike down British Imperialists; exterminate the foreigner". [1]

The question of American ships transporting troops for civil war
and at the same time demanding American protection, if fired upon
or attacked, seemed to liberal foreigners in China at the time to
be an absolute violation of the spirit, if not of the letter, of the
treaties. Burkhart had notified MacMurray that he had been
approached by American shipping interests [2] as to the position the
American Government would take concerning official naval protection in case of attack. In reply to MacMurray's reference of the
problem to him, Stimson replied [3] that he should advise such ship
owners "that the degree of protection this (the U.S.) Government
can afford them in their normal activities will be adversely affected
to the extent that they allow themselves to become involved in
Chinese military operations".

On October 17th, Cunningham sent a very important message
to Stimson, via MacMurray, in which he pointed out the great
increase in anti-foreign crimes and murders. [4] He cited a number
of kidnappings, where brigands held foreigners for ransom, cases
of mistreatment which almost resulted in the death of the persons
involved, and the case of three Catholic missionaries of the French
Mission who were murdered. He pointed out that, despite the fact
the French Government had protested strongly, the murderers were
still at large, and that there had been no apprehension or punishment of the brigands involved in any of these cases.

He said that in addition there had been eight foreigners murdered
since April of that year in the interior and added a cogent statement
which is of particular interest in a study of China of that time.
He stated that despite the protestations by the Nationalist Government that they were able to guarantee "protection for foreigners in

---

[1] F.R.U.S., 1929, II, p. 477.
[2] Op. cit., p. 481.
[3] Loc. cit.
[4] Op. cit., p. 482.

the event of extraterritoriality being abolished", it was obvious that "the lives of foreign subjects are ruthlessly taken" and that there was no question that such cases were on the increase. "So far no remedy has been found by Nanking to counteract the activities of organised gangs of bandits who are responsible for the outrages and who appear to have established themselves in every part of the country in spite of the presence of a large standing army supposedly united under the direct control of the Chief Executive of the country". This statement is of especial interest to us because it was one of the big problems facing the foreign nations, from the establishment of the Kuomintang Government onwards — the problem of abolition of extraterritoriality.

On the 25th, the Minister, in acknowledging receipt of a dispatch containing a statement of the Commander of the Yangtze Patrol, advised Cunningham [1] that Stimson had discouraged transport of troops for the Nationalist Government. The commander had said that he would not afford protection "to such vessels as contract to carry members of the military forces of China, or arms, ammunition, or any other non-commercial article, such as opium". The commander was carrying out an order of the Commander-in-Chief of the Pacific Fleet, in this. MacMurray told Cunningham he would refer the opium question to Stimson.

Stimson replied on December 9th, [2] that the treaty of 1844, as well as that of 1880, between America and China, prohibited traffic, by Americans, in opium; that furthermore by an act of Congress in 1887, it had been made a misdemeanour for an American citizen to traffic in opium. Stimson also referred to the question of protection of ships transporting arms and ammunition. He said that he could see no objection to witholding naval protection from such ships, since it appeared that there was great risk of involving such ships in Chinese military operations.

This was a very wise move on Stimson's part, but even more, it was a just one. It would be certain to involve such American ships in trouble with the opposition to the Nationalists for whom

---

[1]   *Op. cit.*, p. 483.
[2]   *Op. cit.*, p. 495.

they were hauling the men, arms and ammunition. Unquestionably
the opposition would resort to any means within its power to
precent such assistance, thus forcing America into a position of
intervening in the internal affairs of China. Here Stimson was
following traditional American policy.

On November 9th, Lockhart notified [1] Stimson that the Reverend
Kreutzin, an American citizen, had been kidnapped and held
for $ 10,000 ransom, and that he had taken up the case with
the Chinese authorities. On the 12th, Lockhart notified Stimson
that the Chinese authorities had sent a military expedition to rescue
Father Kreutzin. On the 14th, MacMurray sent a telegram to Stimson to say that he had requested the Minister for Foreign Affairs
to make every effort to save Father Kreutzin. [2] On the 17th, word
was received that the bandits had reduced the amount of ransom
and that the Catholic Fathers felt certain of securing his release
within a few days. [3] On December 2nd, Lockhart reported the
release and safe arrival of Father Kreutzin at Tayeh.

Such a case serves to show the policy of America in dealing with
China at this time. It must be admitted that Stimson's attitude was
a reasonable and tolerant one, that he did not take a harsh attitude,
nor try to make an unfair use of the treaties. He realised that the
situation was serious, not for the foreigners alone, and that the
National Government was in a difficult position; he felt that sympathy and understanding were the only solutions to the problem.
If the Foreign Powers had taken such a sympathetic stand and
if the Chinese had been as ready to respond at the opening of the
19th Century, as they were in 1929, the story of China might have
been very different.

On December 30th, Lockhart sent a dispatch to Perkins, the
Chargé d'Affaires, in which he enclosed a letter from Father
O'Shea. The latter said that the National Government had "done
little in south Kiangsi to justify its declarations to protect foreign
lives and property" and that his own mission had suffered great
loss because of "the inefficiency and culpable neglect of the

---

1   *Op. cit.*, p. 484.
2   *Op. cit.*, p. 485, footnote 10.
3   *Op. cit.*, p. 486.

young government". O'Shea stated that he wanted the Nanking Government notified that he intended to file claims for all damage done to the mission property. He also requested that "that government be urged to send reinforcements to south Kiangsi". [1]

On January 25th, 1930, a telegram was received from O'Shea in which he said that the Red armies had occupied a place only 50 miles from Kanchow, the location of his mission; the local general had only 500 men and admitted his inability to defend the city. "General begs you urge Nanking send re-enforcements immediately, situation grave". Perkins stated that he had taken the matter up with General Ho Ying-chin at Hankow, and he sent a copy of the record both to Stimson and to O'Shea. [2]

A very reasonable and sensible observation closed Perkins's wire to Stimson: "Legation does not feel that it can properly, at intervals of a few months, request the Nanking Government to send an army to Kanchow for the protection of the mission". He stated that because of the chronically disturbed conditions in the area he "believe(d) that you should advise Americans at Kanchow to evacuate as soon as they can safely do so". [3]

On March 11th, O'Shea wired Burkhart: [4]

> Urgent. American Consul, Hankow. All Kanchow soldiers leaving for Fukien. Last regiment ordered to leave in two days. Entire Southern Kiangsi defenseless. Chu and local Reds awaiting chance to enter Kanchow. Please urge Nanking order General Chin Han-Ting leave Northern brigade here until other troops replace his. Our egress blocked on arrival (all sides?).

Burkhart notified the Foreign Minister, sending him a copy of the telegram and requesting that he make it possible for the Americans to withdraw safely. But Perkins recommended that the Department consult with the appropriate Catholic authorities in the United States advising them to have the Americans at Kanchow withdraw, because of the disturbed conditions in southern Kiangsi, and "the difficulties in the way of the Nanking Government's extending

---

[1] Op. cit., p. 504.
[2] F.R.U.S., 1930, II, pp. 82—3.
[3] Loc. cit.
[4] Op. cit., pp. 93—4.

protection, and the manifest impropriety of the Legation's having repeatedly to urge at brief intervals that an army be sent to or maintained in Southern Kiangsi in order to protect the mission". The Foreign Minister informed Johnson, new Minister to China, that instructions had been sent General Ho to send troops to suppress the Communists, and that the 35th brigade would leave one detachment at Kanchow to offer protection.

On March 21st, Hornbeck, Acting Secretary of State, wrote to the Reverend J. J. Burke, General Secretary of the National Catholic Welfare Conference, advising him to order the evacuation of the missionaries from Kanchow, temporarily — as soon as arrangements can be made to give them safe conduct, in view of conditions there. He requested Burke to telegraph this order at once. [1] On the following day, March 22nd, Johnson wired the Chinese Foreign Minister (it must be remembered that the Legation was still in Peking) that word had come from an American at Nananfu: "Kanchow besieged by Reds; very grave danger, Americans trapped; send help quickly." Johnson requested him to "urge upon the proper authorities the necessity of speedy action to protect Americans at Kanchow". [2]

On the 25th, Jenkins received this telegram from Father Young at Namyung, Kwangtung: "Forced to flee, Reds approach. Impossible obtain news Kanchow." Jenkins wired Johnson that a copy of the message was immediately turned over to local authorities, who said that, while they had no official reply from Kiangsi to an earlier wire (concerning O'Shea), they had received a reliable private wire from Nanchang, Kiangsi, saying that Kanchow was safe. [3]

On the same day, C. T. Wang wired Johnson: "Kiangsi Provincial Government inform me that strong measures are being taken to suppress the Communists. Will you instruct your nationals to remain where we station Government forces and not to go about without first informing local authorities? Trust Your Excellency will see the importance of this request". Johnson added to Hornbeck

---

[1] *Op. cit.*, p. 95.
[2] *Op. cit.*, p. 96.
[3] *Loc. cit.*

that he was "respectfully renewing" the request for evacuation, as he had in his wire to him on March 12th. [1]

Hornbeck wired Johnson that he had communicated his request to the Catholic authorities and that, confidentially, the latter stated that they were taking steps to comply with the request. [2]

On the 26th, in reply to his request of the previous day, Jenkins was notified by the Governor of Kiangsi that troops were dispatched to Kanchow and that that city seemed safe. [3]

On April 22nd, Cotton, Acting Secretary of State, wired Cunningham, [4] at Shanghai (for the Minister) that he had a report from Jenkins, at Canton, that two American priests had just arrived from southern Kiangsi, reporting that there were 25 foreigners at Kanchow, including 19 Americans, many of them women and children, unable to get out. They stated that the Communist forces were again converging on Kanchow and were threatening to kill all foreigners. Jenkins was urging the Cantonese authorities to send relief troops, but feared that they would not do anything about it. He urged that Chiang Kai-shek be asked to order the Governors of Kiangsi and Kwangtung to co-operate in the relief of Kanchow.

Cotton stated:

> Department is gravely anxious with regard to this situation and believes it warrants your making immediate and urgent representations to the Nanking authorities asking them to take every possible measure for the protection and rescue of this group of foreigners, the majority of whom are Americans.

On the 23rd, [5] Lockhart notified Stimson that he had requested General Ho Ying-chin to take up with Chiang Kai-shek on his arrival at Hankow, the following day, the urgent problem of adequately protecting the foreigners who were awaiting further instructions at Kanchow. He said that he was unable to tell from Jenkins' telegram, whether the situation described was the same about which there had been much correspondence a month earlier,

---

[1] Op. cit., p. 97.
[2] Op. cit., p. 98.
[3] Loc. cit.
[4] Op. cit., p. 103.
[5] Op. cit., p. 104.

but added that, since the two priests walked most of the way from Kanchow to Canton, it was more than likely that the situation described by them was the same.

This anomalous situation was, however, soon cleared up. On the 24th, [1] Jenkins wired Stimson that Father Moehringer, one of the priests who walked from Kanchow to Canton, had received two letters from Kanchow, dated April 6th, one of them from O'Shea, the other from Father Cahill, both of whom stated that "the outcome at Kanchow was very uncertain and that there was no hope except in God".

Moehringer stated that while he was in Lungnan, Kiangsi, on the 13th, he was reliably informed that all the larger cities south of Kanchow in Kiangsi province had fallen to the Communists who were closing in on Kanchow from two sides, with an estimated force of 7,000 men, besides large groups of bandits and disaffected Nationalist and provincial troops, scattered through the region. The 70th Regiment of General Chin Han-ting was supposedly still at Kanchow, but since they were a small force, and had not been paid for over five months, would not be able to defend the city unassisted, and would likely refuse to fight. He said that the 71st Regiment had mutinied and disappeared. He was certain that the telegraph wires from Kanchow had been destroyed by the Communists and that all means of communication between Kanchow and the outside were in the hands of the Communists. He re-affirmed the fact that there were twenty-five foreigners there, including eight American sisters, of whom four had come in from surrounding country districts.

Jenkins stated that the Chinese authorities had promised to consider plans of sending a relief expedition into Kiangsi, provided Kiangsi forces would co-operate. He urged the Legation to impress upon the Nanking Government the urgency instructing the authorities in Kwantung and Kwangsi to co-operate in relieving southern Kiangsi.

Both the Legation and the State Department "put the heat on" the Nationalist Government and on Ho Ying-chin, simultaneously.

---

[1] F.R.U.S., 1930, II, pp. 104—105.

The result was a personal note from Ho to Lockhart: [1] "The communist brigands will be promptly exterminated; at present Kanchow is very safe and quiet and no danger will arise; General Chin Hanting has been telegraphed to render protection to American life and property." Ho wound up by hoping that Lockhart would entertain no further anxiety concerning Kanchow.

The following document is so important that it is necessary to quote it *in extenso*: [2]

> "1. In mail despatch of April 10 American Consul General, Hankow, encloses letter to him from Bishop O'Shea at Kanchow, dated March 28th, with the comment, 'in spite of the fact that he is apparently of the considered opinion that there is very little hope for peace in Kiangsi Province under existing conditions, Bishop O'Shea does not mention leaving that area or issuing instructions to his subordinates to evacuate to places of greater safety.' From the correspondence it is not wholly clear to the Legation whether the Americans at Kanchow would have been able to withdraw within the last few weeks since the Bishop states, 'the country side is still too unsafe for travel.' There is, however, no indication that Bishop O'Shea has, since the original warning given him in January by the American Consul General at Hankow, manifested any intention of withdrawing or that he has at any time applied to the Chinese authorities for a military escort to enable him to effect the withdrawal of the Americans under his charge.
>
> 2. As having a possible bearing upon the attitude of the American missionaries at Kanchow, the following excerpt is quoted from a memorandum of a conversation at Peking on April 10 between Minister Johnson and Archbishop Constantini, the Apostolic Delegate in China:
>
>> 'I said that it was impossible for the American Government to afford protection for Americans living in the interior of China under these conditions and that for many years it will be impossible for any Chinese Government to afford protection in isolated places particularly in times like the present when the government itself is under attack. I said that I felt that all American citizens should remember this in establishing themselves in interior of China and govern themselves accordingly.

---

[1] *Op. cit.*, p. 106.
[2] *Op. cit.*, p. 107.

The delegate stated that he well understood the matter; that
of course my responsibilities were the responsibilities of the
agent of the state and that my thoughts must be the thoughts
of the state while his views were the views of the Holy See.
He said that their belief was that their missionaries were
like soldiers in the trenches. They must of course not take
any unnecessary risk but on the other hand if it were necessary for them to die they were prepared to die. He said
that he quite understood the difficulties that any foreign
government would be under at any time in furnishing protection at all places.' "

Jenkins wired Stimson [1] that he had been assured by Cantonese
officials that there were sufficient troops in Kiangsi to protect
Kanchow, but admitted that there had been no direct communications, and that there was no news of the present situation. He
further suggested that, if Lockhart had not already done so, he ask
Ho what means he had of communicating with Kanchow, and
whether he could send O'Shea a message through Chinese sources.
He had the inescapable "feeling that the situation in Kanchow is
or will soon be very dangerous and that the Chinese authorities do
not know what is developing there".

On the 30th, Lockhart did as Jenkins suggested, [2] and was
assured by Ho that the situation was quiet in Kanchow and that he
could communicate by land, wire and wireless apparatus with
Kanchow, whereupon he asked him to ascertain O'Shea's situation
and let him know.

On May 1st, Johnson talked with the Chinese Foreign Minister
about the Kanchow situation; [3] "...I told him that my Government was extremely agitated over the safety of American citizens
in the city of Kanchow .... I said that reports had reached us
that the lives of these Americans were in danger and that the
American Government had instructed me to ask that the Chinese
Government do something to relieve this situation and make it possible for these people to get out of there." Wang promised to send
a telegram to the area. Wang added that it was Ho's opinion that

---

[1]   Op. cit., p. 108.
[2]   Loc. cit.
[3]   Op. cit., p. 109.

there were sufficient troops at Kanchow to protect and hold the city, and that no reinforcements were being sent to the area.

On May 2nd, Stimson wired Johnson that he had talked to Burke [1] and discussed the long document anoted *in extenso* on the preceding pages. He stated that he also discussed with him the withdrawal of missionaries "and it was explained to him that American citizens by continuing to remain in exposed positions contrary to official advice to withdraw are likely... not only to endanger their own lives, but also the lives and interests of other American citizens, and to create complications for the Chinese Government and people and for the American and other Governments". Stimson also instructed Johnson to elaborate and emphasize these considerations in a conversation with Archbishop Constantini as soon as a suitable occasion arose, if he had not already done so.

On May 22nd, Stimson informed Johnson of a long conversation which he had had with Burke [2], in which the latter stated that he "... did not believe the Church would instruct them to withdraw, that he thought whether or not they did withdraw would depend largely on their own discretion and estimate of the situation.... Father Burke was informed that the Department felt that it had done everything it could to place its views before the Catholic authorities and that a situation might develop in which it would be highly desirable to know definitely what attitude the Catholics at Kanchow could be expected to take regarding the question of withdrawal". Stimson suggested that Lockhart have Ho contact O'Shea and find out under what circumstances "these Americans, any or all of them, would act in accordance with American official advice to withdraw".

On June 19th, it was learned through Ho Ying-chin [3] that the Americans at Kanchow were safe, and adequately protected; nevertheless it was known that the families of many Chinese officials were withdrawing from the area to Kiukiang, and that some foreigners were also evacuating from the interior of Kiangsi, under military escort, to Kiukiang.

---

[1] *Op. cit.*, pp. 109—110.

[2] *Op. cit.*, pp. 122—3.

[3] *Op. cit.*, pp. 134—5.

Johnson stated that as soon as communications were restored he would contact O'Shea and enquire about the welfare of Americans there, and "as to whether and in what circumstances any or all of them would act in conformity with American official advice to withdraw". He also sent a message to Lockhart: "Commander in Chief telegraphed June 10 that Nanchang will probably be evacuated within 10 days if Chang Fah-kwei maintains his advance and that Communists would then control entire province of Kiangsi. In this eventuality, are there any further measures which suggest themselves to you on behalf of American citizens at Kanchow?"

Lockhart's answer was prompt: [1]

> Inasmuch as the Americans resident in Kanchow and in that vicinity have more than once been advised to withdraw to a zone of safety I can offer no further suggestion as a possible means of relief except that it might be advisable to continue to urge the Nanking authorities to supply adequate forces for the protection of American life and property in the Kanchow area. So far as can be ascertained Chang Fah-kwei does not appear to be making any headway towards either Nanchang or Hankow at present.

On the 4th of August, the Foreign Minister, Wang, asked Price to notify the legation that: [2]

> A telegram has been received from Chairman Lu of the Kiangsi Provincial Government stating that Brigadier General Ma withdraw from Kanchow . . . in order to avoid danger.
> You are requested immediately to instruct your nationals to leave Kanchow temporarily; otherwise, if untoward incidents occur the Chinese Government will assume no responsibility.

On the following day Lockhart wired Johnson [3] that he had wired O'Shea to evacuate and to notify the other Americans to do likewise.

On August 14th, Jenkins wired Stimson [4] that Catholic priests and sisters arrived safely at Canton from the interior. The priests

---

[1] F.R.U.S., 1930, II, p. 136.
[2] Op. cit., p. 161.
[3] Op. cit., p. 162.
[4] Op. cit., p. 168.

said that the garrison forces were being withdrawn, leaving Kanchow entirely to the tender mercies of the Comrades. Furthermore the General said that foreigners could not safely accompany the army who would be having to skirmish.

O'Shea's attitude, under any circumstances, was that the National Government had promised to protect foreigners and that he would stay until they admitted to him that they were no longer able to protect him. Jenkins said: "I drew attention of the priests to the fact that the Department had already urged Bishop and other Americans to leave Kanchow and said I frankly could not understand Bishop's position."

On the 14th, Lockhart wired Johnson: [1] "I respectfully suggest that O'Shea and other foreigners could withdraw with National troops and that the Legation may wish to request Ministry of Foreign Affairs to thus or otherwise afford them safe conduct to places of security."

Johnson immediately dispatched to Adams at Nanking the following wire for delivery to Wang: [2] "I have the honor to request that if the forces of Your Excellency's Government have not yet withdrawn from Kanchow, Kiangsi, the American citizens and residents be given safe conduct and permitted to accompany the troops out. An early reply is requested."

On August 14th, Jenkins was notified by the Cantonese authorities that they had had no response to their wires concerning O'Shea and the other Americans at Kanchow, but that General Ma's troops had probably left Kanchow and that the city was in grave danger, if not already occupied by the Communists, and that under the circumstances the Cantonese could do nothing more.

On August 21st,[3] Johnson received from the Ministry for Foreign Affairs a telegram, informing him that the Kiangsi Provincial Government had ordered all foreigners to evacuate with the troops, "but American missionaries there telegraphed this Ministry expressing their unwillingness to evacuate with the troops. This is not what was expected. . . . I have requested the Kiangsi Provincial

---

[1] *Op. cit.*, p. 169.
[2] *Loc. cit.*
[3] *Op. cit.*, pp. 174—5.

Government by telegraph to exhaust effort and devise means to effect a rescue and extend protection."

Johnson stated that in a conversation with the Vice-Minister for Foreign Affairs the latter had told him that in the very long telegram received by the Ministry from Kanchow, Bishop O'Shea had not only refused to leave the town, but had furthermore demanded that additional troops be dispatched there in order that he could remain in safely. The Vice-Minister also informed Johnson that he believed the Communists to be already in Kanchow by that time.

On August 15th, [1] Burkhart had General Ho sent the following radio message to O'Shea: "Legation has requested Ministry of Foreign Affairs to afford you safe conduct out of Kanchow to place of security in view of Government's decision withdraw troops from Kanchow. Please notify other Americans." He stated that he would take no further steps in the matter except under instructions from the Legation or Department.

Johnson told Stimson: [2] "In view of the above there would appear to be no further action which the Legation might appropriately take at this time."

On October 22nd,[3] the Consul at Hongkong notified Johnson that a Father McGillicuddy had come to his office and informed him that he had had a letter from O'Shea on the 9th, informing him that he and seven other priests wanted to leave, but were unable to do so safely. McGillicuddy said that he was unable to get messages through to the wireless station and feared for their safety because of the recent capture of Kian by the Communists.

What happened to the priests when they actually did fall into the hands of the Chinese Communists is shown by the following telegram which is especially interesting because of some names in it which have since become much more widely known than they were in 1929:[4]

"October 22, 4. p.m. Catholic priests have arrived at Kiukiang from Kian and report the Fathers referred to in my

---

[1] Loc. cit.
[2] Loc. cit.
[3] Op. cit., p. 203.
[4] Loc. cit.

October 21, 3. p.m. were tied together, paraded and beaten by Communists. No destruction of property at Kian had occurred up to 14th but considerable looting. Communist army which invaded Kian was led by Chu Teh, Mao Tse-tung and Peng Teh-hwai. [1] The refugees left Kian 14th, travelling via Changshu; were arrested many times by communist soldiers but released on showing safe conduct issued by communist leaders at Kian who released Fathers for the purpose of permitting them to go to Kiungchau (*Kiukiang?*) to raise ransom of ten million dollars. Priests observed no Government troops going to relief of Kian." [2]

Hornbeck wrote a letter to Burke on October 21th, which is so revealing that it will be quoted in full. Here he more or less sums up the troublous conditions of that day in China, and shows the problems the Consuls and Legation were up against:[3]

Washington, October 29, 1930

Sir: The Department refers to correspondence conducted with you in the past in regard to the safety and welfare of American missionaries in the interior of China. The Department has availed itself of your good offices to transmit to the interested American missionary organizations with which you have contact information regarding these matters.

At the present time, great areas, particularly in central China, are without dependable agencies for the administration of justice or even the protection of life. American citizens who continue to reside in these regions cannot escape the risks incident to this disturbed state of affairs. In fact, in some instances, they seem actually to prove an incitement to lawless action, either as furnishing a supposed means for involving the constituted authorities in difficulties with foreign nations, or as a means of possible profit through demands for ransom.

The American citizens in China whose safety is most menaced by the activities of lawless elements in interior regions are, for the most part, those engaged in missionary and cultural enterprises. Information reaching the Department indicates that in many cases a great deal of liberty is allowed by the parent organizations to their representatives in China in deciding whether the missionaries concerned shall, when danger

---

[1] Communist leaders Chu Teh and Mao Tse-tung are today the minions of Russia.

[2] F.R.U.S., 1930, II, p. 203.

[3] *Op. cit.*, pp. 207—208.

threatens, remain at their posts, or shall retire to places where they can be protected or from which they can be evacuated. In these circumstances, it has been found that members of missionary organizations are sometimes unwilling to relinquish, even temporarily, the duties entrusted to them. In response to advice from the Department's officers in China that places of safety be sought, the reply is sometimes made that the persons warned are grateful for the solicitude of their Government but that danger exists practically everywhere in China, that it attaches especially to the missionary vocation, and that the writers feel a moral obligation to remain at their posts.

The Department's purpose in addressing the present communication to you is to request that a suggestion be transmitted from the Department to the various missionary organizations concerned that the decision in regard to evacuation in the face of threatening danger be not left by them entirely to their representatives in the field. It would be gratuitous at this time to cite specific instances in which American citizens in the interior have, in the face of consular advice, chosen to incur serious risks, or to list the instances in which disregard of consular advice has resulted most unfortunately. It is the Department's desire to reiterate the suggestion previously given that American missionary organizations exert such authority as may be theirs in the matter and that the decision in regard to withdrawal from danger be left in a less degree than appears to have obtained in the past to the discretion of the persons immediately concerned.

It is sincerely hoped that missionary organizations in the United States, taking account of the difficulties in the situation and of the serious complications which injuries to American citizens cause both for and among the Chinese people and Chinese authorities themselves and for and between the American and the Chinese Governments, will take the position that it is the duty of their representatives in China to adopt all reasonable precautions to avoid capture or death and in the face of danger to err, if there seems to be doubt, on the side of caution.

The Department believes that this Government's officers in China have been and are unremitting in their efforts to provide for the safety of American citizens in their various and respective districts. These efforts will be continued.

Very truly yours,

For the Secretary of State:

STANLEY K. HORNBECK.

Chief, Division of Far Eastern Affairs.

On November 24th, [1] the Mayor of Canton notified Jenkins that the Chairman of the Kwangtung Provincial Government was in receipt of a telegram from the Chairman of Kiangsi stating that the American Catholic Missionaries at Kanchow had been officially requested to evacuate and proceed to Kwangtung under safe transit, but that they had refused to do so on the grounds that the city was still safe. They requested, however, that the authorities continue to extend protection to them and their property.

Thus finishes our story of O'Shea. We do not know what happened after that. His name does not appear further in our records. Presumably he stayed on to plague the Japanese when they took over the area. One can well imagine that the Japanese had their hands full with the obstreperous and doughty Father. One can visualize them sending a detachment of troops which were badly needed elsewhere to protect him and his Mission and having to apologise to him for their inadequate number. Doubtless he was quite a headache to Tojo and it is to be wondered whether or not the latter was as long-suffering as the State Department, the Legation, Consulates, and Chinese Foreign Ministry and Ministry of War.

The Reverend Bert Nelson was kidnapped in Kwangsham, Honan, by the Communists on October 5th, 1930. On the 7th, he was forced by his captors to write a letter demanding $ 300,000 ransom. [2] The case was taken up with the Foreign Ministry, by the Consul at Nanking, on the 16th. On the 20th, Johnson notified Stimson that he was very worried about the safety not only of Nelson, but of other Americans resident at exposed points, because of the brutal murder, by beheading, of two English women missionaries after their captors had failed in bargaining to secure $ 100,000 ransom. The Chinese authorities had made no effort to secure the release of these women and were making none to secure release of Nelson. Johnson asked Stimson to inform the Chinese Minister of the deep concern of the American Government over the case of Nelson. He felt that only Stimson's effort might save him. Johnson had himself taken up the case with the Foreign Ministry

---

[1] Op. cit., p. 215.
[2] Op. cit., pp. 197—198.

two days previously, and had been promised that everything possible would be done to effect his release. On the 21st, wires were sent to two local military commanders to effect his release.

On the 24th, a group of missionaries was captured by the same Communist army and held for ransom. Two of these made private arrangements for their own ransom with the bandits, the Lutheran Mission supplying the money, the persons concerned assuming responsibility for repayment to the Mission. The Communists released one, a woman, but refused to release the other after having received the money. The sort of trick they used to extort the money is illustrative of the Communists and their psychology. In one of the dictated letters the missionary was forced to say: "We two are held here because of financial difficulties and ask $ 400,000 for our release. On one side we ask the Consulate to help, on the other to approach Chiang Kai-shek to recognize the responsibility of protecting missionaries ...." It would be difficult to imagine anything more cynically dishonest and immoral. The Communists are telling Chiang to pay them for stealing Westerners, whom he, and China, are under treaty obligation to protect. They admit here the very thing they have been most vociferous in denying — the validity of the treaty system. They are here acting in character as communists. Nothing is sacred, nothing has meaning or value, unless it serves their doctrinaire ends. If they stir up a crisis and it backfires, they can slink off into anonymity. The Government, and hence the people, cannot. The country must suffer and pay for the irresponsibility and treachery of the Communists.

The bandits demanded $ 30,000 for the release of Nelson and Tvedt, the other missionary, minus the $ 3,000 paid. On the 5th, Lockhart was told that the Chinese Government was doing everything possible to suppress the Communists and bandits and save the missionaries, but that there was not much hope. It was reported that Nelson had died of disease.

On the 28th of November, however, Nelson wrote to Ho Ying-chin: "Our captors and guards impatiently urge us to request the immediate paying of the balance on peril of our lives." New representations were made to Ho Ying-chin to save the two. Ho replied that he had ordered a General Li Ming-chung to effect their release.

On December 4th, Lockhart received a wire from a Dr. Skinsnes at Sinyangchow: "Letter from Tvedt and Nelson dated November 26 stated that Communists now talk of ($) 5,000 in medicines or ($) 10,000 in cash. Both offer to pay all they have to obtain freedom. Would you advise an offer of ($) 3,000?"

Lockhart sent the money by two trusted servants of the two men. After a failure to contact the captives from Hankow, the servants went to Sinyangchow, from which place they believed they could reach them and Consul Clark was sent by the Legation to help Skinsnes secure their release.

It seemed as though the release of Nelson and Tvedt was about to be affected, but their two servants who were carrying $ 3,000 from Sinyangchow to Hwangan were unable to reach their destination because of brigands and returned to Sinyangchow. Dr. Skinsnes attempted to send the money through persons having contact with the 5th Red Army. The amount of ransom had, in the meantime, been raised to $ 10,000. The missionaries were reported to be well at that time, and Consul Clarke, having determined that Dr. Skinsnes was doing all in his power to secure the release of the missionaries, returned to Hankow.

On January 20th, 1931, it was learned by the American Minister in a letter from the captives that the Communists had taken Nelson and Tvedt to Anhwei and that the Chinese authorities there were being urged to effect their release. Johnson recommended that the case again be brought to the attention of the Nanking authorities.

It now began to look as though the missionaries might never be rescued. On March 9th, Skinsnes sent a copy of a letter to Lockhart stating: [1] "We have just been bound and whipped and told to make haste with the ransom money or there would be worse things to follow." The chit-coolie [2] who delivered this message told Skinsnes the location of the ransom office as well as the location of the missionaries. He said that the missionaries "looked fair but had been beaten some".

---

[1] F.R.U.S., 1931, III, p. 938.
[2] Messenger-servant.

Perkins stated that this case was being given great publicity in the Hankow area and had been taken up by the Press. He was convinced that the only method of saving the men was the payment of the ransom money demanded and "that this must be done quickly". He advised a personal appeal to Chiang-Kai-shek and the lodging of an emphatic diplomatic protest by Stimson. He advised that the Secretary lodge the protest with Dr. Wu.

This brought immediate reaction in Washington. On the day of receipt of the cable Hornbeck informed Dr. Wu that the American Minister in China had been ordered to demand from the highest Chinese authorities immediate action on the Nelson case and that he hoped Wu would impress upon his government the seriousness and importance in American eyes of this matter. The protest handed to Wu for delivery to his government stated that the missionaries had suffered at the hands of their captors, having been "bound and whipped with bamboo poles and told to make haste with the ransom money or there would be worse things to follow". The protest ended: "We hope that the Chinese Government will make every possible effort to effect the release of these men." [1]

The Department also instructed Adams to "make urgent representations to the Ministry of Foreign Affairs", and if he thought wise to make "a personal appeal to President Chiang Kai-shek with regard to the treatment accorded by Chinese bandits to the Reverend Mr. Nelson and with regard to the long-continued failure of the Chinese authorities to effect Nelson's release".

The Americans now began to bring all the pressure at their command to bear upon this case. Lockhart saw General Ho Ying-chin and urged upon him the importance of the matter.

Things again seemed hopeful. On the 17th, Skinsnes received a letter from the prisoners stating that they were in good health and no longer tortured; the information of their place of captivity was immediately sent to the Chinese authorities. But as could be expected, things did not stay bright for long, as a telegram from Skinsnes indicates: "Messengers provided with Kwangshan magistrate's pass and on strength of this pass escorted by local militia were robbed by comrades of escort," giving the name of the

---

[1] F.R.U.S., 1931, III, p. 939.

magistrate and head of the militia. After this robbery the Americans took a much less tolerant attitude. The Chinese government realized that the robbery would be recognised abroad for what it really was, a legally arranged theft, which would cause a loss of face from the highest circles of the government down. The Chinese government ordered the commanding general in an adjacent area to the place were the missionaries were held, to "lend cooperation to a brother of Nelson and two other gentlemen who left for Macheng this morning by motor car with an escort of one officer and two men. The persons proceeding this morning are carrying personal letters from General Ho (Ying-chin) to General Hsia at Macheng."

It would have seemed that the party above referred to, armed with a letter from the Minister of War, would have been whisked through with no obstacles whatever. Their authority, however, was not enough, for they wired Nanking reporting the refusal of the Macheng authorities to do anything. The wire was informative of the existing situation in China. In it Nelson said that upon his arrival he first interviewed the Vice-General, who told him: "This is not our business and we cannot do anything." He tried to see General Hsia, who refused to see him, but sent word that "what the Vice-General said is just the same as though he had said it." Nelson stated that more pressure from Hankow was imperative. As a result of this wire the Minister of Foreign Affais ordered General Hsia in a wire "to advance against Red brigands and effect release of Nelson and Tvedt". Lockhart was asked to find out whether or not such instructions were received by Hsia and what actions he took upon them. The repercussions seemed to be immediate, because the following day Nelson's brother wired from Macheng that General Hsia had left for Hankow. On the 7th of April, Skinsnes received letters from Nelson and Tvedt, dated March 26th, stating that the medicines had been received and that the Communists were now demanding $ 20,000 for their release. On April 20th, Tvedt was released on the payment of $ 6,500 by mission authorities, and it seemed that the prospects were good for the release of Nelson also, in the near future. But again, just when it seemed that Nelson was about to be sent back, the Communists again raised the ante, demanding "gramophone records, tennis rackets and balls, basket-balls, chess boards, wrist watches, fountain pens, footballs, fresh fruit and ammunition and other things".

Lockhart reported that "some of the above not including fresh fruit or ammunition, are being sent today to Sungpu. Nelson is well and brigands have promised to release him on receipt of $ 10,000 less amount expended for articles sent today. If the brigands keep their promise Nelson should be released within a week."

The go-between soon returned to Hankow and reported that "Red brigands declined to release Nelson and are insisting on delivery of 30 tins of gasoline and in addition two sewing machines. Go-between returned to Sungpu yesterday morning taking with him two sewing machines and 30 tins of gasoline. He was accompanied to Sungpu by Nelson's brother." Since active military operations had been launched against the Reds in this area by governments troops, several days ago, and several Communist strongholds captured, it was hoped that Nelson's release might be secured before military operations reached the area where he was held captive.

The communists evidently thought Nelson to be a man of great importance because they made a further demand of $ 50,000 for his release. "In the latest attempt to procure Nelson's release, Dr. Skinsnes sent, in compliance with bandits' demands, 9,000 bolts of cloth and 100 miles of telephone wire upon receipt the bandits again declined to release Nelson. They desired insulated telephone wire and larger pieces of cloth." The "chief of the Commission of Foreign Affairs of the Soviet Government for the Hupeh-Honan-Anhwei district" addressed an open letter to Adams in which he said that Nelson was "a very valuable captive whom they wished to utilise for the solution of some difficult problems of supplies faced by the Communists" and that since the death and losses of the labourers and peasants in that region had been very great "the quantity of supplies received by the bandits for Nelson's release was insignificant compared with the Communists' losses in other parts of China" and proposed that five political offenders be exchanged for Nelson and threatened that "failing this 'we can only proceed by the extreme measure of revenge (requiting) upon the person of this missionary Bert Nelson, measure for measure the treatment accorded to our revolutionary fighters' ".

We do not know the fate of Nelson, since the records available do not again mention him.

After this time, as in the case of Extrality, trouble began to die down in the interior, and anti-foreignism was not used to such a great extent by the Kuomintang as an instrument of policy. Naturally when the people were not agitated by propagandists, they quickly settled down into friendly relations with the few foreigners in the interior who had not been evacuated at the orders of their organizations and governments. The individual Chinese had little reason to dislike the average westerner in his midst, rather the contrary. Most of these foreigners were missionaries, teachers and doctors, usually connected with Missions. They were, for the most part, kind and friendly to the Chinese who turned to them for medical and sanitary advice and help, and they often helped in other ways too. When the government was in trouble it could not continue its double game of using and abusing the foreigners to the same extent as before, and by the autumn of 1931, it was indeed in trouble with the Japanese invasion of Manchuria and needed all the international goodwill it could get. Of course things did not clear up over night; the cases troubling the Legation and Consulates were much the same, except that they were on a smaller and less serious scale. There were isolated atrocities and outrages, mostly on the part of Communist armies and bandits, but they were no longer of a magnitude to endanger international relations, or threaten conflict.

It is ironical that China should have had to be in such an unhappy position as she was in December 1931, in order that relations with other nations might be amicable. Perhaps if Japan had not overrun Manchuria and attacked Shanghai, there would have been fresh waves of general anti-foreignism. The Japanese onslaught ultimately threatened all non-Japanese foreign rights in China and many individual Westerners were destined to suffer under the brutal rule of the Kempeitai, but the immediate effect of the Japanese invasion was to make the Chinese mend their ways in dealing with the nations to which they now looked for sympathy and support.

CHAPTER XII

THE CASE OF CAPTAIN NAKAMURA

On the night of September 18th, 1931, Japan attacked China by beginning hostilities in Manchuria. The friction between China and Japan had been increasing for years. There was no doubt in the minds of most people at that time that Japan was the aggressor, was entirely unjustified in her actions, and was, unless stopped by the Western powers, on the way to the seizure and annexation of Manchuria. Many thought that it might be the beginning of the seizure of the whole of China unless the Powers intervened. Now that the story of that episode has been told by time, by many documents in the possession of the State Department, recently released, and by captured records in Japan, it is interesting to try to recapitulate it.

The main pretext seized upon by the Japanese for their action was the execution, called by them murder, of a Japanese spy, Captain Nakamura, who was seized in the Solun region of Northern Manchuria. This region is far outside any area which had ever been claimed by Japan under any pretext. It was, in fact, in the Russian "sphere", along the Chinese Eastern Railway.

On the night of September 18th, 1931, Japan attacked China.

It must be understood that this was merely the flimsiest pretext for the attack. The tension went back to the Sino-Japanese war in 1894—as a matter of fact its causes can be traced far back in the history of the two nations. One must remember Hideyoshi's desperate war, the Mongol attacks, the war of the T'ang and even earlier clashes. But for our purpose the rise of nationalism and the renaissance of the historical dream of expansion and world domination, which began to take form in the last two decades of the 19th century; the defeat of China and the resultant treaty of Shimonaseki; the forced return of the Liaotung Peninsula (by Germany, France and Russia); Japan's defeat of Russia in 1904 are more important. All these concomitant factors culminated in the notorious "21 Demands". From this date, 1915, onward, tension mounted daily.

Japan forced China to yield against her will many of the most important points of the "21 Demands". As China became stronger, she tried to mullify these concessions, at Versailles and again at Washington. When she found that the Western Powers would not help her in this, she began to circumvent the "treaty" in every possible manner. Chang tso-lin began to build parallel railway lines to syphon off the revenue of the S. M. R. He built a new seaport, Hulutao, and established competitive Chinese industries, as we shall see later. Many points China claimed to be illegal because extorted by duress, of others she denied either the validity or their existence. Japan had to have more space, more natural resources, more outlet for capital and for her skilled technicians and white-collar classes. It was imperative that she expanded industrially. This meant that she must bring Manchuria completely within her orbit—that she must seize Manchuria.

The Nakamura case had nothing to do with the Japanese attack upon China. It just happened to coincide with the rise to power and dominance of the war party, the jingoes and expansionists, but since this is the pretext used by Japan for her attack let us examine it and see what are the salient facts.

It is interesting to review various statements concerning the Nakamura case. There seems to be agreement on a few points; that he was seized and executed by the Chinese in Northern Manchuria, where he was traveling on a visa which listed him as an "agricultural expert", and that he was a captain on regular duty with the Japanese army and a member of the General Staff. In a report to the Secretary of State, N. T. Johnson, then American Minister to China, reports:

> .... that Captain Shintaro Nakamura, of the Japanese
> General Staff, and said to be a spy, was executed by Chinese
> soldiers of the Khingan Reclamation Army, in the bandit-
> infested Solun region of Manchuria, where he was traveling
> presumably to investigate the interesting reclamation, coloniza-
> tion and agricultural enterprise which is being carried out in
> this area, but very possibly to collect political and economic

information that would be of interest to the Japanese General Staff. [1]

In another report to the Secretary, dated August 20, 1931, Vincent, the consul at Mukden, made a more elaborate report explaining something of the circumstances of how and why Nakamura happened to be where he was at the time of his seizure and execution.

> Sir: I have the honour to submit for the information of the Legation a brief account of the execution of the Japanese army captain, Nakamura and his party between Taonan and Solun, by Chinese soldiers. The details of the incident were given me by Mr. Hayashi, Japanese Consul General at Mukden.
>
> Early in June Captain Nakamura obtained from the Mukden Special Delegate of the Ministry for Foreign Affairs a "huchao" for travel in Manchuria. This "huchao" excluded the territory between Taonan and Solun (Hsingan Colonization Area) from travel by the Captain. At Harbin, however, a second "huchao" was secured which, according to the Japanese Consul General, gave the desired permission to travel in the Taonan-Solun area.
>
> Captain Nakamura conducted "investigations" along the Chinese Eastern Railway at Manchuli, Tsitsihar, Angangchi, and Hailar. He secured the services of a Mongolian and a Russian interpreter, and also that of a Japanese named Isugi, a retired Japanese army sergeant who kept an inn at Angangchi. This party of four left Pokotu on the Chinese Eastern Railway about the middle of June, their immediate destination being Taonan. On June 27th the party were arrested by Chinese troops at a place called Suokungfu, a small place east of Solun between that town and Chalaite Wangfu. Although the place and manner of execution have not yet been fully established, it is believed that the party were taken to Solun where they were shot on July 1 st and subsequently burned. The execution was carried oud by order and in the presence of Kuan Yu-heng, commanding the 3rd Regiment of the Hsingan Reclamation Army during the absence in Mukden of Colonel Chao Kuan-wu, the regular commander....
>
> Mr. Hayashi assured me that the negotiations were entirely in his hands in spite of rumours to the effect that the Japanese military authorities were to interfere in securing a settlement. He deplored the attitude of military officials, mentioning a call

---

[1] F.R.U.S., 1931, III, p. 9.

which Major Mori, a Japanese army officer, had made upon General Tsang Shih-yi on July 17th. Major Mori is of the Japanese General Staff Office and was sent to Mukden by the Japanese Army apparently to investigate the case. He informed General Tsang Shih-yi of how seriously the Japanese Army viewed the incident and gave out the following report:

'In dealing with so serious a case, nice diplomatic courtesies could not satisfy the Japanese Army, and I am here to see for myself what amount of sincerity is shown by the Chinese side handling the case. It goes without saying that, once we are satisfied of lack of sincerity on the Chinese side, the Japanese side might enforce its demands'.

This incident is believed to be the first . . . where a Japanese army officer has been arrested and executed by the order of the Chinese military authorities. The Japanese press in Manchuria is making much of the incident and Mr. Hayashi tells me that the outspoken indignation of the military authorities in Japan is exciting the Japanese populace. He did not indicate what action might be taken in the event the Chinese did not meet the demands he has presented but I was led to believe that he is seriously concerned over the effect which protracted negotiations might have on Japanese feelings.

In discussing the general Sino-Japanese situation in Manchuria, Mr. Hayashi did not try to minimize its seriousness. He stated that while that portion of Japanese public opinion which was demanding a 'strong policy' in Manchuria did not represent a majority of the people, nevertheless irritation with Chinese tactics and Foreign Office policy was growing, particularly among the members of the military party and the Japanese residents in Manchuria. The Japanese authorities in Manchuria were taking every precaution to avoid a conflict in Manchuria but the possibility of some unexpected Sino-Japanese conflict developing into an incident of major importance forced them to view the situation with grave concern. [1]

As in most disputes of this kind, it is difficult without a judicial trial or independent investigation on the spot to arrive at a conclusion about what really happened because both sides lie, give garbled reports, conceal and twist facts. Obviously Hayashi was giving Vincent the official Japanese version, that which they wished believed in Washington. Let us now look at a statement given by

---

[1] Op. cit., pp. 1—3.

the other side. The documentary evidence now available shows
that it was at any rate largely true:

> "Captain Shintaro Nakamura was a Japanese military officer
> on active service, who met his death at the hands of Chinese
> soldiers in the interior of Manchuria... The Japanese Gov-
> ernment admitted that he was 'travelling in Inner Mongolia
> by order of the General Staff', but it is very curious that an
> army officer should be engaged on an authorised mission in a
> foreign country while keeping secret his professional identity, and
> posing as an agricultural expert interested in technical research
> — unless of course his mission was one of military espionage.
> The purpose of his journey has never been revealed but that
> he was actually engaged in spying admits of no doubt in view
> of the fact that notebooks found on his person contained data
> concerning military positions, strategic locations, and other
> matter relating to the conduct of military operations...... It is
> no secret that Japan's designs against China's domains included
> not only Manchuria but also Mongolia, and from the fact that
> this officer was on his way to Inner Mongolia it may be in-
> ferred that he was not only a spy, but was sent by the Japanese
> government to suborn Mongolian chieftains from their al-
> legiance to the Chinese government. This conclusion is borne
> out by the increasing activities of Japanese agents in Mongolia
> since the occupation of China's North Eastern territories......
>   In view of the obviously illegal activities of Nakamura di-
> rected against the Chinese Republic, it is not to be wondered
> that he should meet his end at the hands of over-zealous Chin-
> ese soldiers, who probably were under the erroneous im-
> pression that they were lawfully entitled to execute a spy who
> had been caught in *flagrante delicto*...... As soon as China
> was able to connect Nakamura, the military man, (of whom
> there was no record by the authorities granting the passport)
> with Nakamura, the 'agricultural expert', investigators were
> detailed to make the necessary enquiries".[1]

The point made above, that Nakamura was admitted by the
Japanese Government to be an officer on active duty and at the
time "traveling in Inner Mongolia by order of the General Staff"
but under false identity, i.e. as an agricultural expert, is well taken.
"Is is," indeed, "very curious that an army officer should be en-

---

[1] "China Today" Series, *The Puppet State of Manchukuo* (Shanghai 1935),
pp. 72—3.

gaged on an authorized mission in a foreign country while keeping secret his professional identity... unless of course his mission was one of military espionage." There is no doubt that he was a spy.

A point of great interest in the study of Sino-Japanese relations of this period is whether Shidehara and the Japanese Foreign Office were in fact acting in good faith in their protestations of Japan's peaceful intentions toward China and respect for her sovereignty in Manchuria, and later in their claims that the civil government was not a party to, and were ignorant of, the aims and plans of the military in Manchuria. In the document of Hayashi's conversation with Vincent quoted *in extenso* there is grave room for doubt. Such statements as that he (Hayashi) "was seriously concerned over the effect which protracted negotiations might have on Japanese feelings", irritation with Chinese tactics and foreign office policy, "some unexpected Sino-Japanese conflict developing into an incident of major importance", could easily be considered as future explanation for measures of which Hayashi had previous knowledge. If this is true, it would certainly seem that his superior, Shidehara, must have had the same knowledge. At any rate one of the terms later set forth by Japan for settlement of the Manchurian conflict was "Recognition and reaffirmation of treaty rights", and this seems to be a predetermined move to force China into an untenable position, for if she acquiesced, her sovereignty would be seriously jeopardized. This was the crux of the whole issue. Japan claimed certain treaty rights. China claimed that some of the treaty rights did not exist and that others were illegal or had been extorted by force. Hence it is clear that she could not sign such a document as Japan proposed.

Hayashi's conservation with Vincent clearly foreshadows Japans's next move, the invasion of Manchuria, which began September 21, 1931. In passing, it is pertinent to mention that Hayashi's conversation with Vincent quoted above, although taking place a month earlier, clearly is a "rung in the ladder" of the rapidly moving events, leading to Japan's invasion of China and ultimately to the attack on Pearl Harbor.

One constantly sees it stated that the civil government was innocent and was fighting against the military party, that Shidehara was ignorant of the army's intentions. It seems fair to say that he

represented the moderate element of the Japanese government and
that he was against aggressive action if Japan could have all the
advantages of trade, industry and territorial and commercial exploitation without using force. To deny, however, that he had any
foreknowledge or suspicion of the plans and intentions of the
military is to fly in the face of facts. The theory does not square
with later events, nor with what can be read between the lines of
many of his statements of the time. This matter will be referred to
in greater detail, but let us now turn to the preliminary steps leading
to the invasion and the diplomatic correspondence relating thereto.

Mr. Stimson, Secretary of State 1929-33, published a book, *The
Far Eastern Crisis* (third edition 1936), in which he set forth his
views and explains American diplomatic policy in relation to the
crisis. This book was a highly interesting work at the time of its first
publication, but is doubtly so now that many of the documents upon
which it was based are available for study. It is very revealing to
compare his arguments in the book with the record of official policy
and the Secretary's interpretation of events which we can study for
ourselves. In this case we have an exceptional opportunity to follow
an evolution of diplomatic policy in very recent history and to check
against the original documents the official explanations of the
government of the day.

Mr. Stimson says [1] that the State Department had known of the
strained relations between China on the one hand, basing her case
upon her titular sovereignty and the massive Chinese population in
Manchuria, and on the other hand "the interests of Japan arising
out of her claimed treaty rights along the South Manchurian Railway". He refers to the Nakamura case and says: "The Japanese
army were resentful and were agitating for forcible action in reprisal.
Investigations were going on and there was reported to be a very
sharp division between the army authorities and the foreign office
in Tokyo as to the steps which should be taken." He says that
when news of the clash in Manchuria reached him he recorded in
his diary on Saturday morning, September 19, 1931:

> "Trouble has flared up again in Manchuria. The Japanese,
> apparently their military elements, have suddenly made a
> coup. They have seized Mukden and a number of strategic

---

[1]   Stimson, H. L., *Far Eastern Crisis* (New York, 3rd ed. 1936), pp. 31—32.

towns all along and through Southern Manchuria. The situation is very confused and it is not clear whether the army is acting under a plan of the government or on its own".

He says that the alleged cause of their military action, an alleged act of sabotage by the Chinese on the South Manchurian Railway, diminishes to such small proportions as to suggest its actual non-existence. He points out that the Japanese had acted with such promptness and celerity as to make it obvious that they were acting under a previously arranged strategic plan.

Discussing this aspects of the question Willoughby [1] points out that the investigating committee sent out by the League of Nations found that the circumstances did not justify the claim of the Japanese officers that they were acting in self defence, and that even if they thought they were, that could only be a partial mitigation of their personal culpability, but did not lessen the responsibility of the Japanese Government for their acts. He adds: "It is further to be noted that the Commission, while concluding that an explosion of some sort did occur on or near the South Manchuria Railway tracks near Mukden, on the night of September 18th, expressed no opinion as to who had been responsible for that explosion. Thus it may have been the act of a Japanese *agent provocateur* for all that the Commission has to say."

Let us now follow the development of the Japanese aggression and the reasons given therefore as evidenced in diplomatic documents issued by the State Department within the past few years. There are two sets of documents issued by the State Department covering the same period. One is the regular issue: *Papers Relating to the Foreign Relations of the United States, Japan 1931—1941,* published in 1943 in two volumes — of which we are only interested in Volume I; the other is a subsequent for 1931 in three volumes, of which Volume III is entitled *The Far East,* issued in 1946. It is

---

[1] Willoughby, W. W., *The Sino-Japanese Controversy and the League of Nations* (Baltimore 1935), pp. 25—6.

Willoughby was one of the greatest experts on Far Eastern foreign affairs in his day. He was Professor Emeritus of Political Science at Johns Hopkins University, a representative at the Washington Conference and author of a number of books and articles on China, among which are *China at the Conference,* an account of the Washington Conference, and *Foreign Rights and Interests in China,* 2 volumes, 2nd ed. 1927.

obvious that these two volumes cover the same period, but the
latter is largely an issue of documents which for diplomatic reasons
were not published during the war. An attempt will be made to
refer to the two sets of documents chronologically, as nearly as
possible. [1]

Hayashi's conversation with Vincent has already been mentioned.
This was the prelude, as it were, to what would occur within four
weeks. The conversation took place before August 20.

On September 11, 1929, Johnson, American Minister to China,
wrote a memorandum which was subsequently forwarded to the
State Department, noting a conversation with Dr. Ferguson, who
was a trusted adviser to the Chinese Central Government, in which
Dr. Ferguson stated that he felt very much concerned about the
situation developing between China and Japan. He considered "that
Japan was bound to take drastic action vis-à-vis China very shortly.
He said his information was that Japan would occupy Manchuria
within the next three months. He said that a high Japanese official
had made a tour of China for the purpose of investigating the
situation here and had reported to his Government that the opportunity for taking this action had now arrived and he had recommended it". Johnson had remarked that it was fantastic that
Japan should take such a step, for Japan could exploit Manchuria
without the liability of administration, which would remain on
Chinese shoulders. Dr. Ferguson replied that he considered his
information authentic. It is interesting to note that Johnson saw fit
to disregard this conversation and the memorandum thereof until
October 1, when he transmitted it with Dispatch 1203. It arrived at
the State Department on October 26. It would doubtless have made
no difference to the action of the State Department in the light of
its later reactions to really serious matters. But it cannot be argued
that it was simply gossip and unimportant. Any statesman or
person wishing to be informed authentically about anything in
China could get no more reliable source than Donald or Ferguson,
when either of these men saw fit to give inside information.
MacMurray and the press realized this and considered themselves
fortunate to get a hint from either.

---

[1] In future F.R.U.S., 1931, III, will be used as the citation for the second
of the two works listed above. The other will be F.R.U.S., Japan 1931—1941, I.

On October 12, Johnson sent a very interesting report to Stimson, quoting a dispatch from Vincent at Mukden:

"There is good reason to believe that internal Japanese politics are more responsible for the present threatening aspect of Sino-Japanese relations than anything that the Chinese have done or left undone with respect to the case. It is my opinion that relations between Japanese Army and the Japanese Foreign Office (representing non-Army elements in the Government) are as much strained just now as relations between China and Japan, and that the Army authorities are quite as willing to have the negotiations fail as the Foreign Office is anxious to have them succeed." [1]

This was indeed a cogent statement and one which was generally understood by the well-informed world opinion of the time.

On September 12, 1931, Peck, Consul-General at Nanking, received from Dr. M. T. Z. Tyau, Chief of the Chinese Department of Intelligence and Information, an aide-mémoire setting forth various "provocations in Manchuria in order to provide excuses for the use of force, as well as an intensive propaganda campaign designed to blind the eyes of the world to the facts of the situation". [2] The aide-mémoire set forth a number of facts calculated to counteract this propaganda. Four principal points were made, to show the difference between Japan's public protestations of goodwill, pacific intent and defensive action and her real intentions: (1) At a military commanders' conference in June, 1931, it had been decided to increase Japanese forces in Northern Korea by two divisions and place the Japanese garrison in Manchuria on a full-strength basis. (2) The Japanese, having been unable to make a success of colonizing Manchuria themselves, were doing so with Koreans whom they encouraged to emigrate and protected in Manchuria; by this time they reached almost one million in number and were creating a grave problem, as the Wanpaoshan affair had showed. In 1931 a group of Koreans, under Japanese military protection, had seized five thousand *mow* of Chinese land in Wanpaoshan and dug a canal causing great damage and loss to the Chinese. The Chinese had repeatedly protested, but instead of giving justice the Japanese Consul at Changchun had sent a

---

[1] F.R.U.S., 1931, III, p. 4.
[2] *Op. cit.*, p. 6.

detachment of police to protect and help the Koreans in their illegal activities. The Japanese had been using every type of propaganda and lie in the Korean press to stir up the Koreans against the Chinese. A massacre of Chinese in Korea had been the result. (3) During this massacre, which had lasted nine days, from the 1st to the 9th of July 1931, the Japanese did not act to stop the slaughter, despite official Chinese protest. A hundred and fifty Chinese had been killed, 340 injured, and 70 reported missing, while the property losses suffered by the Chinese, directly and indirectly, amounted to no less than three million yen. (4) During and after August 4, 1931, the Japanese had staged military manoeuvres in Huening, and on the 12th, a party of 34 soldiers crossed the border into China and began surveying for construction of bridges; on the 15th the troops had mined the Tumen River and, manning steam launches, patrolled the unmined sections of the river. Thirty Japanese crossed into Chinese territory and began practising with machine guns. [1]

Copies of this report were sent to the British and to the League of Nations. Peck notes that "the *Aide-Mémoire* handed to me for the American Legation was typed on plain paper, bore no seal or other sign of its origin and was enclosed in a 'Waichiaopu' [2] envelope which bore no address." [3] This was presumably due to Chinese fear that Japanese agents would get to know of it. The document began: "The military clique in Japan has of late been clamoring for a drastic policy towards China, particularly in regard to Manchuria and Mongolia. At the Military Commanders' Conference the Minister of War publicly drew attention to the possibility of what he termed grave developments in Manchuria and Mongolia, and urged the necessity of preparedness...".

Vincent's analysis quoted above proved to be the correct one. Internal Japanese politics were indeed more responsible for the situation than anything the Chinese had "done or left undone" and the War Office was not only "quite as willing to have the negotiations fail as the Foreign Office is anxious to have them succeed," if, indeed, the Foreign Office was sincerely anxious or determined to see that they did.

---

[1] *Op. cit.*, pp. 5—7.
[2] *Waichiaopu* means Foreign Office.
[3] F.R.U.S., 1931, III, p. 5.

There had been another cabinet change in Japan and the war party was now in power. They were determined to carry out their plans if it were possible to do so. If they had initial success they would move forward. If they were thwarted by foreign Powers they could always stop and say that they had only taken emergency action. But if they could succeed in playing off one foreign Power against another or in lulling Washington long enough, they could present the world with a *fait accompli*. It would then indeed be difficult to force their withdrawal.

They had, we now know, and even Stimson then understood, put into action a carefully concerted plan which had been worked out in great detail. The Lytton-Commission recognized that in its report. Oral reports and unofficial reports emanating from the Tokyo trails prove this beyond doubt, if further proof were needed. Unfortunately there are no documents available for citation since the testimony of the Tokyo trials has not yet been released. In 1931-3 well-informed lecturers at UCLA (University of California at Los Angeles) said from the platform that this was an integrated military invasion. J. B. Powell and Mr. A. De C. Sowerby, in their publications in Shanghai said this openly and clearly. Only the diplomats were fooled or pretended to be—Stimson was certainly duped, despite the fact that *aide mémoires* at the time show that he understood the facts but could not or would not recognize that he understood the facts and their implications.

Of one thing we may be certain—to repeat—the Nakamura case was only a convenient excuse for Japan's invasion of China, since Manchuria was part of China as much as Texas is a part of the United States—but it is doubtful if even the most sanguine expansionist in Japan dared hope for the quick success which the Japanese scored in Manchuria. The military clique had seized the reigns and was responsible to no one. They had the puppet Japanese emperor as firmly in their grip as the shoguns had had his ancestors in theirs. The police, press and schools were under their thumb. They could mould and control public opinion. The military clique was on the move on a broad and open highway with nothing to stop them—except Pearl Harbor. Yes, Captain Nakamura was a convenient martyr. His death had nothing to do with the invasion. Japan struck when she was ready.

CHAPTER XIII

THE MUKDEN INCIDENT

On September 19th, 1931, Johnson sent to Stimson the news of Japan's first military move:

> Mr. Donald just called me by telephone and said that Marshal Chang Hsueh-liang had received a telegram from Mukden stating that . . . soldiers had left the Japanese area and proceeding southeast of Mukden had commenced firing with rifles at the east camp and at the arsenal. He said they were also using a cannon and were apparently firing shells on the city at the rate of one every ten minutes; that one had landed somewhere near the Japanese monument. He said that at that time it was reported that some seventy Chinese soldiers had been killed in the east camp but they had no information as to what damage had been done in the city. He informed me that Marshal Chang Hsueh-liang had issued orders restricting troops to barracks and depoting all arms and had forbade any retaliatory measures.
>
> Mr. Donald stated that he had received a personal message to the effect that firing was continuing at one o'clock this morning and that Japanese soldiers had been seen marching in the direction of the west gate of the city, the inference being that the Japanese were making a move to occupy the city of Mukden. Mr. Donald stated that their information was that apparently the Japanese military had got completely out of hand at Mukden, that the Japanese civilian authorities, namely the consul general, were powerless to do anything. [1]

On the same day the Japanese newspapers announced that a state of war existed between the two countries, but a member of the Foreign Ministry told Forbes, Ambassador to Japan, that the truth seemed to be that there had been a minor clash between Japanese South Manchurian Railway guards and Chinese soldiers over damage to a section of the track just north of Mukden, which the

---

[1] F.R.U.S., 1931, III, p. 10.

Japanese had since occupied. He assured Forbes of Japan's determination to obtain a peaceful settlement. [1]

In this way Japan gradually occupied Manchuria. Always making
peaceful declarations, and always moving in deeper, and always
finding a new excuse for each new aggressive act. In every such
case the world was assured that this move was different from the
last, that this time Japan was going to give up or that she was going
to withdraw immediately or that it was a temporary necessity. But
Japan never withdrew, once she occupied an area. She only allayed
the suspicions of the powers, who wanted to have them allayed,
who did not wish to recognize an aggression because that would
have meant taking some action and no one wanted to take any
action except Japan. On the 19th, Yingkou was occupied by soldiers,
and warships moved in. [2] Then Kowpangtze was occupied, [3] cutting
Manchuria off completely from the rest of China. [4] On the same
day Wellington Koo came to Johnson and confirmed all the rumors
and reports which had been pouring in, of seizures and occupations
and sounded him out about America starting discussions looking
toward bringing the matter before the League under the Convenant,
the Washington Pact, art. VII, or the Kellogg Pact. [5] The Japanese
occupied Changchun, Antung and Newchang on the 19th. [6]

At a press conference on the same day [7] Stimson said that the
Japanese soldiers had seized Mukden against the will of their
government representative. He reiterated the statement, as he was
to do many, many times in the future. This was to become a sort of
incantation with him. In reply to a question of whether or not this
action of Japan's came under the Four-Power Pact of 1921, the
Secretary thought not, since, from the reports coming in to the
Department, it was not a clash of governments, but a clash of
subordinates of governments, and therefore it would not come under
the Kellogg Pact or any of the other treaties. In reply to the remark
of a correspondent that "clashes between governments usually grow

---

[1] *Op. cit.*, p. 11.
[2] and [3] *Loc. cit.*
[4] *Op. cit.*, p. 12.
[5] *Loc. cit.*
[6] *Op. cit.*, p. 14.
[7] *Op. cit.*, p. 15.

out of smaller things", Mr. Stimson admitted that "it might lead to something that would call for the invocation of the Kellogg Pact or other Treaties, but it certainly is not yet an act of war by one Government against another, according to the press despatches". When pressed for an official statement which could be attributed to the Department by the press, Mr. Stimson authorized the statement that "the Department is following the matter carefully, but on the news thus far received there seems to be no ground for indicating any violation of the Kellogg Pact". [1]

Late on Saturday afternoon, [2] September 20th, 1931, at a session of the League of Nations Council in Geneva, the Japanese delegate to the League, Mr. Yoshizawa, at the request of the President of the Council, made a statement, in which he said that his information was very meager, but that he had requested further information from his Government and would keep the League informed. He declared that his Government would doubtless take appropriate steps to localize the incident, so that it would not lead to more serious consequences, "and to effect an appeasement of the situation".

Dr. Sze, the Chinese Delegate, spoke immediately after the Japanese and expressed grave concern at the "highly regrettable incident", adding that the information thus far at hand indicated that the Chinese were not responsible for the incident. He also said that he would pass on to the Council any authentic information which he obtained. Since no other member spoke, it was obvious that the President was attempting to allay world apprehension concerning the threat of war by these public declarations of representatives of the two countries concerned.

The following quotation is a paraphrase printed in the State Department documents of a part of a telegram from Gilbert, American Consul at Geneva, to the Secretary of State. This paraphrase has evidently been made by the editor of these documents from a longer paper: [3]

This morning Dr. Sze called on me to say that he was aware of my following in a strategical way the Council's proceedings,

---

[1] Op. cit., pp. 15—16.

[2] Op. cit., pp. 17—18.

[3] Op. cit., pp. 18—19.

so he thought the Chinese position in this matter might be of interest to me.

I was told by Sze that the chief delegates of certain powers had met informally and privately prior to the Council's meeting on Saturday and had more or less decided against having the question brought up before the Council. This attitude Sze attributed to Japanese influence. Certain delegates after the meeting approached him as to whether he intended to present the question, and for reasons to be explained later in this telegram, he would not say what he planned to do. He gave as his excuse that he was receiving messages from Nanking which might control his action. In consequence of his reply, another meeting was held by the same delegates, and following this (in this case apparently as a result), the question was presented to the Council by the Japanese delegate. This Japanese action, incidentally, is interpreted here as a Japanese desire (as they do not know Sze's plans), by taking the initiative, to prevent bringing up the aspect of good faith. However, it resulted in allowing the Chinese delegate to make a move without initiating it in a way which might be interpreted to be tantamount to an appeal to the Council.

I learned from Sze that he was not able and probably would not be able during the present Council session to communicate to it any more authentic information regarding the Mukden situation, since he had been informed by Nanking of the cutting by the Japanese of communications from Mukden to Peiping and Nanking, thereby preventing his getting any information from Mukden. Sze attributed this Japanese cutting of communications as an act to prevent the true facts becoming known before the Council's meetings have concluded. He also revealed to me that instructions from his Government on the position he should take at Geneva had not yet been received; that his action would be governed by these instructions, but that he would put off this action as long as he could, even if directed to present the question to the League.

After the above statements, it became apparent why Sze had come to see me. The press in Europe has published articles under a Washington date line about the United States considering the relationship of the current situation to the Four-Power Pacific Treaty's provisions. Sze said he felt that action under this treaty or under the Kellogg Pact of 1928 would be better for China than League of Nations action, since the stronger position of Japan in the League would militate against China. According to Sze, Japan can use its position by employing its relations to questions of Europe as trading points.

Sze has no wish to fall between two stools, but if there is a possibility that Washington may take the action mentioned above, Sze does wish to avoid an appeal to the League, especially as he feels that possible American action might be prejudiced by prior League action. From the foregoing it will be noted that neither Japan nor China has as yet requested the League Council to act in this matter.

On September 21, 1931, Johnson sent a wire to Stimson outlining events in Manchuria. It will be of interest to summarize this telegram to show the opinions of the American Minister at that time and also the tactics which Japan would use in the future to gain her objectives by military force while maintaining that she was being driven to act in self-defense or that she was perfectly willing to withdraw her forces from occupied areas as soon as China settled all outstanding issues. She was trying to place China in a position where she would have to settle all issues to Japan's satisfaction. This would in effect take the dispute out of the jurisdiction of any international body and constitute recognition by China that Japan had acted in self-defense, hence legalizing Japan's aggression.

No one appears to be able to give satisfactory reason for chain of incidents which began about 10 o'clock on the evening of September 18th and which by steady progress have resulted in putting all of Manchuria south of Changchun and east of the Peking—Mukden Railway line under Japanese military control.... It is my belief that it was this incident [1] which precipitated the chain of events above referred to.... For some two or three weeks past Japanese soldiers have been carrying out daily and nightly maneuvers and sham fights in and around the railway settlements along the line of the South Manchuria Railway from Changchun to Liaoning, using blank cartridges....

Guests in hotels state that during such sham fighting Japanese soldiers would enter hotels, seek out vacant rooms, plant machine guns in windows and on roofs and immediately commence firing to the disturbance of everyone. It is my present belief that much of this was deliberately staged for the purpose of accustoming the populace to the maneuvering of Japanese soldiery day and night and to the sound of machine and other guns.

Japanese statement .... is to the effect that this chain of

---

[1] The Nakamura aiffair.

incidents was not precipitated by the Nakamura affair but was started because of clash between Japanese guards and armed Chinese soldiers attempting to break South Manchuria Railway tracks.

It seems to me absurd to believe that mere destruction of railway tracks would warrant occupation of Manchuria, and to imply that chain of events above mentioned was accidental or occurred on the spur of the moment leaves out of consideration the fact that whole series of incidents involving military occupation of places as far apart as Changchun, Newchang, Antung, Kowpangtze and Hulutao implies a degree of staff work which could not (have been?) improvised. Furthermore it is our understanding here that Japanese military headquarters were transferred almost immediately from Port Arthur to Mukden.

. . . I understand that Japanese military believe this necessary to restoration of their popularity. [1]

Johnson states in the same report that he had been reluctant to put much faith in the statement of Dr. Ferguson's (quoted above) and other similar statements that Japan intended within three months to occupy Manchuria, but that, now it had transpired, he could not help feeling that it had been the result of careful planning. He said that he was without information what Japan planned to do next, but felt that before she withdrew from points now occupied she would demand and get a satisfactory settlement of all questions outstanding with China, at least as regards Manchuria. He added that the Japanese then occupied all South Manchuria and that train service was open from Peiping to Mukden, but only on a Japanese travel permit. [2]

In another telegram Johnson told the Secretary of State that Japan's acts amounted to planned aggression and as such came under the Kellogg Treaty to which the U.S., Japan and China were adherents. He concluded by saying that the powers signatory thereto owed it to themselves and to the world to pronounce themselves in regard to Japanese aggression, which must fall under any definition of war and was carried out in utter and complete disregard to Japan's obligations. [3]

In a memorandum of September 22nd, 1931, Stimson noted a con-

---

[1] F.R.U.S., Japan 1931—1941, I, pp. 2—3.

[2] *Op. cit.*, p. 4.

[3] *Op. cit.*, p. 5.

CHRISTOPHER, Conflict in the Far East   15

versation with Debuchi, the Japanese Ambassador. This is interesting because it gives the view which he still held in 1936, when the second edition of his *Far Eastern Crisis* was issued, namely that Shidehara and the civil government of Japan were completely innocent and ignorant of any plans of a military nature.

> I explained that as he well knew, I had the utmost confidence in Baron Shidehara and his desire for peace and correct international relations. I told him that I had learned from Dr. Hornbeck's report of what Debuchi had said Sunday—that there was a sharp cleavage between Shidehara and some of the militaristic elements of his government. He said that that was so. I said that what I was now doing was seeking to strengthen Baron Shidehara's hand and not to weaken it. The Ambassador said he understood that perfectly. I then took the memorandum which had been prepared (a copy of which is annexed) and read it very slowly to the Ambassador, paraphrasing the language into more simple words wherever it seemed at all necessary in order that he should fully understand it. He repeated many of the sentences, showing that he did understand. When I had finished I said that this was not to be taken as a formal note or an official action on the part of my government, but as the memorandum of a verbal statement given to the Ambassador for the purpose of enabling him to understand and report to his government how I, with my background of friendship towards Japan, felt towards this situation. [1]

The Secretary then asked him to postpone his imminent departure for his leave in Japan. He explained in detail what a bad impression it would create in America if the situation in Manchuria was not restored to the *status quo ante*. Debuchi admitted that he fully realized that and said that he was surprised at the moderate tone of the American press so far, which he attributed to the care Stimson had taken in his press conferences. In departing he asked Stimson whether he would first notify him if the time ever came when he did wish to act officially. Stimson told him that he would try to do so.

It is difficult to know whether Stimson's moderation at such an advanced stage was wise or not, but there was little he could have done, had he been so minded. It must be remembered that this was the depth of the economic depression and that Hoover was already

---

[1] *Op. cit.*, p. 6.

becoming very unpopular, he was being more or less personally blamed for the depression, and naturally his administration shared in his unpopularity. Stimson might have taken a more vigorous tone and even suggested serious consequences if Japan did not back down immediately. It seems that it might have had some effect at that stage, but it is not at all certain. It must be remembered that the Japanese Embassy was not ignorant of the internal condition of the country. In the final analysis nothing America could have done, alone or in conjunction with other Powers, short of a threat backed by readiness to go to war, would have had effect. It is doubtful whether even economic sanctions, and a trade boycott with severance of diplomatic relations, would have had the effect of a threat backed by the readiness to go to war. If the United States had been prepared to go to war Japan probably would not have risked it, but war was utterly out of the question at the time.

Japan could not have picked a more opportune moment to begin her aggression. The entire economy of the Western world was tottering. It is doubtful whether any Western Government in the autumn of 1931 could have led its country to war without serious domestic consequences leading to a fall of the Government in a parliamentary democracy, and perhaps even more drastic consequences in a country such as America, which does not have the safety valve of turning out the Government of the day between Presidential elections. It is possible that some form of revolution would have taken place in America.

In any case it would have been impossible to threaten war for the simple reason that the President of the United States cannot declare war without the consent of Congress, and there would have been no change in the prevailing political situation of his obtaining such consent, especially after 1932.

Taking into consideration the limits within which Stimson had to form his policy, it is very interesting, nevertheless, to see how he played the cards he had. Obviously the good opinion and friendliness of America were extremely important to Japan. It goes without saying that she would have preferred to be able to carry out her aggressions in Asia without interference from any other Power. Short of that, her tactics were to stall for time, create new diversions, advance new legalistic and semi-legalistic arguments, which, however specious, would consume time, while she went ahead on new pretexts with her designs in Manchuria. As we shall see, she took advantage of every possible moot point of international law, and in this case there was even some question where the sovereignty of Manchuria lay; at that time there were sincere and reasonable people in whose minds honest doubt was raised on this point.

As suggested in the telegram from Gilbert, the Consul at Geneva, there was the strong possibility that Japan would be able to make deals with some of the principal Powers of the League, "employing its relations to questions of Europe as trading points", in return for their non-interference, if not official acquiescence, in Japan's schemes. This however was not possible in Japan's relations with America, which was not a member of the League, and it was of the utmost importance for Japan to ward off America's interference for as long a time as possible. Even American disapproval, without any active steps in diplomacy, would be aired in the world press and would inevitably influence other Powers, putting them more on their guard and making them more careful not to do anything which America might interpret as sanction for Japan's actions. They would not wish to do anything which, in case any of them were to need the support of America at a later date, would prejudice their chances of being able to make an effective appeal to American opinion. But over and above such influence, the United States might take the initiative, as she had in the Sino-Russian conflict, to get the Powers to act, either under the League Covenant, or, as Japan feared much more, under one of the treaties to which all concerned were signatories, the Nine-Power Pact or the Kellogg Pact.

If, however, Japan could hold off concerted action long enough, she would then be in a position to present a *fait accompli* to the world. This would be quite another matter.

The memorandum which Stimson read to Debuchi at the meeting mentioned above, is the first clear statement of his official attitude to the incidents in Manchuria:

> Without going into the background, either as to the im-
> mediate provocation or remote causes or motivation, it appears

that there has developed within the past four days a situation in Manchuria which I find surprising and view with concern. Japanese military forces, with some opposition at some points by Chinese military forces, have occupied the principal strategic points in South Manchuria, including the principal administrative center, together with some at least of the public utilities. It appears that the highest Chinese authority ordered the Chinese military not to resist, and that, when news of the situation reached Tokyo, but after most of the acts of occupation had been consummated, the Japanese Government ordered cessation of military activities on the part of the Japanese forces. Nevertheless, it appears some military movements have been continuously, and are even now in process. The actual situation is that an arm of the Japanese Government is in complete control of South Manchuria.

The League of Nations has given evidence of its concern. The Chinese Government has in various ways invoked action on the part of foreign governments, citing its reliance upon treaty obligations and inviting special reference to the Kellogg Pact.

This situation is of concern, morally, legally and politically to a considerable number of nations. It is not exclusively a matter of concern to Japan and China. It brings into question at once the meaning of certain provisions of agreements, such as the Nine Powers Treaty of February 6, 1922, and the Kellogg-Briand Pact.

The American Government is confident that it has not been the intention of the Japanese Government to create or to be a party to the creation of a situation which brings the applicability of treaty provisions into consideration. The American Government does not wish to be hasty in formulating its conclusions or in taking a position. However, the American Government feels that a very unfortunate situation exists, which no doubt is embarrassing to the Japanese Government. It would seem that the responsibility for determining the course of events with regard to the liquidating of this situation rests largely upon Japan, for the simple reason that Japanese armed forces have seized and are exercising *de facto* control in South Manchuria.

It is alleged by the Chinese, and the allegation has the support of circumstantial evidence, that lines of communication outward from Manchuria have been cut or interfered with. If this is true, it is unfortunate.

It is the hope of the American Government that the orders which it understands have been given both by the Japanese and the Chinese Governments to their military forces to refrain from hostilities and further movements will be respected and that there will be no further application of force. It is also the hope of the American Government that the Japanese and the Chinese Governments will find it possible speedily to demonstrate to the world that neither has any intention to take advantage, in furtherance of its own peculiar interests, of the situation which has been brought about in connection with and in consequence of this use of force.

What has occurred has already shaken the confidence of the public with regard to the stability of conditions in Manchuria, and it is believed that the crystallizing of a situation suggesting the necessity for an indefinite continuance of military occupation would further undermine that confidence. [1]

On September 24th, Stimson wired Neville, the Chargé d'Affaires in Japan that the State Department was giving most careful consideration to the situation and informed him that he had received from the Chinese Chargé d'Affaires a note claiming that "in this case of unprovoked and unwarranted attack and subsequent occupation of Chinese cities by Japanese troops" Japan had deliberately violated the Kellogg Pact. The Chinese Government had urgently appealed to the American Government "to take such steps as will insure the preservation of peace in the Far East and the upholding of the principle of the peaceful settlement of international disputes".

On September 24th, Stimson sent a cable to Johnson setting forth the policy of the Department. He pronounced himself in favor of sending identical notes to both China and Japan. Because of the extreme importance of the remainder of the message it will be necessary to quote most of it verbatim; only thus can the working of his mind be fully revealed in all its nuances. His reading of the situation would have little or no significance for us now if it were simply the opinion of an individual on current events, but the opinion of a Secretary of State influences policy, and any misinterpretation is a serious matter. Of course, Stimson had not the knowledge of the facts which we have now; he was dealing with a contemporary event and had no hindsight to guide him; he was

---

[1] F.R.U.S., Japan 1931—1941, I, pp. 7—8.

working in the void, in the unknown, as it were. But all statesmen
have to make judgements on situations as they arise and not all
statesmen of the time seem to have been so misguided as Stimson was
in this affair. This is not to say that he was unfitted for the office
he held. Quite the contrary, he is one of the very few Secretaries
of State of really high caliber the United States has had. Attention
has already been drawn to the peculiar circumstances of the time,
the financial and political situation, the effects of the world-wide
depression, the unpopularity of the Hoover régime, and the
narrow choice of alternatives. Yet, allowing for all this, his policy,
in certain respects, seems to have been extremely ill-advised and
inadequate, if not inept. He did not make enough of the weak hand
he did hold. Not only did he not bluff, he at all times underbid
his hand, and lost the bid. He was much concerned with what the
Japanese would think of him, and how they would react, too
frightened that he might weaken the civil and strengthen the military
element in Japan, too nervous of inflaming Japanese sentiment and
hurting the notorious Japanese "sensitivity".

At the outset let it be conceded that he was wise to consider
these points and to weigh their importance, but their importance
should also have been weighed against other considerations and
not allowed to determine policy as they did. It must be remembered
that Stimson acted as a brake on pressure against Japan for
several months after the tempest in the Japanese teapot about
Nakamura, and the pretension that the alleged destruction of a few
yards of railway track by the Chinese entitled Japan to take control
of South Manchuria in self-defence. It must also be remembered
that in each conference he made a theme-song of his friendliness
for Japan and his desire to protect Japan. The Japanese were very
astute in taking advantage of all this good will. The Japanese have
been noted from their earliest recorded history for the combination
of trickery with violence, from the massacre of the Earth Hiders, [1]

---

[1] Sometimes called Earth Spiders or Earth Huggers. Perhaps aborigines who
dwelt in caves, and opposed the conquest of Japan by the invaders, now known
as Japanese. Jimmu, the first emperor, according to the mythological histories
Nihongi and Kojiki, Nihongi, p. 123, Kojiki, p. 171. Kojiki says: "When (Jimmu)
... reached the great cave at Osaka, earth-spiders ... eighty bravoes were in
the cave awaiting him. So then the august son of the Heavenly Deity commanded

who had been invited as guests to a banquet by Jimmu, the first so-called emperor, down to the attack on Pearl Harbor. Her actions in 1931 were in character. Is it beyond reason that the Japanese Ambassador soon realized this weakness of Stimson and played upon it while stalling for time, time which Japan was using to extend her conquests and dig herself in, time in which to present a *fait accompli?* It is more than likely that the Foreign Office officials in Tokyo were well aware of the fact that they could "use" Stimson while proceeding with their own designs. One is almost tempted to say that Stimson's trouble was that he had never read the *Nihongi* or *Kojiki,* [1] or studied the history of Japan, or made himself familiar with the career of Hideyoshi Toyotomi. [2]

To one reading through the documents, it seems that there never was any nation so abused as Japan was by China. One can sum up the whole Japanese case by saying that Japan wanted Manchuria and was able to use specious arguments to tie up the Powers until she had accomplished her aims. It seems too ridiculous to dignify the Japanese diplomatic correspondence with Washington by introducing it as serious documentary evidence. It is enough to refer to a statement communicated by the Japanese Embassy to the State Department. [3] This declared that the Japanese Government had constantly pursued a policy of friendliness to promote the interests of both countries; conduct of Chinese officials and individuals, unfortunately, had often irritated the Japanese national sentiment; unfriendly acts in Mongolia and Manchuria in which Japan was interested in a special degree, were beginning to make

---

that a banquet be bestowed upon the eighty bravoes. Thereupon he set eighty butlers, saying: 'When ye hear me sing, cut (them down) simultaneously'... Having thus sung, they drew their swords and simultaneously smote them to death."

[1] *Nihongi* and *Kojiki,* explained above, mythological histories of the origin of the Japanese and seizure of Japan, the former translated by Aston, W. G. (London 1924), the latter by Chamberlain, B. H. (Kobe 1932).

[2] The greatest Japanese leader—the only peasant ever to rise to high place in Japan before the Restoration and one of the few really great men Japan has produced. He was born in 1536, died 1598. His project was a similar one to the design of Japanese policy from 1931 to 1945; he planned to conquer Korea, China and Indonesia, but never got further than Korea.

[3] F.R.U.S., Japan 1931—1941, I, pp. 11—12.

Japan think China did not reciprocate in like spirit; in such an atmosphere some Chinese soldiers had destroyed track and attacked railway guards on September 18th, midnight; since there were only 10,400 Japanese soldiers and 220,000 Chinese soldiers, the Japanese, to forestall attack, had had to disarm the Chinese soldiers; soldiers in surrounding areas were also disarmed "and the duty of maintaining peace and order was left in the hands of the local Chinese organizations *under the supervision* [1] of Japanese troops". [2] Most Japanese troops had already been withdrawn into the railway zone; some detachments still remained in Mukden and Kirin and a small number in some other places, but nowhere did military occupation "*as such*" [3] exist; the cabinet had taken a decision that aggravation of the situation should stop and had so informed the commander of the Manchurian garrison on September 19; it was true that a detachment had been dispatched from Changchun to Kirin on the 21st, but not for military occupation, only for flank protection. "As soon as that object has been attained the bulk of our detachment will be withdrawn"; the four thousand men sent from Korea to Manchuria to reinforce the garrison, the total number being still less than the number set by treaty, cannot in any way be regarded as Japan's having added to the seriousness of the international situation. "It may be superfluous to repeat that the Japanese Government harbors no territorial designs in Manchuria."

Stimson's memorandum for Johnson of September 24, 1931, begins by saying: "For your personal information, I want to give you . . . a picture of the policy of the Department." After stating that he was sympathetic to the idea of sending identical notes to Japan and China, he proceeds: [4]

> However, the idea of sending a military commission to Manchuria to establish the facts disturbed us. At the time of the dispute between Bulgaria and Greece this was done by the League with success. Entirely different, however, are the conditions in the Manchurian situation. The issue in the

[1] Italics mine.
[2] F.R.U.S., Japan 1931—1941, I, p. 12.
[3] *Loc. cit.* Italics mine.
[4] *Op. cit.*, pp. 10—11.

Bulgarian-Greek dispute was a line dividing the two countries. In Manchuria, since the Japanese troops are in that section of China under treaty provisions, no such issue arises. Moreover, even as a fact-finding body, the Department has felt very strongly that a commission sent to Manchuria could have little success without the consent of both the Chinese and Japanese. That the Japanese nationalistic element would be immensely strengthened and that it would unite Japan behind the military element, is our principal fear concerning such an imposed commission. The civilian arm of the Government in Japan, we believe, is opposed to the adventure in Manchuria, and the Department feels it is important in every way to support this element. It was our suggestion to Geneva, therefore, that there was a greater possibility of obtaining the consent of Japan if the composition of the commission to be appointed were to be along the lines of our suggestion of two years ago to China and Russia. In other words, the commission should be one appointed by both parties involved in the dispute. The League has adopted this suggestion and, if Japan accepts, at present intends to establish a commission consisting of two members appointed by Japan, two by China, and three by the League Council. This commission we understand would be purely fact finding and have very narrow terms of reference. However, if it can be brought about between the Japanese and Chinese, we believe there is a much greater chance of reaching a solution —in view of Oriental psychology—by direct consultation. The Department feels at the same time that inevitably the dispute is of interest to the world, and that it would make a travesty of the various treaties of which Japan and China are both signatories to allow Japan to consolidate the occupation of the Manchurian cities. Since in this matter the League has already taken action and since as members of the League both parties have agreed to submit to the action therein provided, this Government would be inclined to favor, in case direct conversations are unsuccessful between the two parties, action under article 11 and subsequent articles of the League Covenant signed by both Japan and China.

The treaties of 1922 and the Kellogg Pact still remain and might be invoked in case this action should be unsuccessful.

It is rather interesting to follow some of Mr. Stimson's logic. For instance he says the Japanese are in Manchuria by treaty provisions, but certainly that is begging the question, for the treaty did not give them the right to wage an aggressive war and occupy the territory under a military and civil government set up by themselves. His idea about having the consent of the Japanese to any investigation is equally odd. Judges do not ask the consent of the accused in order to try them, and granted that there is a difference, one must still allow that the purpose of the League of Nations was to preserve peace and, if necessary, to impose conditions upon an aggressor which the aggressor obviously would not like. Further, Stimson's statement about uniting the Japanese people behind the army seems rather strange to anyone who is familiar with Japanese history. The masses have practically never had any motive power of their own, except occasionally in famine riots. Japan has always been an oligarchical government, traditionally that of a feudal military aristocracy. The people have never had anything to say except what they were told. By holding off action, Stimson was simply giving the military and nationalist element time to whip up national sentiment for their own purposes. The people would follow where they were led. There was no important mass public opinion in Japan, as we in the West know it. Delaying and allowing the army to gain more territory in Manchuria was simply giving the military jingoes in Japan more fuel with which to feed the flames. The apparent world-wide fear of Japan's power strengthened the extreme nationalist propaganda of Japan's mission to rule the world in the name of the Sun-Goddess, Amaterasu, and the *Kodo* or "Imperial Way". Naturally, when the army could present as an accomplished fact to the people a large addition to the Japanese Empire, the threat that it was about to be taken away from them by America or the League could be represented as a danger of attack on Japan and used to work up patriotic frenzy. Hence by trying to delay concerted action to stop Japan, Stimson was bringing about exactly what he wished to avoid. His feeling about the civil government being opposed to the adventure in Manchuria led him astray, for whatever opposition there was, it was not sufficiently resolute to put a brake on the militarists as long as the latter were clearly getting away with it.

In his constant reference to supporting the civil element he was, in reality, aiding the aggression, for while the diplomats were dealing in sweet reasonableness, the soldiers were not being idle; they were driving ahead full speed on a round-the-clock schedule.

They never stopped their activity to see what would be the outcome of the chit-chat going on in the Embassies and Foreign Offices of the world. They let the diplomats bring up moot points and discuss them, make enquiries and conclude tentative agreements, which, meanwhile, gave them, the men of action, more time to consolidate and expand.

Stimson's reference to his plan for arbitration in 1929 over the Chinese Eastern Railway dispute sounds rather hollow. What did China get from his proposals? What can any one party to a dispute get from an arbitration when the other side holds a gun to his head during the arbitration? The Powers knew Russia held the gun and that the conclusion was foregone. Yet everyone piously and cynically pretended that it was a victory for peace. Now Stimson was suggesting the same mockery over again. It would indeed have been a repudiation of treaties and of honour, explicitly to permit Japan to consolidate her occupation, not only of the Manchurian cities, but of the whole of South Manchuria, eventually of all Manchuria and North China. Yet that was exactly what such a policy led to.

As to America's preferring action under Article 11, or any other article, of the League Covenant, she had no right to such a preference. She had refused to join the League or to participate in the comity of nations on any but her own terms; of what concern, then, was any article of the Covenant to Stimson or to America? It is interesting to notice the way the telegram finishes in a limp. "The treaties of 1922 and the Kellogg Pact still remain and *might* [1] be invoked . . . ." Here indeed were treaties which America did have a right to invoke, but Stimson preferred to take action under an article of a pact to which America was not a signatory. It was a question of "let's you and him fight".

On September 31st, 1931, the Council of the League adopted a resolution in which it [2] (1) notes the replies of Japan and China to the appeal addressed to them and the steps taken in response thereto; (2) recognizes the importance of Japan's statement of having no territorial designs on Manchuria; (3) notes Japanese

---

[1]   Italics mine.
[2]   F.R.U.S., Japan 1931—1941, I, pp. 13—14.

representative's statement that his government is withdrawing and will continue as rapidly as possible the withdrawal of troops into the railway zone; (3) notes the Chinese representative's statement that his Government will assume responsibility for the safety of the lives and property of the Japanese as the troops withdraw, and the local Chinese authorities and police are re-instated; (5) notes that both will prevent spread or aggravation of the incident; (6) urges both to hasten restoration of normal relations and execution of above undertakings; (7) requests both to furnish the Council, progress reports; (8) decides to meet again in Geneva on October 14; (9) authorizes the President to cancel meeting if no longer necessary.

On October 8th, Neville notified [1] Stimson that the Japanese General Staff had issued a declaration stating that it would be impossible to withdraw the Japanese to their original stations, because of atrocities committed by defeated Chinese troops. Neville said that he believed the Japanese were becoming increasingly irritated with developments in China and might have to take other steps to protect Japanese lives there.

In a memorandum sent to the Under-Secretary of State by Shige-mitsu, a copy of one sent to China, the argument was advanced that the Manchurian incident was nothing but the outcome of deep-rooted anti-Japanese feeling in China which had become especially provocative in the recent challenge to the Japanese troops compelling them to protect themselves. The responsibility for the situation naturally lay with China. The Chinese engaged in boycotts of Japanese goods and Chinese secret societies had recently gone further and decided to cancel contracts and prohibit all transactions between the two countries. This campaign, though unofficial, reflected a national policy of the Chinese government.

On October 9th, Stimson wired Neville [2] to see Shidehara and ask him whether or not it was true that the Japanese Government had given its assent to the statement issued by the Japanese General Staff, that it was impossible for various reasons to withdraw Japanese troops to their original stations or even to the contiguous

---

[1] *Op. cit.*, p. 14.
[2] *Op. cit.*, p. 17.

territory, and whether or not it was true that bombs had been dropped on Chinchow by Japanese planes. The following day Neville replied [1] that Shidehara had just informed him that "the bulletin issued by the General Staff was not a Government pronouncement". In answer to the other question Shidehara had replied: "Information had reached the commanding general that there was a large concentration of Chinese troops in that vicinity and Japanese Army planes had been sent to make a reconnaissance, They had been fired at by Chinese troops and had replied by dropping bombs on the barracks." Shidehara added that the affair was of no importance.

On October 11th, Stimson wired Neville [2] that he was not satisfied with Shidehara's reply about the bombing, saying that he thought it of the greatest importance and that the Japanese statement was quite inadequate. He pointed out that Chinchow was more than fifty miles from the Japanese railway zone and was in a zone where the Chinese had every right to have troops, that he was unable to see what right Japanese planes had to fly over the town, thus provoking attack, or what right they had to drop bombs. He pointed out the seriousness of bombing an unfortified and unwarned town, an act which was deprecated even in war. He stated that Japanese military authorities were quoted in usually reliable press sources as saying that this attack was intended to prevent Chang Hsüeh-liang from establishing his new capital there and resuming his authority in Manchuria. He added that the explanations given by Japan for this act were quite at variance with the commitments undertaken by her on September 30th, 1931, with respect to the resolution of the League Council, and that he was constrained to regard the bombing as of very serious importance and "would welcome any further information from the Minister for Foreign Affairs which would throw light on it".

This episode of the Chinchow bombing showed in a striking way not only Japan's complete contempt for her commitments, for the rights of other nations, and for international law, but also the utter futility of Stimson's policy. By her action Japan revealed not only her cynical disregard for international law and world opinion, but her

[1] *Op. cit.,* pp. 18—19.
[2] *Op. cit.,* pp. 20—21.

determination to pursue her appointed end, the seizure of Man-churia, while the Powers protested and discussed the niceties of diplomacy. Even though Stimson was held back from really drastic action by the domestic and international situation, at least he could have stopped the pretence of believing that Japan's actions might be honourable in intention, or due to a temporary situation which could be cleared up by the usual diplomatic correspondence between honourable nations. He could have "got tough" with Japan by letting her know immediately that he would do everything in his power to back the League and the signatories of the agreements to which America was also a signatory. He should have recognized the fact that Japan was now a self-outlawed nation, pursuing a policy of aggression and territorial aggrandizement and hypocritic-ally declaring the purity of her intentions while using diplomatic channels to stall for time. But Stimson still preferred to believe that Shidehara could and would restrain the Japanese army.

On October 12th, Neville sent to Stimson a telegram which is very revealing and further confirms that Japan was refusing to settle the affair on any terms except her own. Shidehara, the man in whose innocence and integrity Stimson has always professed to believe, talked quite frankly to Neville. The tenor of his con-versation seems absolutely to refute the belief that he was ignorant of Japan's ultimate aims. He said that in his opinion the affair would be dragged out as long as China could avoid direct negotiation with Japan. He compared the situation to the Shantung negotiations, when, after the ratification of the Treaty of Versailles, Japan had notified China that she was ready to open negotiations for the rendition of Tsingtao and the Shantung railway to China, but China had refused; the affair had then been protracted until the Washington Conference, where all points at issue had been settled amicably in a short time by direct conversation between Japan and China. He said that the present difficulty could be speedily solved by direct negotiations, but that as long as China had any encouragement to believe that pressure could be applied to force her to yield her position, she would avoid direct negoti-ations. He claimed that Japanese responsibility to withdraw her forces within the railway zone was conditional upon China's safeguarding Japanese lives and property in China, but that China

had made no effort to do so. For these reasons Japan was unable
to withdraw her troops and, until China indicated her intention to
carry out her part of the agreement, he could not see how the
situation could be altered. Shidehara said that, if China were made
to realize that she 'had no chance of settlement except by direct
negotiations with Japan, all the problems would settle themselves
immediately. "Once that is made clear to them," Shidehara declared, "the irresponsible agitation by students and professional
politicians will die down because the Kuomintang will have no
chance to make domestic political capital out of baiting the Japanese.
.... in the meantime Japan would exercise extreme forbearance
and not provoke any trouble." [1] In reply to a statement by Neville
that the Chinchow bombing had aroused much criticism, Shidehara
said he had no further comment to make on that subject.

The statement that the Shantung question had been amicably
settled between Japan and China in a short time as soon as China
agreed to negotiate directly with Japan was dishonest, for the truth
is that China did not then negotiate directly in the strict sense of
the word. In fact she refused until Hughes and Balfour persuaded
her to negotiate on the condition that British and American
representatives should sit in on each conference as observers. Was
Shidehara ignorant of this fact or was 'he merely contemptuous of
Stimson and the State Department because they had been such
dupes for him? He was not ignorant of the fact, because he
represented Japan in those negotiations. Hence it must have been
the latter. What he was proposing, if we may impute any
honor to the man or sincerity to his statements, was, in fact, a
similar arrangement to that made for the settlement of the Shantung
question, that foreign observers should sit in on the negotiations.
Yet this, Japan from 1931 to 1932, resolutely refused. In the end,
in order to prevent such "outside interference" she would shortly
withdraw from the League of Nations.

Confirmatory of this view of Japan's intention was Neville's
observation in the last paragraph of the document quoted above:
"I am pretty well satisfied that the statement I made in my 162" (an
unpublished telegram) "is still correct: direct conversation between

---

[1] *Op. cit.*, p. 22.

the Chinese and Japanese is the only way out, because the Japanese for the present will not welcome interference by any third party."

Shidehara's statement about Japan's inability to withdraw until China indicated her intention "to safeguard Japanese lives and property in fact as well as in name" is a morally dishonest, if not an outright false, statement. China pledged herself to do this before the League Council at the same time that Japan agreed to withdraw her troops within the railway zone. She had been given no chance by Japan to do so "in fact as well as in name". The Japanese proposal for forcing China to negotiate through recognition of the fact that there was, in effect, no appeal open to her, was really a coldly cynical confession to the American representative of Japan's will to coerce a weaker nation by isolating it from all aid. If China were driven to recognize the fact that she was helpless and that there was no international justice for her, she would have to settle on Japan's terms. The "rape of Manchuria" was indeed an apt phrase. The plain truth is that Shidehara was appealing to an American diplomat to help Japan force this realization upon China and to be an accomplice in Japan's aggression. As for Shidehara's remark about Japan's exercise of forbearance, one would have thought that it was Japan which had been invaded by China instead of the other way round.

CHAPTER XIV

JAPAN PLAYS FOR TIME

In a memorandum dated October 12th, Stimson noted that the Japanese Ambassador had brought him a reply to his aide-mémoire of October 10th, to Shidehara. It was in the following terms:

First: Baron Shidehara was strongly of the opinion that the General Officer, commanding in Manchuria, was not in a position to take charge of diplomatic negotiations; and that such a question as the recognition of Marshal Chang's authority in Manchuria was a question for the Imperial Japanese Government.

Second: It was very far from Baron Shidehara's real thought to minimize the bombing at Chinchow; that all he wished to express was that the bombing was an isolated military action which did not reflect the real attitude of the Japanese Government.

Third: Baron Shidehara wished Ambassador Debuchi to assure me that the fixed policy of Japan towards China will not be influenced by a few incidents caused by Japanese military officers in Manchuria, which incidents might be merely the results of temporary states of mind on their part.

Fourth: Baron Shidehara has entirely approved Ambassador Debuchi's explanation of the Japanese memorandum to China (a copy of which was left by Debuchi at Mr. Castle's home the other evening [1]), which was to the effect that this memorandum was merely a precautionary measure and could not be construed as an ultimatum or as evidence of aggressive action on Japan's part.

After conveying these messages, the Ambassador made some personal observations. One was to the effect that the position of the Japanese Cabinet is very difficult; that Shidehara is responsible to the Cabinet and to Parliament and for that reason it was very difficult for Shidehara to say whether he approved or disapproved the action of the Japanese military

---

[1] F.R.U.S., Japan 1931—1941, I, pp. 15—16.

in Manchuria or of the act of Japanese airplanes in bombing Chinchow.

I replied that I understood Mr. Shidehara's position. I said that my attitude towards him personally was not modified by the fact that he did not seem to be able to control his general officers, but that on his part he must remember that I faced the fact that these actions by the general officers may affect the safety of the world and must govern my action accordingly. As the Ambassador left I told him that the one important thing I wished him to convey to Baron Shidehara was that the situation in Manchuria was regarded here as most serious, both by our government and the American people, and there should be no mistake about that. I then told Debuchi that I was going to authorize Gilbert to sit with the Council of the League of Nations, if invited, in their discussion on any matters that related to treaties to which we were a party. I told him that my reason was that both for the sake of the effect on the world at large and the relations of this country with Japan I wanted it to be clear that we stood not alone vis-à-vis Japan but with the other nations of the world. [1]

Castle, the Under-Secretary of State, in a memorandum dated October 14th, 1931, noted that Debuchi had told him in great confidence the basis on which Shidehara wished to deal with China.

1. Mutual declaration of non-aggressive policy or action in Manchuria.
2. Mutual engagements to suppress hostile agitation.
3. Reaffirmation by Japan as to the territorial integrity of China, including Manchuria.
4. Japanese subjects in Manchuria to be sufficiently protected by the Chinese when carrying on their peaceful and legitimate proceedings.
5. Arrangements to be reached between Japan and China for the prevention of ruinous railway competition and for the carrying into effect of existing railway agreements. [2]

The memorandum concludes by stating that Debuchi pointed out these five points were all covered by existing agreements. Of course China denied that many of these treaties were either extant or in some cases valid.

In another memorandum also dated October 14th, Castle says

[1] *Op. cit.*, pp. 22—23.
[2] *Op. cit.*, p. 24.

Debuchi asked him if he knew the terms on which the League of Nations would try to operate, i.e. what their proposal would be in the Manchurian matter. Castle replied in the negative. Debuchi said that he feared that the League would attempt to set up a neutral commission, that Japan would consider it an affront to her national honour and could not possibly accept it.

Debuchi said that his government seemed to have become united at last, and that the Minister of War had ordered cessation of advances in Manchuria. He said Shidehara had had to compromise in his stand, but now there was agreement, and the civil as well as the military elements would oppose the neutral commission. "He said .... that the League might ask a definite promise from Japan immediately to withdraw its troops to within the railway zone or to do so within a specified number of days. He said that he felt that to sign a blank check of this kind might be impossible."

Debuchi brought up the Shantung settlement just as Shidehara had done in the last discussion with Neville, quoted above, and said "that he felt something along these lines might create a way out of the situation", referring to Article 3 of the Shantung treaty which established a Sino-Japanese commission to deal with the question. Castle did what Neville had failed to do, and pointed out the essential omission in his statement: the point that the Chinese had only agreed to the negotiation on condition that neutral observers were present. Castle suggested that a similar arrangement might be made in the present case if the League suggested this remedy, and asked Debuchi whether Japan would be willing so to negotiate in the presence of observers. Debuchi replied that he had been studying this angle very closely; the two situations were different in one important respect. It had not, for various reasons, mattered so much to Japan in the first case, but now, because of the national interest in the Manchurian affair, Japan might find it this time a bitter pill to swallow, to accept observers in direct negotiations. In reply to the obvious comment by Castle, Debuchi made a rather peculiar and enlightening statement. "He said, however, that the quality of the observers would be very important; that the League of Nations meant nothing to the Japanese [1] and

---

[1] The italics are the present author's.

that they would not be interested in observers appointed by the League of Nations, whereas they felt that observers in Washington in 1922, representing Great Britain and America, really meant something." [1]

Castle noted that the fact that both Shidehara and Debuchi had brought up the Shantung analogy indicated to him that they were thinking along these lines for finding a possible solution.

It seems here again we can see Japanese method at work and signs of the fact that they had already decided their ultimate course in Manchuria. Both Shidehara and Debuchi, who had been concerned in the Shantung negotiations, had been morally dishonest in their statement of the analogy. They were certainly aware that the Americans realized this. By advancing the analogy they implied they wanted a similar arrangement now, but by refusing the same conditions through specious excuses they showed that they only wanted that part of the arrangement which pleased them, and that they were going to follow their own course, with and through approval of the State Department if possible, but without it if necessary. Here we have a preview of their policy over years to come, their subtle and insinuating strategy, of prevarication, concealing the knife within the glove. It is sad to have to admit how well it seems to have worked with the State Department in 1931.

As final evidence that Stimson was taken in, it is appropriate to quote from his book cited above (p. 214), keeping in mind that it was copyrighted in 1936, hence reflecting his views several years after the incidents referred to:

> At the same time, while the importance of great caution in order not to inflame the passions of the Japanese people was thus in our minds, the other side of the picture of necessity was also clearly before us. If the military should succeed in having its way, if Shidehara eventually should yield to them, the damage to the new structure of international society provided by the post-war treaties would be incalculable ... [2] My problem is to let the Japanese know that we are watching them and at the same time to do it in a way which will help Shide-

---

[1]   Op. cit., pp. 25—6.

[2]   Op. cit., p. 37.

hara who is on the right side, and not play into the hands of any nationalist agitators. [1]

Of Debuchi, Stimson says: "I was very sorry for Mr. Debuchi, whom I believe to have been from the beginning earnestly and sincerely desirous of helping to seek an honorable solution of this matter." [2]

It is certain that Stimson believed in the truthfulness, honor and sincerity of the two diplomats. If they did in fact possess all the qualities of straightforwardness which he attributed to them, his policy is more justifiable, but if not, he was taken in, used as a dupe, and bears some responsibility for the Japanese aggression in Asia at the time and subsequently. The internal evidence seems to indicate that he misjudged them and that they exploited him.

The importance of the passage quoted above from Stimson's book is critical. In the first place, as stated previously, Stimson seems too apprehensive of what the Japanese might think of American policy, of American public opinion. In the second place, he was certainly aware of the probable intentions of the Japanese army. In the third place, he staked everything on his belief in the correctness of his opinion and evaluation of Shidehara, his idea that Shidehara was fundamentally opposed to the traditional ambitions and aspirations of his own country. Even if he were correct in this view he was still too lax, too dilatory, and, as we shall see presently, he delayed the League action, or at least weakened it, at several crucial moments by his wavering and vaccilating policy.

If he were wrong in his evaluation of Shidehara, then we cannot escape the fact that by trying to protect and aid Shidehara for almost ninety days, days in which false promises followed aggressions and new aggressions followed false promises, ninety days in which the Kwantung army expanded and consolidated its conquest, he made it possible for Japan to succeed. Her position at the beginning was precarious, and, uncertain of herself, she was ready to withdraw in face of concerted action, but she was emboldened by each new success and each fresh piece of evidence that her diplomatic strategy was working in America. In fact

---

[1] *Loc. cit.*

[2] *Op. cit.*, p. 75.

Stimson did the very thing he tried to avoid. The aggression began
and succeeded, initially, under Shidehara; while he remained in
office the fluid situation solidified into an accomplished fact on a
large scale. Then the army took over power more directly. They
would not have taken over if the policy had failed, for they would
merely have identified themselves publicly with a national humiliation. As soon, however, as it was apparent that they had succeeded
behind Shidehara's skirts, in acts which, if unsuccessful, they could
have disavowed — for up to December they could have gone back
to the railway zone without loss of face — they were quick to
realize the possibilities for themselves and began whipping up the
emotions of the people to a frenzy, so as to make it appear to one
not familiar with Japanese politics that they were coming to power
with a mandate of the people. When they had manipulated this
morbid nationalism of the people to the point where they were certain
of themselves, the militarists eased Shidehara's Government, that
of the Minseito party, out of power and put in the more amenable
Seiyukai party to carry on their business.

On October 16th, [1] Stimson had another conversation with
Debuchi in which Debuchi told him he knew the League Council
had voted to ask the U.S. to participate in a discussion of the
Kellogg Pact, but he knew no more than that. Stimson told him
that Gilbert was sitting in the conference at the first meeting.
He said he had just talked to Gilbert on the phone, that the
invitation had been made at five o'clock and that Gilbert had sat
in the conference at six o'clock. Debuchi said that the Japanese
objections to America's participation in the conference had been on
purely juridical grounds. Stimson replied that nevertheless Japan
had objected and that this fact, coupled with statements made by
a Japanese Foreign Office spokesman, would lead the whole world
to believe that America and Japan were arrayed against each other.
He added that this situation undid everything he had been working
for since September, and a great deal he and Shidehara had been
working for the past two years. Debuchi admitted this and said
he was sorry. Stimson said he was unable to see how Shidehara
could have permitted his spokesman to make the statement and

---

[1] F.R.U.S., Japan 1931—1941, I, pp. 26—27.

Debuchi said he was certain the spokesman had made a mistake.

On October 24th, [1] the League Council passed a resolution recalling the pledges given by China and Japan, (1) the statement of Japan that she would continue as rapidly as possible the withdrawal of troops into the railway zone "in proportion as the safety of the lives and property of Japanese nationals is effectively assured, and the statement of the Chinese representative that his Government will assume the responsibility for the safety of the lives and property of Japanese nationals outside that zone—a pledge which implies the effective protection of Japanese subjects residing in Manchuria." (2) Recalling that both sides are bound not to resort to aggression. (3) Japan has no territorial designs in Manchuria. (4) (a) Calls upon Japan to begin immediately and proceed progressively to withdraw its troops into the railway zone; (b) Calls upon China to protect the lives and property of Japanese subjects in Manchuria. (5) Recommends that China and Japan immediately appoint representatives to see to the carrying out of these points. (6) Recommends that the two countries, after the evacuation is complete, begin direct negotiations on outstanding issues between them, and suggests a conciliation committee. (7) Adjourn until November 16th, when it will again examine the situation, but authorizes the President to call a meeting at any time he thinks necessary.

There follows in Japanese-American relations for some weeks a long exchange of notes between Stimson and Shidehara, in which Stimson calls attention to Japan's duties and pledges while Shidehara reaffirms these pledges, denies aggressive intent and assures Stimson that the troops are being withdrawn, but excuses new aggressions as not being covered by past promises, or being due to extenuating circumstances.

Finally, on November 6, 1931, Shidehara comes momentarily out into the open and confirms what later happened. He has constantly denied statements by the army and Foreign Office spokesmen which attacked America or indicated potential failure to withdraw, but here he shows us the next step in the game. He told Forbes that "before the withdrawal of troops they wanted an agreement between the Chinese and Japanese, binding on both, affirming the following five principles:

---

[1]   *Loc. cit.*, pp. 29—30.

"1. No aggression on the part of either country against the other.

2. Obligating each country to respect the integrity of the territory of the other.

3. Agreement on the part of the Chinese Government to prevent the enforcement of boycott by violence, and freedom on the part of Japanese and Chinese citizens to carry on their trade wherever they pleased and without intimidation. (He recognized the right of individuals to conduct a boycott by discontinuing purchases or trade relations when and where they pleased.)

4. Protection of lives and property of Japanese and Koreans resident in China. In this connection he said immediate or early withdrawal of troops until these points were agreed upon would result in general disorder and acts of violence against the Japanese and Koreans in Manchuria who would, he feared, be practically driven out.

5. Recognition and reaffirmation of treaty rights." [1]

Here we have a typical Japanese trick similar to that used by Ishii in the unfortunate Lansing-Ishii-agreement. Japan makes a proposed agreement, apparently harmless and straightforward, and slips in a single clause or sentence ceding her a vital point, which she could never get under ordinary circumstances. In the proposal cited above the first four points are mere padding, points on which both parties agree, but she slips in the apparently innocent fifth clause recognizing and reaffirming treaty rights.

That was one of the main causes of the Japanese invasion — the very fact that China denied the validity of some and the existence of others of these so-called treaty rights. Had China signed this agreement, she would have ceded to Japan the principal points over which Japan was now invading Manchuria. China would have made legal what she now denied and Japan would then have some legal claim to the use of force, in the event China refused to negotiate peacefully. China would be recognizing all the concessions wrung from her by Japan by force and duress over the past thirty-five years, including the "21 Demands".

China would be signing away her sovereignty — as it was Japan

[1] Op. cit., p. 38.

was violating her sovereignity by military aggression. The result would be the same, but under the circumstances the onus was on Japan. China was the aggrieved party and had a right to go to an international tribunal for justice — not that it would do her any good. If she signed this article she would be willingly surrendering not only her sovereignity but her right to appeal, or what amounted to the same thing.

Three days before the League Council's invitation to America on October 16th, to join in its meetings, Stimson had held a long telephone conversation with Gilbert in Geneva. It had been known for some time that America would be invited, but Stimson was very worried about the implications of acceptance. In the conversation with Gilbert, Stimson tried to clarify the situation, both for himself and for Gilbert, concerning the line to be taken, and took care to avoid commitment of America to definite proposals. Following are pertinent parts of the telephone conversation: [1]

> Secretary: In case you are invited to come in I want you to understand this. I want you to be very careful so as to avoid the danger which Drummond feared. [2] In invoking the Pact of Paris, in case it is invoked, I have always had in mind that it should be done as a warning only, or as a caution against a future act of war which has been anticipated or feared and not at all as implying a decision that such an act has already taken place. I agree with Mr. Drummond that it would be dangerous to invoke the Pact of Paris in such a way as to indicate that war has already taken place. I want you to state that emphatically to the Council if it comes up. Do you understand?
>
> Gilbert: I am quite certain that I do understand.
>
> Secretary: You see if those people say that an act of war has already taken place it would open the whole question of sanctions, with which we have nothing to do.

In the remainder of the telephone conversation, Stimson instructed

---

[1] F.R.U.S., 1931, III, pp. 178—82.
[2] Op. cit., p. 178.

Gilbert to avoid discussion of the Nine-Power Pact. In reply to a request from Gilbert for an opening statement drawn up by Stimson, he authorized Gilbert to go ahead on his own, but finally agreed to try to get a statement to him in time. Stimson said that the telegrams coming at the time indicated that Japan was showing a more conciliatory attitude and seemed more inclined to the Council plan. He told Gilbert that he did not want anything he, Stimson, said to indicate that he thought that it was wise "in all events and regardless of consequences to push ahead with an invocation of the Pact". Stimson took great pains to let Gilbert know that he did not wish to involve the country in any altercation with Japan, or commit America to any drastic action:

> "About the only instruction I can give to you is that it has seemed that it might become advisable to do it, but that ought to be a matter of discussion, and it ought to depend upon what the facts are at the time it finally comes up. All I wanted to have understood was that we stood ready to consider it, in such a discussion, as a matter which, in case it should be decided to invoke it, we would feel that we could join, and join in the way in which I have suggested — as a warning to the future and not as a decision as to the past."

On October 13th, Stimson sent Gilbert an opening which he should read: [1]

> "I thank you for your invitation, at this moment of deep international concern, to sit in your deliberations and participate in your discussions as far as the Pact of Paris to which my country is a party, is concerned. My country does not seek to intrude into or express any opinion in respect to such measures as you have under consideration as representatives of the League of Nations. Acting independently and through diplomatic channels my Government has already sought to signify its approval and moral support of your effort in this capacity to bring about a peaceful solution of the unfortunate controversy in Manchuria. In your deliberations as to the application of the machinery of the Covenant of the League of Nations we can, of course, take no part.
> But the Pact of Paris, bearing as it does the signature of

---

[1] *Op. cit.*, pp. 184—85.

the President of this meeting together with that of our former Secretary of State as joint proponents, represents to us in America an effective effort to marshal the public opinion of the world behind the use solely of pacific means in the solution of controversies between the nations of this earth. We feel not only that this public opinion is a most potent force in the domestic affairs of every nation, but that it is of constantly growing import and influence in the mutual relations of the members of the family of nations.

The timely exercise of the power of such opinion may be effective to prevent a breach of international peace of world-wide significance. We assume that this may be the reason why the invocation of this treaty has been suggested by this conference, and I have been directed by my government to accept your invitation in order that we may most easily and effectively take common counsel with you on the subject. It is our earnest hope that by its action its conference may assist in the fruition of the efforts which are being made by the disputants themselves to adjust by peaceful methods their own differences."

On October 14th, 1931, Castle noted in a memorandum a conversation with Debuchi in which the latter referred to an American communication to the League reading: "The Council has formulated conclusions and outlined a course of action to be followed by the disputants; and as the said disputants have made commitments to the Council, it is most desirable that the League in no way relax its vigilance and in no way fail to assert all the pressure and authority within its competence towards regulating the actions of China and Japan in the premises." Debuchi said this had created more or less of a sensation in the Japanese press because of the use of the phrase "to assert all the pressure and authority". The trouble came from the use of the word "pressure", which the Japanese press had interpreted as meaning something beyond moral pressure. Castle reassured the Ambassador by denying this. [1]

Again we get a glimpse of the State Department's indecision and lack of firmness. Why should America not exert all the pressure possible on Japan, who had repeatedly broken her pledges and carried out the worst aggression of the century up to that time? It is rather ironical that America should have been put on the

---

[1] *Op. cit.*, pp. 190—1.

defensive by Japan, but it seems to have been in keeping with the policy of the day. America did not come out unequivocally and lay down a charge or a challenge. She always nullified what might have been such by pretending that she was only repeating what she had heard, but that if such and such things were true, it was, or might become, serious. Stimson always left an escape clause.

On October 14th, Gilbert notified Stimson that he had delivered his message (the suggestion of a procedure similar to that used at Washington to solve the Shantung case) to Drummond; the latter had informed him that Briand had advanced a similar idea in the morning and that the Committee of Five was considering it. [1] He also reported that Sze had come to him to deny the rumor which he thought Japan was spreading, that China had agreed to direct negotiations. [2] In another dispatch Gilbert told Stimson that Briand was discussing with a few Council members an "ingenious plan" to send neutral observers along with the Chinese armies as they took over from the Japanese in Manchuria. Japan was opposed to neutral observers, but this procedure would make impartial observation possible. The observers could report on the manner in which the Chinese carried out their obligations, and Japan could hardly object to such an arrangement. [3]

On October 14th, [4] the Secretary wired Neville more or less to the effect that he did not seem clear about the Department's policy. Stimson said that America ". . . is attempting neither to 'sit in judgment' nor to 'force a settlement'. When you say the two parties concerned must themselves find a solution, you are quite right. All that the League of Nations is trying to do, and the United States concurs heartily with this aim, is to have the hostilities cease in order that Japan and China may be able to arrive at their own solution without recourse to war". He told Neville he thought it important to impress upon Shidehara the fact that a peaceful solution concerned the world and that, if Japan did not recognize this, she would find world opinion almost solidly arrayed against her, but that he should recognize that America had no desire to judge or to suggest terms

---

[1] *Op. cit.*, p. 190.
[2] *Loc. cit.*
[3] *Op. cit.*, pp. 191—92.
[4] *Op. cit.*, p. 194.

of settlement, but only to prevent war and assist in a peaceful solution by direct negotiation between the two.

On October 15th, [1] Johnson sent Stimson the first authentic report of the Chinchow bombing, made by Colonel Margetts on the spot. This report was in response to a cable from Stimson to Johnson on October 11th, [2] requesting him to send someone immediately to Chinchow to make a full report of the incident, "number of casualties, the damage to property etc.". The report stated that at about 2 p.m. on October 8, without warning twelve Japanese planes flew over Chinchow, circling the city once and then heading for the radio station where they began bombing. "It was mere accident that two foreign missions and the railroad hospital which flew two Red Cross flags were not directly hit by bomb . . . . fragments were found in all three compounds." Sixteen people had been killed, twelve seriously wounded, of whom three had died at the time of the report, and thirty slightly wounded. The University, which was serving as the provincial Government headquarters, had apparently been the main objective. "Although the raiders may have had a military mission evidently little attention was given to modern conventions of ordinary humanity or protection of personal property."

On October 16th, [3] Stimson again briefed Gilbert, so nervous and fearful did he seem. "Since the receipt today of the invitation from the Council for you to attend its meetings, I think it well to repeat, for the purpose of absolute clarity, your instructions, which are as follows:

> "You are authorized to participate in the discussions of the Council when they relate to the possible application of the Kellogg-Briand Pact, to which the United States is a party. You are expected to report the result of such discussions to the Department for its determination as to possible action. If you are present at the discussion of any other aspect of the Chinese-Japanese dispute, it must be only as an observer and auditor."

On the same day the Secretary called Gilbert on the telephone

---

[1] F.R.U.S., 1931, III, p. 196.

[2] *Op. cit.*, p. 157.

[3] *Op. cit.*, p. 203.

again. [1] The burden of his conversation was constant repetition
of the fact that under no circumstances was the Kellogg Pact to be
invoked at Washington, that it must be done there, at Geneva, but
under no circumstances by America. Rather than have it referred
back to Washington, he would drop the whole matter first. He also
showed again his characteristic reaction to Japan when he said: [2]
"The incidents which took place yesterday in the objection of Japan
to our coming in would be very disastrous. If we should take over
the invocation of the pact here, Japan would believe that we have
gone into it to do that very thing instead of on the invitation of the
League. She would resent it and believe that we have something
behind our actions and it would set back the cause of the settlement
of this thing very much. The people at Geneva must understand
that. Japan's action in objecting to our sitting with the League has
very much changed the situation and it has made it necessary to
proceed with the utmost delicacy so far as we are concerned." In
reply to a statement by Gilbert that the Japanese had come to say
that their objection was on purely juridical lines and that they were
sorry they had to take such a position, Stimson said: "You know
that is nonsense." [3] To another of Gilbert's statements that the
Japanese said the action was in no way directed against the United
States and that they would be very happy to have her there,
Stimson said: "That is eye-wash." [4]

---

[1] *Op. cit.*, pp. 203—7.
[2] *Op. cit.*, p. 206.
[3] *Loc. cit.*
[4] *Loc. cit.*

CHAPTER XV

JAPAN DEFIES THE WORLD

On October 19th, 1931, Stimson ordered Gilbert in a telephone conversation to withdraw from the meetings of the League Council:

Secretary: ... I am sending you instructions today that in view of the fact that the Kellogg Pact matter seems to be disposed of, we think that it is wise for you to withdraw from the meetings. They are now taking up matters which belong peculiarly to the League and we all think here that in view of that fact and in view of present tension with Japan it would be better for you to withdraw .... Of course, make your position clear that you stand ready and available for consultation at any time there is need of it; but your presence there in case they should discuss other matters under the League covenant alone is open to misconstruction both here and in Japan ....

Gilbert: I understand perfectly. I would like to say something. The Japanese came to see me today and told me they had prepared a statement which the Japanese wish to make at the opening of the next public meeting of the Council, in which they wish to say that their objection to the United States was entirely on juridical grounds. I prepared a brief reply. Briand wished them to say something at the Council of that sort favourable to the United States to relieve the tension. It was also arranged by Lord Reading. They are very anxious that that statement on the part of the Japanese should be made public and that I should make a reply.

Secretary: What kind of a reply?

Gilbert: It would seem most unfortunate for me to withdraw before the Japanese have had the opportunity to say that.

....

Secretary: Read me your statement.

Gilbert: 'I have heard with deep gratification what the representative of Japan has said, and I wish to assure him that I heartily appreciate the spirit in which he has spoken. I have never had any thought of attributing this decision in this matter to other than juridical considerations, but it gives me great pleasure to be able to hear him say this himself, and to reassure him that on my part they may have no fear of my interpreting his attitude in any other light. The sentiments he has expressed as to the friendship and amity between our countries are cordially reciprocated. The long period of friendship between our people and the people of Japan is among the happiest stages in our history. It is furtherest from our minds that that record will ever be broken.

Secretary: That is the end of the statement? That is all right. I am very glad to have you stay until that is done, provided it is done right off.

Gilbert: I cannot say when the next meeting is to be held. Briand and Reading have all worked on the Japanese very hard to get them to make the statement.

Secretary: Let them say it before they get into the other matters. I will tell you what I am afraid of. The resolution which they are working on now contains certain matters which in my opinion will probably not be adopted by the Japanese and will probably lead to a new dead-lock.

Gilbert: ... There is no intention now of any kind to present a resolution which would be in the form of a public ultimatum for the acceptance of Japan and China. It is all being worked out in private conversations to reach a possible solution and that is the plan they are working on now ....

Secretary: I understand, and I am very glad to hear it. I want you to know my views. That is going to take a long time. They are not going to accomplish a resolution which will be acceptable to both the Chinese and Japanese without long and laborious negotiations. In the meanwhile they are attending to something which relates purely to the League of

Nations and not to the Kellogg Pact and it is
something which conceivably may make a deadlock
or renew trouble at any time in which Japan may
be strongly arrayed against the League .... [1]

It this same telephone conversation Gilbert suggested that, if he
were to let it leak out to the press that he was no longer attending
secret meetings of the Council, a formal withdrawal would not be
necessary. But Stimson was adamant that it must be publicly known
that he was not sitting in on any future secret meetings. Gilbert
answered that he was only following the Secretary's former
instructions, to which the Secretary replied, in effect, that he was
now changing them. The Secretary then instructed him to go to
the next public meeting and let that be the last one. After reiterating
his desire that Gilbert should not attend further meetings, Stimson
said that he wanted above all things to avoid any misunderstandings with Japan.

His final instructions to Gilbert were to notify Lord Reading and
then to withdraw in the most graceful manner possible.

Shortly thereafter, on the same day, Lord Reading called Stimson
by trans-atlantic telephone and expressed his apprehension that
Gilbert's withdrawal from the Council be regarded as a sign of
American disapproval of the League's action, thus causing international confusion and strengthening Japan's hand. Stimson
advanced, as his principal reasons for the step, protection of his
Government against adverse public opinion and avoidance of the
implication that there was a clash between the United States and
Japan. However, he finally agreed to permit Gilbert to attend one
more public, and one more private, meeting in his present capacity
and to limit his further attendance to public meetings — in a seat
reserved for observers. [2]

The following day, in another telephone conversation between
Gilbert and the Secretary, Gilbert reported that there was great
apprehension on the part of Briand and the others at the manner in
which he was being withdrawn.

Briand was very deeply concerned at this move because he felt

---

[1] F.R.U.S., 1931, III, pp. 242—3.
[2] Op. cit., pp. 248—58.

that Japan would consider it as a great diplomatic victory due to pressure applied in Washington, and that it would further strengthen the Japanese position and foredoom the efforts of the Council. He said that there was also great concern over the international reaction to the news. The Secretary replied that he was unable to see how all these things could result from the change in attendance at the secret meetings.

In response to Gilbert's suggestion that he be allowed to remain in the public meetings, Stimson said he had agreed to let him continue, provided he changed his seat. It seems that one has here an excellent example of the inconsistency which has dominated American diplomacy. One might say that it was the result of national, political and diplomatic inexperience and immaturity. Obviously Stimson was operating under a great handicap in many ways, and it is much easier to see what one should have done in reviewing an incident which is already past, than it is to know what to do at the time. However, it would be difficult to deny that Stimson's action shook the already weak faith which European diplomats had in America's conduct of foreign relations. It would also be difficult indeed to deny that it greatly strengthened the militarist element in Japan, and encouraged their future aggressions.

On October 21st, General Tanaka called on McIlroy, the American Attaché in Japan, and told him very emphatically: [1] "I ask you to cable your Secretary of War that the fighting men of Japan will not permit the League of Nations or America to intervene in any way that might weaken Japan's position in Manchuria." This sort of talk was only to have been expected as a result of the inept handling of diplomatic affairs on the part of America.

On October 22nd, at midnight, [2] the Acting Secretary of State wired Gilbert at Geneva that the State Department had a report on the situation at Geneva from which he quoted:

> " 'The Japanese delegation is unofficially telling people that after the Secretary of State's explanation to Japanese Ambassador indicating that America would not join in economic sanctions, Japan would not continue to object to the presence of American representative in Council meetings. Japan's tactics

---

[1] *Op. cit.*, p. 283.
[2] *Op. cit.*, p. 299.

seem to separate Washington from Geneva just as she successfully did in September. Officially she is taking stiff attitude
in negotiations with Briand.' You may tell this to the Secretary
General or M. Briand or Lord Reading. You may state that
there has been no statement by the Secretary on either
joining or refusing to join in action which the League may
take or propose. The American Government is in no way committed, either affirmatively or negatively, in this connection."

On October 28th, Drummond informed Gilbert [1] that a new
situation had arisen in Japan, as Tokyo press reports had issued
new Japanese demands, making it now uncertain exactly what Japan
was claiming, but leaving an opening for her to take further action
by thus appealing to home opinion. He told Gilbert that he felt
that the League must immediately make a counter-move and
implied that he was uncertain as to where America stood. He said
he believed that Japan was stiffening her attitude and that her next
move would be the establishment of a puppet government in Manchuria.

On November 3rd, Peck, [2] Concul General at Nanking, informed
Stimson that a Chinese official had shown him a Reuter telegram
dated Washington, October 31st, attributing certain remarks to the
Under Secretary of State, Castle. Because of the ambiguity of this
report the Acting Minister of Foreign Affairs requested Peck to
enquire:

1. Whether Castle said that under treaties guaranteeing
   integrity of China the United States would feel compelled
   to disapprove permanent Japanese occupation of Manchuria; and

2. If so, what were the treaties in reference;

3. Whether the fact that the United States did not endorse
   the League resolution which demanded that Japan evacuate
   occupied areas in Manchuria by November 16th should be
   taken as implying that the United States did not approve
   of that stipulation. Doctor Lee [3] observed that the United
   States had announced its approval of previous actions taken
   by the League (in) connection with the present controversy.

---

[1]   F.R.U.S., 1931, III, p. 341.
[2]   *Op. cit.*, p. 357.
[3]   Chinese Acting Minister of Foreign Affairs.

It is obvious to anyone reading these documents, that one has here the fine hand of Japanese diplomacy. Japan is using one of the most ancient political stratagems of the Orient, and one which China had mastered many centuries past "to divide the barbarian and rule them" by rousing mutual suspicion.

In keeping with this policy the Japanese Vice-Minister for Foreign Affairs informed Chargé Neville that the Japanese government was preparing a statement for the League Council Meeting on November 16th, informing him that he could not divulge its contents but hinting that America should not associate herself with the League resolution, since the Japanese public believed that the other Powers, primarily Britain and France, had "put through the resolution with the sole purpose of damaging Japanese interests in China". He implied that, since America had had nothing to do with framing the resolution she should abstain from associating herself therewith, and argued that the strength of the American position lay in the fact that the United States had refused to pass judgment upon Japan in the Manchurian crisis.

This was obviously a move on the part of Japan to influence America to dissociate herself from the League resolution and the notifications which would soon be distributed internationally by the Council Powers. This would greatly strengthen Japan's hand.

At this point Stimson adopted the stand that Japan should not refuse to evacuate prior to concluding negotiations on past controversies unrelated to the present struggle. But Japan was already moving ahead again, on November 5th, she began a new military offensive on the Nonni River. This was practically the end of all hope to stop Japan, who by now realised that because of America's refusal to take a definite stand, the League Council was paralysed.

Japan had taken a great chance and won an empire. It is difficult to realise, even after having read the documents, how she was able to gull Stimson and stall the Council so successfully. It is fully apparent now that at any time prior to November, by stiff action and co-operation among themselves, the Powers could have made Japan back down. It seems, however, that Japan was at that time the only nation who fully realised the fact, and she was careful to continue exuses and assurances to cover each new move. After the attack on the Nonni River she excused it on the ground that the

Japanese Army had determined to repair the bridges and had sent troops to protect the construction gangs; these men were said to have been attacked by the Chinese with machineguns and field artillery. "Baron Shidehara very deeply regrets this incident. He reiterated the definite intention of the Japanese Government, however, to withdraw all the troops as soon as the construction work was done.... The Ambassador says that there is no intention of sending troops to Tsitsihar." [1]

Despite this assurance, fighting did break out near Tsitsihar the following day. In the meantime the Japanese had forced the withdrawal of the Chinese and were now in possession of large new areas of Manchuria.

It is needless to point out that the Nonni River is far from any sphere of interest which Japan had ever previously claimed in Manchuria and that the bridges which she proposed to repair were not on the SMR, but on the CER, in which she had no legal rights! Even if the Chinese had attacked the Japanese on the Nonni, they would have been perfectly within their rights.

Within a few more days, fighting broke out in Tientsin and it seemed that Japan was provoking a situation whereby she should not only bring off a new coup but gain a foothold in the eighteen provinces.

While the Council pondered, Japan moved on to new conquests. In this way she not only consolidated her position but was enlarging her conquests far beyond her fondest hope.

On November 28th, 1931, Stimson sent a telegram to Forbes informing him that it had recently been called to his attention that General Honjo's army had moved southward from Mukden and was encamped near Chinchow and that Japanese bombing planes were operating in that area. The secretary expressed bewilderment at this in view of the assurance given him by the Japanese Foreign Office. His information indicated that the Japanese were planning a large scale attack. Stimson reiterated that Shidehara had assured him that he and the Japanese Minister of War and the Army Chief of Staff had agreed that there should be no military operations in that region and that military orders had been issued to that effect. [2]

---

[1] F.R.U.S., 1931, III, p. 385.
[2] F.R.U.S., Japan 1931—1941, pp. 53—4.

On November 28th, Stimson wired Forbes concerning the attack made upon him by the Japanese press. He said: "The statement quoted therein as having been given out by me is untrue in every particular. No such attitude by me towards the Japanese Government has ever been expressed either in public or private." He further stated that Debuchi knew that Stimson had used every endeavour to prevent an unpopular press in America towards Japan. [1]

On December 10th, Stimson wrote a memorandum in which he stated that he had sent for the Japanese ambassador and discussed with him the Wellington Koo proposal to withdraw troops from Chinchow to Shankaikwan pending general settlement of the Manchurian question provided Japan guaranteed to the U.S., Britain and France that she would not occupy this area, leaving Chinese civilian administration and police intact. [2] He explained to Debuchi his version of the misunderstanding that had arisen between the two countries over this proposal. He had arrived at the following conclusions:

1. that Koo had not intended that the suggestion be taken as an offer, but had made it to sound Japan;

2. that the proposal had not been accepted by Shidehara although Stimson believed Shidehara had intended to imply careful consideration of the proposal;

3. that there had been a possible misunderstanding by the Council of Yoshizawa's definition of a neutral zone, and it had not been realised that Japan had made the limitation based upon the Koo offer.

Stimson felt that Japan was herself "inching up on the original situation." Stimson impressed upon Debuchi that he wished to avoid a misunderstanding which might lead to renewed hostilities, and said he had so telephoned Dawes the previous night; Dawes had replied that morning, informing him that he had taken up the matter with Sze, Matsudaira, Briand and others, and it seemed to him that

---

[1] *Op. cit.*, p. 54.
[2] *Op. cit.*, pp. 58—9.

there had been a misunderstanding and that "a fresh start could be made". Stimson told Debuchi that, although he had taken this step, it in no way changed his opinion that Honjo's army should not renew aggression, which would be entirely unjustified. He further informed Debuchi that he had information from his own military officers on the spot that China was not making military preparations, and that the Chinese troops were in their usual quarters. [1]

On December 10th, the Council of the League of Nations adopted a resolution in which it:

1. Reaffirmed the resolution passed on September 30th, whereby China and Japan declared themselves solemnly bound; hence it called upon them to take all necessary steps to execute the plan, to withdraw the Japanese troops from the railway zone.

2. Considering that events had taken a serious turn for the worst since October 24th, it noted that the two parties undertook to adopt all necessary measures to avoid further aggravation of the situation and refrain from any initiative possibly leading to further conflict.

3. Invited the two parties to keep the Council informed as to the development of the situation.

4. Invited the Members of the Council to furnish the Council with any information received from their representatives on the spot.

5. Without prejudice to the accomplishment of those measures, decided to appoint a commission of 5 members to study on the spot and report to the Council any circumstances threatening peace or goodwill between them. China and Japan each had the right to nominate one accessor to assist the Commission and both countries were to afford the Commission freedom to obtain any on-the-spot information required. It was understood that any negotiations initiated between the two parties would fall outside the scope of the terms of reference of the Commission, nor would the Commission have any right to interfere with the military arrangements of either party. The Japanese Government was not entitled to take advantage of the appointment and

---

[1] *Loc. cit.*

deliberations of the Commission to evade the undertaking given by her in respect of the resolution of September 30th, regarding the withdrawal of Japanese troops within the railway zone.

6. Authorised the President to summon the Council when he felt necessary, prior to its next meeting, January 25th, 1932. [1]

On December 11th, 1931, Stimson issued a statement reviewing the Japanese aggression and expressing America's gratification at the action of the Council. He declared the interests of the American people in the League's objectives, the prevention of war and the finding of a peaceful solution of the Manchurian problem, and added that, as a fellow signatory with Japan and China of the Kellogg-Briand Pact and the Nine-Power Treaties, America had a direct interest in, and an obligation under, the undertakings of those Treaties. He then summarised the official American view of the meaning of the league resolution which was to the effect that it reaffirmed the solemn pledge of Japan to retire within the railway zone as quickly as possible. He praised the appointment of a neutral commission as a constructive step.

He said that the ultimate solution of the Manchurian problem must be worked out in some manner between the two countries concerned, but added that America was concerned that the methods employed in the settlement should be made in harmony with existing treaties, and not of a kind to endanger world peace, and that the resulting settlement must not be the result of military pressure. He made clear his view that the League's adoption of the new resolution in no way constituted an endorsement of any action so far taken in Manchuria and that as one of the signatories of the treaties referred to, America could not disguise her concern over the events which had transpired. [2]

On that same day an event occurred which, if Stimson were right in his evalution of Shidehara, was the most ominous in the tragic sequence of events which had occured in Manchuria. Shidehara's government fell. In a conversation which he had that day with

---

[1] *Op. cit.*, pp. 59—60 paraphrase.
[2] *Op. cit.*, pp. 60—62.

Debuchi, Stimson said that he had been notified of the resignation of the Japanese government. He then went on to complain to Debuchi that "it was being asserted against me that I had assured Debuchi that America would not use the boycott, and I asked him whether he had gained any impression in our talks which would lead him to believe that I had given such assurance . . . . Finally, I had a press clipping of an account of a speech by Henry Cabot Lodge to that effect, and I dictated a letter of inquiry addressed to Debuchi based upon that, asking him whether anything had ever occurred in our interviews to give him the impression that he had received any such assurance from me." Stimson told Debuchi that he realised the latter would feel hurt at the receipt of such a formal letter asking for a reply and so, instead, he would just read it to him and ask him to answer yes or no. After having heard the letter, Debuchi took a pencil and wrote "No. K.D." on the letter. Stimson noted in his memorandum: "I gave him a copy of what I had written, and I told him that I felt very badly even to press him like this but he could realize the matter was serious and that I had been made very angry by the accusations." [1]

Why did Stimson find it necessary to abase himself like this before Debuchi, the representative of a country which was on trial before world opinion for one of the most shameless aggressions thus far recorded in modern diplomatic history? One has the feeling constantly, throughout these documents, that Stimson is on the defensive with Japan and continuously finds it necessary to explain himself, to justify his own and his country's actions, to apologise to Japan for Japan's having made it necessary for him to say anything which might seem condemnatory of Japan.

To recapitulate for a moment, on November 10th, in a telephone conversation with Dawes, Ambassador at London, Stimson had instructed him to attend the League Council meeting when they convened in Paris, to discuss the Manchurian crisis. He sent Dawes because as the former Vice-President, it was felt that he would have more weight in dealing with men of Briand's calibre than an ordinary ambassador. [2] And he seemed to feel too that it

---

[1] F.R.U.S., 1931, III, pp. 677—8.

[2] Op. cit., p. 407.

indicated America's concern in the matter to have a man so eminent in America, as General Dawes, to represent the American Government. [1]

But there were two things which were overlooked at the beginning: first, that Dawes was bitterly hostile to the League, and secondly, that the instructions, issued him initially, gave him no chance to help in imposing discipline on Japan, even if he had been a supporter of the League. In the conversation on the phone Stimson told him:

> We do not want anybody to sit on the Council. We do not want you or anybody else to actually sit in the meetings of the Council but we want them to come to you.

In this one sentence Stimson summed up the weakness and ineffectuality of America's whole role in the affair. In stating that he disagreed with the deadline date of November 16th, for Japanese withdrawal, he said:

> . . . we have simply reserved our independence of action and judgment in respect to that and in *respect to all matters*. [2]

It was the fact that the United States did reserve her independence of action in all matters which made it impossible for the Powers ever to know where she stood or what she would do. They never knew how far they could depend on her. Either Stimson should never have taken a hand in the matter at all in connection with the League Powers or he should have followed through with them after deciding upon policy. If he was not willing to do that, he should have acted as a lone wolf all along, and have demanded as one signatory to another of the Kellogg and Nine Power Pacts that Japan back down. But instead of this he nursed the Japanese along, and made it possible for them to extend and consolidate their aggressions.

Furthermore, he had told Dawes that America wanted settlement by pacific means only. He deterred the League, and encouraged Japan by his willingness to carry on endless correspondence even after he know it to be hopeless. He implies this in his book, *Far Eastern Crisis*, when he says he began to get rumors of a new military movement against Chinchow, on November 22nd, which

---

[1] *Loc. cit.*

[2] Italics mine.

he followed by vigourous protests on the 24th and 27th. These protests were momentarily successful, resulting in the return of troops to Mukden, the point of departure for Chinchow. He says that these two steps "constituted the last effort on the part of the Foreign Office and the Minseito Cabinet to keep their country in alignment with world opinion. It became every day more clear that their tenure of office was brief and their hold upon official power rapidly falling. The army soon began to recover from its rebuff and to claim that it had been tricked into withdrawal, in reliance upon corresponding promises of the Chinese to withdraw their army beyond the Great Wall, which had not been kept."

There is one aspect of the Manchurian crisis which has been too little dwelt upon by historians. This is the influence of Hoover. There are several points to take into consideration. He was a wealthy and successful business man, and apparently cynical and intolerant of what he considered weaklings or weaknesses of the usual sort. He had been in China as a young man and had firsthand knowledge of the people and country. He was a Quaker, and would have been expected, ordinarily, to have been opposed to war, although it is questionable whether a man of his type would have let religion interfere greatly with more practical considerations. A better surmise is that he felt a sneaking admiration for aggressive Japan, who, like himself, had come so far in so short a time, largely through clever initiative, that he thought intervention would not be smart domestic politics, that China was far away and that even if Japan did tear off a strip or two, our trade rights would be respected by Japan. Added to all these things, his Quaker background may have had a small influence, especially since it made such a convenient bedfellow with all the other reasons for not doing anything. At any rate, as we shall see, he was to play a most helpful role for Japan. This is evident in the following message, in the form of a memorandum to Stimson: [1]

It seems to me that two or three more points might be put up to Mr. Dawes for consideration:
First: It is obviously impossible for the Japanese to with-

---

[1] *Op. cit.*, pp. 431—432.

draw their troops on the one hand or the Chinese to restore order on the other, unless some form of properly established civil government is set up in Manchuria. The Japanese will not have Young Marshal Chang in view of his failure to preserve order hitherto. It would seem that the solution of this end of the problem lies in the setting up of a civil government which will be recognized by the Japanese that would be responsible to the Nanking government. It would seem also that the Nanking government ought to be glad to get rid of the young marshal and establish its full and final authority over Manchuria, and that therefore if something in the nature of a viceroy of Manchuria could be appointed by the Nanking government and accepted by the Japanese the whole question of the establishing of civil government and order would fade out of the picture, as then the Japanese could proceed to withdraw as fast as he had established the situation, and the Nanking government could quite well agree to support the new viceroy in obtaining control of the troops and other agencies in Manchuria.

The second point ... is that if these people would be prepared to negotiate the specific provision, that the negotiation should be carried out in the spirit of the Kellogg Pact. It might do away with the necessity to have foreign observers at the negotiation. Both sides would be quick enough to appeal if there was any infraction.

It seems almost needless to discuss this memorandum because of its utter lack of realism, its assumptions and consequent over simplifications.

There was no proper civil government in Manchuria precisely because the Japanese had destroyed it and adamantly refused to permit the re-establishment of any other which would not be a Japanese puppet, as shown by the Chinchow aggression. The Young Marshal had preserved Chinese peace only too well for the liking of the Japanese, instead of having failed. Hoover was accurate in his forecast about the setting up of a civil government acceptable to Japan, but it would be responsible to Japan only. It had nothing to do with China. His evaluation of Chang Hsueh-liang is totally wrong; without Chang's consent and leadership, Manchuria would never have come under the Nanking Government at all. As for pacifying Manchuria, Chiang Kai-shek was not even able to pacify the eighteen provinces. His statement that the

Japanese could proceed to withdraw, assumes that they wanted to. Yet the average man in the street in America knew, and the press proclaimed, that Japan had one intention, and only one: aggression and territorial annexation. As for appealing, if there were an infraction in bi-lateral negotiations, without foreign observers, what did he think China had already done before the Council, and what good would an appeal have done if China had ever been so stupid as to agree to that? For that matter what good was it doing as it was, and before the most powerful international body on earth? To whom, then, could China have appealed? Uni-lateral negotiations was the thing Japan had fought for from the first, for China to negotiate alone with Japan while she held a cocked pistol to China's head. And this man was the President of the United States, and was better than many, many of his predecessors. No wonder Pearl Harbor occurred!

In line with Hoover's advice, Japan was evidently thinking along the same lines, but much more realistically. Stimson received a report from Johnson, at Peking, on November 13th: [1]

> Rumors are persistent here of an imminent attempt ... to make Pu-yi Emperor. Credence is given the reports by the manufacture locally of imperial dragon flags and by Japanese consular confirmation of the departure of Pu-yi from Tientsin. The Japanese Consul General at Mukden has informed the American Consulate General that the Japanese Government disapproves of the movement and is certain that it is doomed to failure even if it is temporarily successful.

As was to have been expected. Dawes' failure to take at least as active a part in the Council proceedings as had Gilbert, a mere minor official, immediately came up for protest. Briand protested that "it would be generally considered to indicate an attitude by the United States of less cooperation than previously with the League's purposes in this situation and a decided injury to the League's prestige and influence". [2] Dawes' answer to Briand was at first that his participation would be considered at home as an advance from co-operation on the Manchurian matter (under the

---

[1] F.R.U.S., 1931, III, p. 433.
[2] *Op. cit.*, p. 444.

Kellogg Pact?) to an alliance of the United States with the League; finally he agreed that if Briand wrote him a special invitation to attend, after several meetings, stating that they were discussing the Manchurian matter under the Kellogg Pact, he could then attend. [1] Stimson agreed to this procedure, in a telephone conversation, when Dawes told him he no longer considered action necessary, since speeches were to be avoided until the Japanese domestic situation had settled down.

This foolish move of Washington's, not to have a representative attend the meeting at Paris, almost immediately had world-wide repercussions. Johnson notified Stimson on November 16th, that Koo had just come to see him regarding the rumours at Nanking that there was an understanding between the U.S. and Japan on the Manchurian question. Johnson stated that they had "grown from the fact of the decision by the United States not to send an observer to the League Council meeting in Paris but to send Ambassador Dawes who will take no part in the Council meetings. This, it is being said, is a concession to Japan." Johnson discussed these rumours with Koo who said "that the American decision against sending observers had caused a good deal of speculation in high official circles". [2]

On November 16th, Sir John Simon [3] in a conversation with Dawes, advanced some personal ideas for solving the conflict in Manchuria:

"1. Nanking Government to give to Japan solemn and formal assurance that Japan's treaty rights in Manchuria would be respected.

2. China to address a note to the members of the League represented on the Council, plus the United States of America, undertaking to these powers that China would strictly observe the above undertaking.

3. A further term of the arrangement indicated in paragraph 4 (1) above would be that the Nanking Government agrees with Japan to set up at once a technical commission for the

---

[1] *Loc. cit.*
[2] *Op. cit.*, p. 459.
[3] *Op. cit.*, pp. 460—2.

purpose of entering upon a working arrangement between the South Manchuria Railway and the Chinese railways in Manchuria so as to put an end to unfair competition.

4. Japan to undertake to withdraw her troops within the railway zone contemporaneously with the above arrangements being entered into."

On November 17th, [1] Stimson wired Johnson that the Department had several times referred to the methods of the Shantung negotiations, but did not want this to come officially from the United States, and he denied that America had any sort of rapproachment with Japan.

In his discussion with Simon, Dawes had quite rightly pointed out that there was no agreement of what the treaty rights of Japan in Manchuria were. He reminded him that China had protested against the Twenty-One Demands in 1915, and that the United States had gone on record against any treaties which in any way impaired America's rights, or the open door. Since the first point fell, the other had no substance, since they depended upon it. But, if conceivable, that could have been agreed upon, the proposal would in effect, according to the last part of the second point, give Japan control of the Chinese railways and greatly enlarge her sphere, above anything which she had ever claimed.

The following day Stimson pointed this out in his objection, and showed that it would amount to forcing China to ratify treaties, the validity of which she has always denied. He pointed out that this was the very thing the Council meeting was all about, that if China were to have done that in the beginning, the matter would never have come before the Council. He used to say that he thought the most hopeful solution was the "presence of neutral observers and that, if pressed hard enough, Japan would consent to them. If Japan refuses, it will be necessary to outlaw her and let her sizzle for the time being under the influence of a good Chinese boycott and feeling against her all the moral pressure of the world. The Japanese Army has been as hardboiled as an Easter egg, and if finally our views have to be publicly stated, they will be sufficiently forcible to crack the egg. If Matsudaira knew this it might help." [2]

---

[1] Op. cit., pp. 464—5.

[2] Op. cit., p. 471.

Here for the first time Stimson is talking like he meant business. This is the line he should have taken from the beginning. Had he done so, it is certain that the history of the Far East since 1931 would have been far different, and almost certain that there would never have been a Pearl Harbor and its horrible aftermath. But he did not see fit to do it that way and one must note even here that he is not addressing a Japanese, but an American diplomat, Ambassador Dawes.

On December 11th, Stimson wired Forbes informing him as follows of the alleged promises made by Koo: [1]

The American Minister at Nanking telegraphed Department on November 24 as follows: "In view of alarming reports current as to imminent Japanese action at Chinchow Dr. Wellington Koo, Acting Minister for Foreign Affairs, has this evening told me and my British and French colleagues that his Government wished to sound our Governments out and if feasible make a formal proposition along following lines:

'In order to avoid any clash China is prepared as a temporary measure pending a general settlement of the Manchuria question, if Japan insists on withdrawal of troops in the Chinchow area to do so up to Shanhaikwan, provided Japan gives guarantees satisfactory to Great Britain, the United States and France, not to go into that zone leaving the Chinese civil administration intact including police.'

"In view of critical situation we undertook to commend this to our respective Governments and ask for a speedy reply."

On December 8, the American Minister at Nanking cabled the following:

"Chinchow situation. The suggestion made tentatively by Koo regarding Chinchow transmitted to the Department in my telegram of November 24, midnight, was apparently communicated by the French Ambassador to the Japanese Government which seems to have received it as a firm offer on the part of the Chinese. In spite of the fact that Koo's intention was merely to sound out the American, British, and French Governments, and that he made his offer contingent upon Japan's giving guarantees to those Governments, the Japanese have chosen to take this stand and now insist stoutly that if the Chinese fail to evacuate Chinchow, they will be guilty of

---

[1] F.R.U.S., Japan 1931—1941, I, pp. 62—65.

breach of faith as the Japanese have withdrawn their military forces east of Liao. It is the contention of the Chinese that no such offer was ever made on their part and therefore they are under no obligation to evacuate Chinchow, last stand in the Manchurian area of the Nationalist Government. It is my understanding that the Japanese maintain their withdrawal was due to the offer by the Chinese, and I have been told that the Chinese Government through Shigemitsu has been informed by the Japanese Government that the situation will become difficult unless the Chinese withdraw their troops."

Stimson stated that he had wired Dawes immediately and ordered him to see Briand, and notify him of the discrepancy between the tentative proposal and Japan's subsequent contentions.

Dawes informed Stimson that he had investigated the matter and that it appeared that there had really been no offer and no acceptance *de jure*, that Koo's offer had been a tentative one, but that Shidehara gained the impression that it was a definite offer. He said that Shidehara's reply to the go-betweens who had informed him of the feeler was acceptance in principle, but with the reservation that the Japanese Government could not give guarantees to the three powers, but would be willing to do so to the Council of the League of Nations. There had been discussion in various quarters but without there having been an acceptance by Japan of Koo's proposal or by China of Shidehara's counter proposal.

Stimson said that the charge that Chinese failure to withdraw from Chinchow constituted bad faith was unjustified on the basis of all information available to him. The alleged proposal was now being twisted and represented to the Japanese people as failure on the part of China to live up to her agreement, but the Chinese, on the other hand, had the impression that Koo's tentative proposal was being misrepresented by Japan and would be used by her as a pretext for further military aggression. He viewed the situation as being that the Chinese troops were on the defensive and not on the offensive at Chinchow, that China could not and would not withdraw them, and that the Japanese were threatening an attack on Chinchow. He added:

> In my opinion, this being the situation, it is imperative that I reaffirm the view which has been expressed by me repeatedly

that if the Japanese Army attack Chinchow, it would be most unfortunate for all concerned and especially for Japan.

It is clear that there has been a misunderstanding ... I find, however, no evidence of bad faith in any quarter ... For the Chinese authorities to withdraw these troops without some definite and satisfactory agreement first having been concluded, it is easy to understand, would be difficult and perhaps politically impossible. They are, after all, on their own soil and we do not have any evidence that aggressive action against Japan is contemplated or could be taken by the Chinese. An attack on Chinchow by the Japanese Army under these circumstances would be regarded as unjustified by the world.

Stimson instructed him (Forbes) to discuss the matter with Shidehara and explain his views. "Inform him that in regard to his absolute sincerity in the whole matter I have no doubt whatever."

This contrasted to the bold line taken by Stimson to Dawes in the telegram just quoted on page 270 supra, is the weakness of the entire policy of the U.S. where any initiative on their part to try to stop Japan was concerned. Stimson was not even willing to let it emanate from the State Department officially that revival of the procedure adopted in the Shantung settlement was his idea. No matter how great a man he is—and it is unquestionable that he was one of our greatest statesmen—he played the part of a weakling in the whole Manchurian affair.

Things had got so bad by November 18th, that even the British Ambassador came around to the Department to enquire if it were true that the U.S. had given out the statement that they would not take part in sanctions if the League passed them. Castle denied it. [1]

On the 18th, Stimson instructed Dawes to reject the Matsudaira substitute proposal, which retained the original points, including the questionable and objectionable fifth, about recognition of Japanese treaty rights. But Matsudaira further wanted a neutral commission to investigate Japan's claims against China in both Manchuria and China proper, while refusing to permit neutral observers even to be present at the negotiations between China and Japan. Where Japan was wrong he refused investigation but demanded a commission where China was on the defensive. Again Stimson shows

---

[1] F.R.U.S., 1931, III, p. 477.

that he is slowly becoming aware of what the press had been howling and the man in the street discussing as commonplace, what travellers and newspapermen just returned from the Orient were saying from lecture platforms all over America, that Japan was playing for keeps and stalling for time to accomplish her purpose. He said:

> Coming from Matsudaira, such a proposition is, in fact, one of the most discouraging things I have heard. It is tending to force me toward concluding that a settlement which this Government can accept in the light of the treaties on peace is, after all, getting to be increasingly hopeless and that the only recourse left may be for everyone to close the negotiations, to make public the whole damning case against Japan, and to rest upon the reaction of public opinion which in the United States would be overwhelmingly against Japan. I shall regret greatly reaching this conclusion, but to me the trend of the latest communications appears to be in this direction. [1]

But even here, while making this admission, Stimson showed his lack of vigour by closing the wire with the remark (in answer to a previous suggestion by Dawes that the more he viewed the situation the more it seemed that the Nine Power Pact was stronger and had more force than the present procedure and offered more hope of a solution) that although he agreed wholly with him, yet:

> ... a full opportunity has been afforded by the Geneva and Paris Conferences to bring to the attention of Japan its obligations under this treaty, and I can see nothing in Japan's attitude to indicate that it would be amenable any more to a direct invocation of this treaty than has been the case already in the negotiations under the Covenant of the League of Nations. [2]

In other words, anything which meat initiative, or a challenge, on America's part was not to be considered. Stimson shrank from any responsibility. He reserved complete freedom of action for America, but would not use it except to do nothing, or to impede the action of others. The conclusion is inescapable that America's policy was the same as it had been since her earliest dealings with

---

[1] *Op. cit.,* pp. 477—8.
[2] *Loc. cit.*

China, demanding rights, but unwilling to enforce them. It was in the earliest days and still remained, "Let's you and him fight".

From this point until January 1st, 1932, events moved swiftly, Japan moved in on Chinchow and increased her military aggression, sending more troops and material to Manchuria. There was a succession of new proposals and counterproposals by both sides, and rejections by the Council of the Japanese moves.

The world press reported many stories of American undertakings kept secret from the other powers, concerning the settlement of the Manchurian crisis; these were followed by American denials. Sir John Simon offered a plan which was rejected by Stimson. In answer to a direct question of whether or not America would agree to sanctions, Stimson replied to Dawes that she "would probably not interfere with an embargo", but Stimson asked Dawes not to be present for a discussion of sanctions by the Council. He stated that he thought the most America could do would be to denounce Japan's aggression and to refuse to recognize any treaties signed under duress. [1] He was very cautious and gave no clear answer.

A few days later in a telephone conversation with Dawes Stimson said that the United States would not offer obstacles to sanctions but again maintained that it would be better for the United States not to participate in an investigation ordered by the League. He added that as long as the League was meeting, America would not invoke the Nine-Power Pact but that if the League failed, the United States who had reserved her freedom of action, would consider doing so.

On December 10th, 1931, the resolution to appoint a neutral commission (that later known as the Lytton Commission) was unanimously passed.

The feeling was very general throughout China that the United States had let China down badly. It was felt that America had tempered the just condemnation of Japan and thus strengthened her moral position. It was natural that his impression should exist not only in China, but in the world at large. It was prevelent in America itself at the time. It seems indisputably just, now, in the light of the available material on the subject.

---

[1] *Op. cit.*, p. 488.

From now on it was realized by all that the situation was hopeless for all concerned, except Japan. A small island nation, which less than a century before had been absolutely isolated from the world for nearly three hundred years, a nation three hundred years behind the West, in material and industrial civilization, had defied the whole world and got away with it. It is incredible how she succeeded. How could she have known that Stimson would be so soft? That Simon and Stimson would clash and thereby make things easier for her? How could she have known that France would back her, not because of a Far Eastern policy, but because of Germany and the Treaty of Versailes, fearing that if she permitted the other powers to go behind treaties she would establish a precedent which Germany might use to set aside Versailles, on the ground that it was wrung from her under duress? Yet even with all the luck Japan had, and with all the timid and selfish and egotistical statesmen she had to deal with, it is still hard, after having read the documents fully, to understand her success. The thought foremost in one's mind is: "How were we all so stupid? how could we have been such credulous fools?" But much more to the point in this year is the query: "Did we learn a lesson, are we repeating the mistake step by step, arguing while others stall us for time to do the same thing Japan did?"

On January 7th, 1932, Stimson sent a pitiful message to Forbes to deliver to the Japanese Foreign office, pitiful because it represented the humiliation and defeat of a strong and powerful nation which had defeated herself by lack of "guts", lack of the manliness to stand up and at least threaten to fight for what she knew to be right. This note represented the moral prostitution and bankruptcy of a nation. It was a whining plea, a recognition of an accomplished fact, implicit in an empty form of repudiation of it. How the Japanese Foreign Office must have laughed that day. This was the first absolute proof they had that America would do nothing, a green light to them to complete their conquest.

> Please deliver to the Foreign Office on behalf of your Government as possible the following note:
> "With the recent military operations about Chinchow, the last remaining administrative authority of the Government of the Chinese Republic in South Manchuria, as it existed prior to

September 18th, 1931, has been destroyed. The American Government continues confident that the work of the neutral commission recently authorized by the Council of the League of Nations will facilitate an ultimate solution of the difficulties now existing between China and Japan. But in view of the present situation and of its own rights and obligations therein, the American Government deems it to be its duty to notify both the Imperial Japanese Government and the Government of the Chinese Republic that it cannot admit the legality of any situation *de facto* nor does it intend to recognize any treaty or agreement entered into between those Governments, or agents thereof, which may impair the treaty rights of the United States or its citizens in China, including those which relate to the sovereignty, the independence, or the territorial and administrative integrity of the Republic of China, or to the international policy relative to China, commonly known as the open door policy; and that it does not intend to recognize any situation, treaty or agreement which may be brought about by means contrary to the covenants and obligations of the Pact of Paris of August 27, 1928, to which Treaty both China and Japan, as well as the United States, are parties." [1]

This memorandum was sent to both China and Japan.

The Japanese answer to this note is one of the most arrogant and insolent to be found in diplomatic documents. It was intended to let America know just what Japan thought of a nation so lacking in pride that it could have permitted the development of the Manchurian crisis to this point. The tone of the Japanese note must have been gall for Stimson. "The Government of Japan were well aware that the Government of the United States could always be relied on to do everything in their power to support Japan's efforts to secure the full and complete fulfillment in every detail of the treaties of Washington and the Kellogg Treaty for the Outlawry of War. They are glad to receive this additional assurance of the fact." [2] To each of the points made by Stimson the same sort of answer was given. After stating that it is unnecessary to point out that Japan has no "territorial aims or ambitions" in Manchuria the note closes with a sentence intended as the lash of the whip: ".... it is agreeable to be assured that the American Gov-

---

[1] F.R.U.S., Japan 1931—1941, I, p. 76.
[2] *Op. cit.*, pp. 76—7.

ernment are devoting in a friendly spirit such sedulous care to the correct appreciation of the situation".

On January 16th, 1931, Yoshizawa, the new Japanese Foreign Minister, called in Forbes and told him in effect that Japan was setting up a puppet Government in Manchuria, claiming of course that the Chinese in Manchuria were doing it on their own initiative. In reply to Forbes' inquiry whether or not the Japanese army were picking men friendly to Japan and other leading questions, which he evidently encouraged him to ask, Yoshizawa gave slyly evasive answers, meaning yes. Three days later he called in all chiefs of missions and gave them the same information.

CHAPTER XVI

THE ATTACK ON SHANGHAI

On January 28th, 1932, the Japanese began aggressive action against the Chinese in Shanghai. This was an extension and result of the Manchurian affair, as far as the Chinese were concerned. It is difficult to analyse Japanese motives for the spreading of the war but it would seem that even from the irresponsible and rabid militarist point of view, it was foolish to attempt a new territorial aggrandizement at this moment. It appears that the cause has to be sought elsewhere. One likely cause, and that suggested by Toynbee,[1] was the Chinese boycott of Japanese goods which had been strongly maintained since the beginning of the Manchurian incident on September 18th, of the preceding year. This boycott was nationwide, but it had its centre in Shanghai. The boycott has always been a powerful instrument in the hands of the Chinese, even when it has not been well organized, but here it was almost perfect. Japanese business was being ruined, and, as Toynbee points out: "....as the weeks passed with no relaxation of the movement and with no possibility of obtaining redress through the courts, the 'demands' made by Japanese nationals in Shanghai to their Government to take direct action to put an end to an intolerable situation became insistent." There was great danger of local Japanese mob action backed by whatever military force there was at hand!

Stimson summed up the situation in a telegram to Forbes on January 27th. He stated that according to official reports, there had been several clashes during the week prior to January 20th, between Chinese and Japanese at Shanghai, in which there had been several deaths and injuries on both sides. Several thousands of Japanese had held a mass meeting on the 20th, and afterwards a parade through

---

[1] Toynbee, Arnold J., Survey of international affairs (Oxford 1933), pp. 476 —715.

the International Settlement, attacking Chinese and smashing shop windows. Another mass meeting was scheduled for the 23rd. On the 22nd, the Japanese Admiral Shiozawa had notified Wu Te-chen, the Chinese Mayor of Shanghai, that, unless certain demands made by the Japanese Consul-General were enforced, the Japanese Admiral would "take appropriate steps to protect the rights and interests of Japan". On the 23rd, the Japanese Consul and the Chairman and the Secretary of the Municipal Council of the International Settlement had called on Shiozawa, who, after a long discussion, agreed to take no military action in the International Settlement without prior consulation with Settlement officials. The Japanese Consul was reported to have promised to communicate the Chinese reply to the Council twenty-four hours in advance of any action.

Stimson said that, while this resumé might be an oversimplification of the situation, it was enough to show that the Japanese, both officials and private citizens, were aggravating a situation at Shanghai, which was already serious, and that the consular and naval officers of the Japanese Government were definitely considering the use of force in the Settlement "as an instrument of Japanese policy". [1]

"The Government of the United States", he went on, "cannot regard with indifference a situation in which apparently a foreign government has authorized the commander of its naval forces at Shanghai to use force, according to his own judgment, to support demands made by the local consular representatives of that government to obtain objectives which are peculiar to that government, without the agreement, request or approval of the local representatives of other governments which have interests and nationals at Shanghai and which, on the basis of treaties and other agreements, have common rights and interests with respect to conditions of trade and residence at Shanghai and are warranted in feeling solicitude with respect to any developments menacing the local situation at Shanghai." Here Stimson is only following traditional American policy. When our rights and interests, especially financial and trade rights, have been threatened we have

---

[1] F.R.U.S., Japan 1931—1941, I, p. 161 seq.

usually got someone else to do something about it, but in this case, because of the estrangement between Stimson and Simon, and because the European Powers did not appreciate our attitude and position concerning the League and its intervention in the Manchurian crisis, there was no one to act for us. Since he could not send Pete to do it, Stimson realized that he would have to do something himself, and he did. Parenthetically, it might be added that if our commercial and trade interests had been great enough in Manchuria, the story there would very likely have been quite different.

The pretences used by the Japanese for stirring up the trouble and attacking the Settlement were several and stretched over a long time. As Toynbee remarks: "The 'spirit of hostility' which had developed between the Chinese and Japanese at Shanghai manifested itself during the first three weeks of January in every possible way. The Japanese were specially 'infuriated' by 'derogatory references to the Emperor of Japan' by a Chinese Newspaper of the 9th January. 'Incidents of violence' were frequent, and a more than usually serious incident of this kind, on the 18th January, proved to be the spark that fired the train." [1] In this incident five Japanese, some of them Buddhist monks, were attacked by members of the Chinese anti-Japanese Volunteer Corps. In reprisal about fifty members of the Japanese Youth Protection Society armed with knives and clubs attacked and burned the factory near which the incident had occurred. These Japanese clashed with Settlement Police on the way home and several were wounded and one died on each side.

But now we come to the real purpose of the impending aggression against Shanghai and the Chinese in surrounding areas. At the mass meeting on the 20th, as we have seen, the Japanese residents requested aid from the Japanese Government. In fact, they demanded that war vessels and military units be sent "*for the complete suppression of the anti-Japanese movement*". [2] This was the real purpose. The demands of the resolution were presented to the Japanese Consul and the Admiral. The former sent a set of demands

---

[1] Toynbee, *op. cit.*, pp. 471—72.
[2] *Loc. cit.* Italics are the present author's.

to the mayor, Wu Te-chen, for immediate acceptance. The first three required of the mayor a formal apology for the riot of January 18th, the immediate arrest of the attackers, and the payment of an indemnity to the injured. It was the last two demands, however, which embodied the real purpose of the Japanese local policy; the first three were only a smokescreen. Wu was *required* to assume responsibility for "adequate control of the anti-Japanese movement.... immediate dissolution of all anti-Japanese organizations actively engaged in fostering hostile feelings and anti-Japanese riots and agitation". This placed Wu in an impossible position. He could expect no assistance from Nanking because they were in so much trouble there that government was practically paralysed [1] and anti-Japanese feeling was so strong in Shanghai that it would have been impossible for any civilian to attempt to enforce the demands; in fact it would have been impossible for a small military organization to have done so. The Chinese were justly infuriated against the Japanese, who were at this time in the process of swallowing Manchuria, and, furthermore, were in the habit of treating the Chinese, individual and official, infinitely more arrogantly and contemptuously than any Westerners did.

Wu replied that he would accept the first three demands, but that it was not possible for him to accept the responsibility for the last two. The Japanese Admiral, in anticipation of this, had published a statement that if the Chinese mayor did not comply with all the demands immediately, he would take steps "to protect Imperial rights and interests". [2]

On January 27th, Stimson [3] notified Forbes that he had received information that the Japanese planned military action near the Settlement including areas in which were located radio sending and receiving stations. This could cut off Shanghai from the world. The Japanese had acted in this way in Manchuria to prevent news from circulating. Stimson instructed Forbes to notify the Japanese Foreign Minister ".... that this Government views with deep concern the possibility of injury to important American interests

---

[1] *Op. cit.*, pp. 272—3.
[2] *Loc. cit.*
[3] F.R.U.S., Japan 1931—1941, I, p. 163.

and would consider any interference with channels of communications to and from Shanghai with deep regret. . . . . this Government earnestly hopes that there is no basis in fact for the reported intention of the Japanese armed forces".

On the 28th, Forbes [1] sent Stimson assurances from the Foreign Minister that there was no intention to interfere with foreign rights in Shanghai, and that proper procedure had been followed to secure permission to land Japanese forces. The Minister had told Forbes that the anti-Japanese feeling in China was the most serious thing his Government had to face and that any Japanese Cabinet which took a weak line with China would fall.

The situation was now becoming more deadly hour by hour in Shanghai. On the 24th, an aircraft carrier and four destroyers arrived in the river; this made ten warships under Shiozawa's command and about 1,300 marines. On the 24th, the injured Buddhist monk died and Murai, the Consul, notified Wu that, "if no reply was forthcoming within a reasonable time or if the reply was unsatisfactory, the Japanese Government reserved the right to take action as required by the circumstances". There had been no time limit so far, but on the 27th, Murai notified Wu that "without fixing a definite day" he expected a preliminary reply "by the 28th January". Later the same day Wu received another message from Murai demanding a ,,satisfactory reply to the demands by 6 p.m. next day, failing which the Japanese would take the necessary steps in order to enforce them". Early on the morning of the 28th, Shiozawa notified the other Powers in Shanghai that he proposed to take action if there was no favourable reply, not later than the following morning! [2] The Municipal Council then held a meeting and decided to declare a state of emergency, beginning at 4 o'clock the same afternoon. They did this for fear of Japanese action if the Chinese refused to accept the ultimatum, and for fear of the reaction of the Chinese populace, if the mayor did accept it.

At 4 p.m. on January 28, Wu notified Shiozawa that he accepted the five demands. Murai told the consular body that Wu had accepted and that it was entirely satisfactory to Japan. [3]

[1]   Op. cit., pp. 163—5.
[2]   Toynbee, op. cit., pp. 474—5.
[3]   Op. cit., p. 476.

But the Japanese navy, jealous of all the fame gained by Honjo in Manchuria were not to be done out of a prize thus easily. The local Japanese press began printing provocative statements in the Japanese Press Union Bulletin, thus further stirring up the Japanese residents and at the same time, by a stupid blunder, the Municipal Council assigned to Japan for protection, under the emergency scheme, the whole north-eastern segment of the International Settlement as well as the Hongkew Park Salient, which extended like a promontory into the Chinese area of Chapei. The Council set a cat to protect their canaries, and they might have been certain that Japan would not miss the opportunity.

The Council decided to enforce the declaration of the emergency despite Wu's acceptance, because they believed that Japan did not want a peaceful settlement but was merely seeking a pretext for trouble. Nor did they believe that the Chinese would take the Mayor's submission lying down. This decision to enforce the emergency meant legally that "authorized by a body representing all the powers with interests at Shanghai", the Japanese troops would at 4 p.m. "go outside the boundaries of the International Settlement and .... occupy a portion of Chinese administered territory which formed part of an area that was believed to be held by a strong force of Chinese troops". [1] Naturally such an action could be expected to start hostilities. Here again, the Council made the mistake of not notifying Wu, who had been anxious to avoid a clash, that the Japanese were to occupy this Chinese sector with the approval and on the advice of the members of the Council. Wu might have done something to forewarn the Chinese soldiers stationed there. As it was, he knew nothing about it.

The trouble started at midnight. The Chinese and Japanese clashed when the Japanese tried to force their way into Chinese territory in Chapei, through gates dividing this area from the Settlement. The Japanese got to the railway assigned to them as a boundary, but were able to occupy only a part of the area. Fighting started and the Chinese, replying to the Japanese use of armoured cars, also brought up armoured cars and in addition an armoured train which fired from the railway. The Japanese tried to dislodge

---

[1] Toynbee, *op. cit.*, p. 479.

the Chinese forces from the railway station, but were not successful, and began bombing it with planes, destroying it together with
the train; they also bombed other vantage points along the railway
overlooking the Japanese area. [1]

The order to bomb was given by Shiozawa, at 4.30 a.m., and as
was to be expected, within a few hours all Chapei was aflame.
"This bombing of a crowded area, without warning, was bound to
cause great loss of life and material damage, and it struck terror
into the hearts of the hundreds of thousands of harmless civilians
whose homes were in Chapei. It was this feature of the Japanese
operations which made the most painful impression upon international public opinion". [2] Toynbee points out that Shiozawa
could plead that the great disproportion of numbers between the
Chinese and Japanese troops made air action inevitable, ".... but
he convicted himself thereby of a fatal error of judgment in the
tacit admission that he had undertaken operations which could
hardly fail to lead to bloodshed with totally inadequate forces".

On the 29th, Stimson ordered Forbes to make a joint protest with
the British Ambassador to the Foreign Minister against the Japanese attack on Shanghai after Wu had accepted the five demands.

> "On the basis of the best information in possession of the
> American Government at the present moment, it appears that
> recent Sino-Japanese negotiations at Shanghai resulted in
> there being sent by the Chinese Mayor of the Municipality of
> Greater Shanghai to the Japanese Consul General, on the
> afternoon of January 28, a reply to demands which the Jap-
> anese Consul General had presented, which reply the
> Japanese Consul General informed the Consular Body was
> satisfactory. Notwithstanding this and although assurance
> had been given by Japanese officials in several instances that
> Japan did not intend to take unnecessary military action, it
> seems that without there having been any change in the general
> situation, Japanese armed forces nine hours later, at midnight
> on January 28, attacked residential and business sections of
> the Chinese Municipality at Shanghai. This has greatly dis-
> turbed the peace of the whole port of Shanghai and interfered
> with the business of the port. It has jeopardized the safety of

---

[1] Toynbee, op. cit., pp. 481—2.
[2] Loc. cit.

the International Settlement. The American Government is frankly at a loss to find justification or warrant for these activities. It feels constrained to protest against the use made in these circumstances of military force, and it is compelled to urge upon the Japanese Government that it restrain its agencies from a course which, causing constant additional loss of life and property, makes more complicated a situation already delicate and occasions apprehension to the governments and people of every country which has interests in and which feels concern with regard to the area thus affected." [1]

In a memorandum of a conversation with Debuchi, Stimson notes: [2] "... by bringing this strong naval force into the port of Shanghai at this time and threatening a landing, the Japanese had created an explosive situation which was bound to result in an explosion and I regretted to say that I could not look at it in any way except as due to the fault of the Japanese." As Debuchi left he handed Stimson a statement by Murai: [3]

> "It is true that the Mayor of greater Shanghai conceded late on January 28th to all demands contained in my note of January 20th and we were anxiously watching for the development in view of various rumors and questionable ability of the local Chinese authorities to control the situation, particularly the undisciplined soldiers and dissatisfied elements. By four o'clock the Shanghai municipal council declared a state of emergency, meanwhile the excited refugees, most of whom were Chinese, poured into the settlement from all directions. The rumor of surreptitious entry of the 'plainclothed corps' gained wide circulation. To make the situation from bad to worse (sic), all the Chinese constables fled from the Chapei district where about 7000 Japanese reside. The excitement of the populace grew to fever-point. As an emergency measure of protecting the Japanese lives and property in Chapei, a Japanese landing force was despatched in accordance with a previous arrangement with authorities of the municipality and British, American and other forces and in conformity with former precedents of similar cases. (The territory in question is a strip of land in Chapei on the east side of the Shanghai-Woosung Railway which by the abovenamed agreement was

---

[1] F.R.U.S., Japan 1931—1941, I, pp. 65—6.
[2] *Op. cit.*, p. 167.
[3] *Op. cit.*, pp. 167—8.

assigned to the Japanese). No sooner had the Japanese landing force appeared on emergency duty near its headquarters than the Chinese soldiers in plain clothes attacked them with hand grenades in the neighborhood of the Shanghai-Woosung railway. This attack served as a signal for the Chinese regulars to open fire on the Japanese force, whereupon the latter was forced to return fire. At about the same time, these disguised outlaws commenced shooting at the Japanese at random in the area mentioned above. They have already claimed a number of Japanese lives in the same area. I made it a special point to ask Mr. Yui, Secretary General of the municipality of greater Shanghai, to withdraw the Chinese troops from the section in question when I received the Mayor's reply yesterday to which he gave his ready assent and assured me that it would be done. Had the Mayor been able to bring the military to coordinate speedily with him we might have averted the unfortunate incident. I am demanding again for an immediate withdrawal in view of what took place and is now taking place. If the Chinese authorities are unable to stop the assault and complete the withdrawal from that section, I see no other alternative but to enforce it by force. I should like to make it clear that this clash is to be distinguished from the question contained in my note of January 20th which was solved for the time being at any rate. I would also like to point out that the wild story about the Japanese attack on the Woosung Fort is groundless. This Chapei incident is entirely a matter of self-defense in emergency in an effort to protect Japanese life and property and indeed those of other nationals including Chinese themselves. I am hoping for a speedy cooperation of the Chinese side to avoid any further conflict or sacrifices and to that end to withdraw its troops."

On the 31st, [1] Stimson notified Forbes that Admiral Taylor had been ordered to proceed on the flagship *Houston* with available destroyers to Shanghai. He added that this was not a threat to anyone and was only intended to protect American lives. Stimson always had to kill in advance the value which any act might have as a bluff, by explaining to Japan that it was not to be misunderstood and had no meaning.

On the same date, [2] Forbes wired Stimson that he and the British and French Ambassadors had all been to see Yoshizawa and

---

[1] *Op. cit.,* pp. 168—9.
[2] *Op. cit.,* pp. 168—71.

protested. Yoshizawa had made a long statement to prove Japan innocent and China guilty. "He claims (1) that collaboration has been maintained in Shanghai with the Municipal Council and with the foreign military and naval authorities; (2) that the clash between the Chinese and Japanese forces bore no relation to the acceptance by the Chinese Mayor of the Japanese demands; and (3) that the Japanese marines took up positions in a sector allotted to them in accordance with joint defense arrangements." [1] Yoshizawa requested American good offices to persuade the Chinese to withdraw their troops and avoid further clashes and asked America to help make peace. He then quoted to Forbes the charges Stimson had made about the bombing and wanton firing in Shanghai and denied them while admitting that "if the facts are as represented to you, your conclusions are absolutely logical and unanswerable".

On the 1st of February, 1932, [2] Forbes notified Stimson that Yoshizawa had said that the Japanese had acted in self defense, but that it might be necessary to counter-attack the Chinese in order to clear them out. In reply to Stimson's statement that the International Settlement must not be used as a base of operations, he said this restriction was inadmissable to Japan. The Shanghai Defense Committees had decided to ask both the Chinese and Japanese to evacuate a neutral zone, and both to withdraw other troops back to their positions of January or to a safe distance so as to prevent trouble. The Chinese accepted the proposal, but the Japanese refused, though the Ambassadors all urged it strongly upon Yoshizawa, "stating that the failure to accept this peaceable solution of the situation would indicate in the eyes of the world that Japan is determined on war". [3] Forbes notified Stimson in the same cable that with the dispatch of the Japanese warships reported that day, there would be a total of 12 cruisers, 2 airplane carriers, 1 seaplane tender, 32 destroyers, 2 river gunboats and 1 mine layer in the Shanghai and Nanking area.

---

[1] Since we are dealing only with the Diplomatic Policy of America in China, there is little place for narration of the events in Shanghai, but to get a vivid impression of what was actually going on, of the Japanese reign of terror and summary executions, read Toynbee, *op. cit.*, pp. 484—5.

[2] F.R.U.S., Japan 1931—1941, I, pp. 172—3.

[3] *Loc. cit.*

On the night of February 1st, 1931, Japan shelled Nanking. On the following morning Stimson sent for Debuchi and pointed out to him that Japan had requested America's good offices to stop the conflict and on that same night they had started firing on Nanking with war vessels. He told Debuchi that this would greatly interfere with the efforts and good offices of America and that the firing should be stopped at once. On the same day he instructed Forbes to call on Yoshizawa and give his reply to the latter's request for good offices, "to induce the Chinese troops not to bring up further re-enforcements and to withdraw the troops now in Shanghai to a safe distance to avoid clashes". He instructed him to read a note and leave it with him: [1]

"Proposal of the Powers for Cessation of Conflict

(1) Cessation of all acts of violence on both sides forthwith on the following terms.

(2) No further mobilization or preparation whatever for further hostilities between the two nations.

(3) Withdrawal of both Japanese and Chinese combatants from all points of mutual contact in the Shanghai area.

(4) Protection of the International Settlement by the establish-ment of neutral zones to divide the combatants. These zones to be policed by neutrals. The arrangements to be set up by the Consular authorities.

(5) Upon acceptance of these conditions prompt advances to be made in negotiations to settle all outstanding con-troversies between the two nations in the spirit of the Pact of Paris and the Resolution of the League of Nations of December 9, without prior demand or reservation and with the aid of neutral observers or participants."

Stimson told Forbes to confer with the British Ambassador, who was presenting an identical note, and go with him to see Yoshizawa.

In a joint conference at which the British and French Am-bassadors were present Yoshizawa agreed to accept the first four points, but refused to consider the fifth. He argued for the good offices depending on the first four and leaving out the fifth com-pletely, since Japan was unalterably opposed to a third party having

---

[1] *Loc. cit.*, p. 174.

anything to do with negotiations between Japan and China concerning Manchuria. The Ambassadors were unable to change the
conditions set forth by their Governments and Yoshizawa said
he would take up the matter with his Government and let them
know the following morning.

Debuchi came in to see Stimson, of his own accord, on the 2nd.
They discussed the five points, and Debuchi repeated that Japan
would accept the first four points, but was unable to accept the fifth,
Stimson said that if they accepted the first four fully and without
reservation and, instead of rejecting, requested more time to consider the fifth, he would be satisfied. They agreed on that and
Debuchi said he had or would so notify his government. Debuchi
claimed that there was more hope, since Admiral Nomura, a great
friend of Admiral Pratt's (CNO U.S.N. 1930-33) and a liberal,
had been sent to Shanghai to take over the command. Stimson
argued for his neutral zone scheme and against the landing of more
troops at Shanghai by the Japanese. Debuchi admitted that he was
right, but said that the report that Japan had dispatched more
troops from the homeland was premature, that his Government
would not do such a thing as to request good offices and immediately
thereafter dispatch troops. In fact, of course, Japan had already
dispatched large land and marine forces to reinforce their units in
the Shanghai area.

There had been serious disputes about Japan occupying the
defence sectors of other powers in Shanghai as well as using the
Settlement as a base. On the night of February 3rd, [1] Debuchi went
out to Woodley, Stimson's home, to tell him that the Japanese were
evacuating the American sectors and that there would be an end of
trouble the Americans had been having with the Japanese in the
Settlement. Stimson said that his information was very different,
and that the Americans were using great forbearance in not firing
on the Japanese. Debuchi said that, while the Japanese warships
were passing the forts at Woosung, they had been fired upon by
the Chinese and had returned the fire, but that he did not know the
results. The truth seems to have been that Debuchi had been sent
in his capacity of personal friend of Stimson's to break the news

---

[1] Op. cit., pp. 177—9.

of the new Japanese tactics in this casual manner, and to lay the blame on the Chinese. Stimson told him that his information was exactly the opposite. The Japanese were firing over the Settlement from their warships, at the Chinese, some shells falling short and hitting the Settlement.

Debuchi asked Stimson whether the United States intended to insist on the fifth point of the proposed agreement. Stimson answered that the president, himself, was extremely firm on this point. Debuchi pressed him very hard to divorce the fifth point from the others, but Stimson replied that they "considered that there was no use in temporizing in stopping individual controversies and conflicts if the cause of the controversy was not ended". Debuchi argued: "Here we were contemplating sending two divisions of land troops to China and instead of that we sent and asked you to use good offices; does not that show we were conciliatory and do you really think you ought to dictate to us on the fifth point." [1] Stimson replied that he was not trying to dictate, but was making what he considered a fair proposition; whether or not Japan had asked us, we should have had to take a hand in the affair.

In this interview one gets a good view of the relation between Stimson and Debuchi. There is something of the spoiled bright youngster, who, when everything else fails, resorts to the sense of fair play and moral justice. He must have thought Stimson even more gullible and malleable than he was. You see, we trusted you and invited you to help us; do you think you should dictate to us? Seldom did Debuchi tell the truth if it was inconvenient. He lied one day and came back the next day saying "Oh, I made a mistake, but let us consider that a closed incident", or "it must be considered closed", or "there is danger in the anger of my people against America". One would have thought that America was a colony of Japan's which had a certain amount of self-government, but had constantly to explain and justify her actions to Japan. Stimson continually let himself be put on the defensive by Debuchi. However, in this conversation Stimson went so far as to tell Debuchi to notify his Government that America, with Britain, was determined to defend the International Settlement but could not

---

[1] *Op. cit.*, p. 178.

successfully do so if the Japanese continued using it as a base of operations against the Chinese; hence they must at once stop using it. This was the nearest Stimson had ever come to being firm or giving an ultimatum to Debuchi. "The evidence that I get today, coming not only from my own officials, but from all of the civil and military officials in the Settlement, is that your troops and your irregulars and your 'ronins' [1] (sic) are violating the neutrality in the Settlement and are using it as a base of attack against the Chinese; that absolutely must stop or otherwise we will all be involved in a great catastrophe. I insisted that he take down these points and submit them to his Government."

On February 3rd, Stimson told Forbes to protest strongly to Yoshizawa against using the sectors of other powers as a base of attack against the Chinese, stating that the Japanese brutality to the Chinese was provoking great hostility among the Chinese against other nations whom they blame for allowing the Japanese to use their sectors "to commit acts of unnecessary violence against the Chinese population". [2]

On the following day Yoshizawa met the American, French and British Ambassadors to give them an answer on the five-point proposal. It was in effect a rejection of all the points and Yoshizawa stated that Japan was sending land troops in addition to the marines. After discussion it seemed that the Japanese Government meant to accept points three and four, but only the first clause of point four. To a blunt question put by the French Ambassador whether Japan still intended to send troops if China accepted all the five points, Yoshizawa replied that she did. [3]

The Japanese wanted war and were going to have it. The mistake of the Powers was in thinking that they did not want war. The Japanese demanded all concessions and conceded nothing. They demanded all consideration for their rights, dignity and sensitivity, but rode roughshod over the rights of others.

---

[1] Feudal warriors in Japan, whose master was murdered and who became a kind of extra-legal desperado; mispelled above. Ronin is plural. F.R.U.S., Japan 1931—1941, I, p. 179.

[2] *Loc. cit.*

[3] *Op. cit.*, pp. 180—82.

From February 3rd, onward, the Japanese began losing to the Chinese in the Shanghai battle. They had expected to overawe the Chinese with superior arms and aircraft, but they failed. They sent up re-inforcements, and were repeatedly driven back. This perhaps, in part, accounts for the determination not to make peace with the Chinese until they had thoroughly trounced them. It was a question of face, and they had certainly lost a great deal, not only before the Chinese, but before the whole world.

On February 6th, Forbes forwarded to Stimson the formal Japanese answer to the five-point proposal: [1]

"I have the honor to acknowledge the receipt of your note number 208 on February 2, 1932, transmitting by instruction of your Government proposals in regard to the Shanghai affair, and to state in reply the views of the Japanese Government in regard to these proposals.

1. It is that the Chinese troops cease immediately and completely their challenging and disturbing activities. If this can be assured, the Japanese troops will also cease warlike activities. If, on the contrary, the Chinese (irrespective of whether they be regular or plain-clothes troops) continue these challenging and disturbing activities, the Japanese forces reserve complete freedom of action.

2. In view of the unreliable actions of the Chinese troops and of the gravity of the situation, the Japanese Government is unable to cease mobilization and preparation for hostilities.

3. The Japanese Government has no objection to its consul and commander entering into negotiations for arranging for separation of Japanese and Chinese forces, and, in case of necessity, for the establishment of a neutral zone in the Chapei district.

4. Assuming that the Manchuria affair is included in "all outstanding controversies between the two nations," the Japanese Government is unable to accede to this proposal because not only is the Manchuria affair distinctly a separate affair, but also because this matter was covered by the resolution of the League Council at the meetings on December 10th. Furthermore, it is the Japanese Government's fixed policy to refuse to accept the assistance of observers of a third country or of participants, in the settlement of the Manchuria affair."

---

[1] Op. cit., pp. 182—3.

On February 6th, Japan asked for an American move in Shanghai for a solution—so that the Japanese would not lose face by making any proposals themselves. Stimson authorized Cunningham, the American Consul in Shanghai, to help in attempting to find a solution, but he told Debuchi that if discussions were going on in Shanghai, they must be considered as having been originated by the Japanese, since they had rejected the American five-point proposal, and hence also good offices. Meanwhile Japan landed new forces at Woosung, for Chapei. Stimson now began to realize that they were holding up the Chinese and the Powers on a pretence that they were seeking a peaceful solution following their first defeat in the Shanghai fighting. Actually they had determined to use military force to gain their point and to restore their prestige and were using this term for mobilization and transfer of troops from Japan to Shanghai. He advised Debuchi therefore, that he felt there was no basis for securing except on terms so humiliating to the Chinese that America could not possibly afford to associate herself with such a settlement. He advised Forbes not to allow his staff to take any initiative in such a settlement and said that there was a feeling in America that we had done everything consistent with our dignity towards conciliating Japan.

On February 14th, 1932, Cunningham sent a protest to the Japanese Consul against using the Nippon Yusen Kaisha wharf in the International Settlement to land troops. He stated that the American Government was opposed to the use by either of the disputants of any Settlement facilities in connection with military operation.

On the 15th, the Japanese Minister received the American, British, French, Italian and German Ambassadors and gave them an exposition of Japan's position, proving that Japan was in the right and the Chinese at fault in the trouble at Shanghai. [1] He said that the Ninth Division would be landing at Shanghai the next day, making a total of 15,000 land troops and 3,000 marines, facing 31,000 men of the Chinese Nineteenth Corps, who were continuing defensive and offensive actions against the Japanese. He made an ominous statement: "It is believed that the Japanese Army will

---

[1] *Op. cit.*, pp. 193—4.

demand the Chinese Army to withdraw and that this step was necessary because as long as they remained where they were they menaced the security of the Settlement and Japanese resident nationals." He predicted that, if the demand were not accepted, the Chinese would be attacked by the Japanese Army; if they withdrew, or alternatively, after they had been driven back a safe distance, equivalent to Chinese artillery range, they would not be followed up, and the Japanese might enter into negotiations for the establisment of a neutral zone.

On the 15th, Stimson had an interview with Debuchi, who told him that there would be no more troops landed at Shanghai, or at any other place in China. [1] He said that the Ninth Division would be the last troops Japan would send to China. He had come to see Stimson specially to deny press reports that Japan was seeking a separate Concession at Shanghai, and was demanding the establishment of neutral zones in other Chinese cities as well as Shanghai. He said that the statement on which these reports were based had been given out by a "very low official in the Foreign Office", a man who had made previous trouble. Stimson said that, if the statement had occurred alone, he would not have given it much credence, but that in this case it fitted in too closely with other statements and other things the Japanese were doing to be disregarded. Referring to the American attempt to mediate, he reminded the Ambassador how the Japanese had refused the fifth point of the Four Powers in their efforts at good offices, "by stating that they would not permit any representative of a third power to participate in any negotiations as to Manchuria".

Stimson said that, as signatories of the Nine-Power Pact, Britain, France and America had a right to participate in any discussions concerning all of China, including Manchuria, which affected the Pact. "He stated that that was true, and he said that the Japanese had no intention of disregarding or not faithfully abiding by the Nine-Power Pact; that Japan had scrupulously kept her treaties." Stimson said that the facts were against his statement, and that it was difficult to reconcile Japan's actions at Shanghai with her duties under the Nine-Power Pact; further, he felt that

---

[1] *Op. cit.*, pp. 194—6.

the statement coming from the Foreign Ministry, that Japan wished to repeal the Nine-Power Pact, must be given more weight than in normal times.

Stimson told Debuchi that he had learned of the landing of the Japanese troops in the Settlement contrary to a promise given by the Japanese Consul there, in response to the last American protest. He regarded this as a very serious matter, as it would provoke the Chinese against all foreigners when they were being attacked by the Japanese with the International Settlement as a base of operations. He stated that he was going to make another public protest and notify the Japanese Government that America would hold Japan financially responsible for all damage which Americans suffered as a result of Japanese use of the Settlement as a base.

On the 17th, Debuchi notified Stimson that his government had authorized the Japanese Commander at Shanghai to order the Chinese to withdraw 20 kilometers from Shanghai.

In Shanghai the Japanese and Chinese Chiefs of Staff met at the suggestion of neutral diplomats and the Japanese orally presented their terms, which the Chinese declared to be unacceptable. After a fruitless discussion the Japanese said they would present their terms in a written communication. They demanded a reply as soon as possible. They sent identic memoranda to the Mayor of Shanghai and to the Commander of the Chinese army, but both said they were unable to deal with such a matter, which was for the National Government alone to handle. They therefore passed on the terms to Nanking. The Chinese Government made a reply pointing out that the prevalence of anti-Japanese sentiment was natural considering Japan's flagrant disregard of China's rights, and making a just summary of the situation. They declared that they refused to comply with Japan's demands and would meet force with force. Japan, however, had not waited for the reply. Long before it was presented she had begun her big attack.

China surprised the world by the defence she put up against Japan, who was forced to rush two more divisions under a new over-all Military Commander, General Shirakawa, to the Shanghai war area. Instead of an easy victory it took the Japanese a hard struggle with all their modern weapons for land warfare, as well as war ships and an airforce constantly bombing, to drive the Chinese back, and then they slipped through their fingers on the night of March 3rd, and retreated in good order. By this time Japan realized that she was held in such odium by the civilized world that she was ready to settle the affair on the pretext that she had accomplished her objective. The Shanghai war was over.

On March 3rd, Stimson ordered Cunningham not to participate, until further notice, in the round-table discussions recently initiated by the League of Nations and at the time sitting in Shanghai, since he felt that the Japanese had instigated the League intervention on February 29th, and accepted the proposals of the League Council for cessation of hostilities as an opportunity to carry out their big offensive. They had had the worst of the fighting until the Council intervened. The two sides accepted the Council's terms and then the Japanese made an all-out drive. Stimson stated that he did not want to be drawn into proposals which would be unfair to China or appear to be an endorsement of Japan's actions.

On March 5th, Stimson in a telegram to Cunningham [1] gave his interpretation of the League proposal as meaning (a) that China freely consented, and (b) that the discussions were to be limited to termination of hostilities, evacuation of armed forces and restoration of peace in Shanghai. Japan had agreed to a restrictive clause: " 'Japan has no political or territorial designs and no intention of establishing a Japanese settlement in Shanghai or of otherwise advancing the exclusive interests of the Japanese'." There was to be no discussion of any former action of the League or prior agreements between Japan and China; the re-establishment of peace and the *status quo ante* in Shanghai was to be the only subject on the agenda. On these terms only Stimson instructed Cunningham and the U.S. military and naval authorities to join the conference.

On March 11th, the League Assembly adopted a resolution which settled the controversy, and in response to this, Stimson sent the following note: "I acknowledge the receipt of your letter of March 11 enclosing for the information of the American Government the text of a resolution relative to the Sino-Japanese dispute which was adopted this afternoon by the Assembly of the League of Nations.

---

[1] *Op. cit.*, pp. 209—10.

"I am instructed by my Government to express to you its gratification at the action taken by the Assembly of the League of Nations. My Government is especially gratified that the nations of the world are united on a policy not to recognize the validity of results attained in violation of the treaties in question. This is a distinct contribution to international law and offers a constructive basis for peace.

"You suggest that I note particularly part 2 of the resolution. In this, the Assembly recalls several resolutions and cites especially its own resolution of March 4, 1932, adopted in agreement with the parties with a view to the definitive cessation of hostilities and the withdrawal of the Japanese forces. My Government, as one of the powers which have special interests in the Shanghai Settlement, has already authorized its representatives at Shanghai to assist, in cooperation with the representatives of other powers similarly situated, toward the consummation of those objectives." [1]

Thus ended the second phase of Japanese aggression in the Far East. During the Shanghai fighting Stimson acted more like a diplomat, and was much more realistic and less easily gulled by Debuchi than over Manchuria. Was it only because of American financial interest in Shanghai or because the issue was more sharply defined?

In looking back on this episode, we can say that it is the only aspect of America's diplomatic policy in China where military aggression was concerned of which Americans do not have to be ashamed, in the period covered by this essay. Certainly Westerners cannot be proud of the blunder which geared Japan's predetermined attack into a fiction of legality by assigning to her the Chapei area to "guard", nor can anyone approve of the international acquiescence in the bombing and murder and pillage of defenceless non-combatant people. But no one nation bears more blame than another for that, and America, while clinging to her historical policy of neutrality, at any rate showed firmness in protecting her commercial, industrial and financial interests and her treaty rights in the largest city of continental Asia.

---

[1] *Op. cit.,* p. 213.

CHAPTER XVII

THE TRIUMPH OF JAPAN

Following the bombing of Shanghai, Stimson, after discussions with Sir John Simon, [1] drew up a rough draft of a statement to be issued by America and Great Britain and possibly other powers. This recapitulated the history of the Nine Power Pact and the Pact of Paris (Kellogg–Briand Pact) and recited the main purposes of both. It asserted that because of the size and population of China the peaceful development of its people was essential to world peace, "and that no programme for the welfare of the world as a whole could afford to neglect the protection of the development of China". The nations had withheld judgment pending the completion of the Lytton Commission enquiry, but had, nevertheless, viewed the Manchurian incident with deep foreboding—the more so, since, when war started, it spread, and no nation could long remain outside the struggle. The spread of the fighting recently to Shanghai, where it involved the vital interests of many nations, was an example of the danger.

The statement roundly blames Japan in diplomatic language for the attack on Shanghai and for the bombing of densely populated and defenceless civilian areas. It was in effect a bitter castigation of Japan. The Treaties had been violated and Japan had refused to honor her committments. She had refused the good offices of the United States, France and Britain, for which she asked, to stop the fighting. Since she refused to permit the presence of third nations, even as neutral observers, in the settlement of the Manchurian dispute, she was actually denying the right of the other signatories to participate in any way in negotiations which deeply concerned those nations, though they had moral and legal rights and responsibilities under the Treaty.

---

[1] F.R.U.S., Japan 1931—1941, I, pp. 80—2.

The statement wound up with a flourish, saying that the signatories do not concede the ineffectuality of the Treaty, if only a certain other nation would not violate it. They insisted that the enlightened policy thus far continued should not be discarded without an "earnest reprobation" from them. They refused to waive their rights to "participate together" in negotiations involving their rights and obligations and the policies represented thereby. They took this occasion to express these views so that they be not mis- understood. They reserved their rights under the Treaty to talk, to discuss, to express "frankly and without reserve" the belief that, if the Treaty be repudiated, the loss to the world would be immeasurable. Therefore they notified one another that they refused to recognize any change created in China by the violation of any part of the Treaty. Oh, yes! as a matter of legality they availed themselves of the rights under Article VII to talk and discuss, in case the Japanese should demand to know their authority for daring to express themselves.

On April 4th, 1932, [1] the Japanese Ambassador notified Stimson that his Government would withdraw from the League Assembly meeting if it insisted on going into the Manchurian affair further than already provided for in the resolutions of September 30th and December 10th. He said that this did not mean that Japan was going to withdraw from the League: he knew that took two years. He did, however, warn Stimson, that because of Japan's peculiar interests in Manchuria, she could not permit outside interference in the questions at issue there, and "particularly that Japan could not permit the application of Article XV of the League Covenant to questions in Manchuria".

In a long discussion Stimson made him admit that Japan was in effect exercising political control over Manchuria and beginning to try to control her finances. Under pressure of a direct question from Stimson, Debuchi had to admit that such actions could not be reconciled with Shidehara's promises. He said that Japan would carry out her obligations under Article VII of the Nine Power Treaty ("to communicate frankly on those subjects"), but he had no comment on Japan's difference in attitude on the two Articles

---

[1] *Op. cit.*, pp. 87—89.

VII and XV. Finally Stimson made him admit that Japan had broken her promises, "but ... that the chauvinist conditions were so acute in Japan that the Government could not take any other position". [1] As usual, when a Japanese is cornered, Debuchi refused to face facts further, or to discuss the matter logically or rationally, but resorted to subterfuge; he evaded the subject and the responsibility. As Stimson says concerning this interview: "... he could only ask me to be patient with his people and try to think of some constructive view of the situation that they were in in Manchuria; that criticism only further inflamed the situation and played into the hands of the chauvinistic elements." [2]

Here is one of the clearest examples of the fallacy and speciousness of the argument of the Japanese. Presumably Debuchi was against all that was happening in Manchuria (according to Stimson this was so), yet he was asking the Secretary of State to take "some constructive view of the situation the Japanese were in in Manchuria". What possible constructive view was there? Why were the Japanese in Manchuria and for whose benefit? What part could sympathetic understanding play, except to give Japan more time to extend and consolidate her gains?

In these interviews we see clear evidence that Stimson and individual Japanese whom he trusted were all being used to further the purposes of the militarists without the knowledge and against the intentions of the latter, or else that the men he trusted were using him as a dupe to further predetermined aims. In either case Stimson was gulled and used as an agent of aggression. He refused to be realistic while it could accomplish anything. It seems that by this time he was becoming a little tougher, but it was too late. The time to have stopped Japan was in September, 1931.

It is necessary to discuss more fully the responsibility of Stimson. It is certainly not the intention here to blacken the reputation or record of one of the greatest citizens and statesmen America has ever produced, but on the other hand we must face the documentary evidence. According to this, Stimson was exploited and deceived by the Japanese. It seems that he lacked guts and initiative, in

---

[1] *Op. cit.*, p. 88.
[2] *Op. cit.*, p. 89.

short that he was a thorough weakling. His worst enemy could not accuse him of either of those sins. As for lack of initiative, it must be remembered that he is a lawyer, and that he was sincere in his belief in the Japanese statesman, Shidehara and Debuchi. Both these factors would logically tend to hobble initiative on his part. But one feels that there is a great deal more to it than this.

The problem is to try to find some other factor. The picture of Stimson as the boob does not fit in with the War Secretary of the Second World War. What is the difference? One gets some inkling of the solution from his book *Far Eastern Crisis,* published in 1936. One feels that even there he is still deceived to a certain extent by Debuchi and Shidehara, but that, though he still believes in them personally he realizes that too much consideration was shown to the Japanese as a nation and that they took advantage of that patience and consideration to carry out the conquest of Manchuria. What then can account for the lack of firmness and insistence on Stimson's part? His belief in the two men is not enough.

Unfortunately such documents as are available do not show political undercurrents. But let us try to reconstruct the situation of that period. Reference has already been made to the world-wide economic depression and the unpopularity of the Hoover administration. It was the second half of Hoover's term and there was a Democratic majority in Congress, just as Wilson had had a Republican Congress in 1918—1920. It is sad but true that men in all countries have often put the welfare of a party above that of the nation. This in part accounted for the fact that Republicans refused to bring America into the League of Nations, regarding it as the handiwork of Wilson. In 1932 there was an even greater urge to turn down anything a Republican President did. America was rabidly isolationist and more concerned with domestic than with international affairs. In fact the author well remembers having heard discussions about supplying the Japanese with scrap iron in 1931—32 and particularly one conversation in which one of the large scrap dealers on the West Coast remarked that it was a question of selling the scrap to the Japanese or of going bankrupt, since there was then no sale for scrap in America, whereas the Japanese were offering several dollars a ton for all they could buy. This same man admitted, in effect, that there was no question in his mind that within a few years we would be getting the scrap back in an entirely different form, in a war with Japan. Such an attitude was general in California at the time. The depression was so black that there was no place for idealism. The short-term interest predominated over everything else.

In considering the policy of America in any period it must always be kept in mind that the Secretary of State could, in the end, only carry out the policy which the President of the United States finally agreed upon. Stimson could formulate no final policy without the consent of Hoover. But we have no direct way of knowing what Hoover's policy was. We can only deduce it from events. It is certain that Hoover was against any strong action which might lead to war. Instead of laying the full, or even a large, responsibility for the actual foreign policy of the United States in 1931—33 at the door of Stimson, we should lay much of it at the door of Hoover. He was finally responsible. If he were displeased with the actions of his Secretary of State, or any other Cabinet Secretary, he could demand his resignation and be certain of getting it. But no President has ever resigned. The President is not responsible except at the Presidential elections. If the people are displeased, they can vote him out every four years, but otherwise the only other effective checks on him are the Congress and the Supreme Court, and the Supreme Court hardly enters into consideration here. It is certain that the Congress of the day was not advocating war. The conclusion is inescapable, therefore, that after allowing for Stimson's patience, his having been taken advantage of by Japanese whom he trusted, and his natural disinclination for war, the main responsibility for our miserable policy in the Manchurian affair largely belongs to Hoover, and was evidently what he ordered. On the other hand his policy was in the long run a reflection of what the people really wanted, just as was Chamberlain's appeasement at Munich—what the English people wanted later—"Peace in our time". Pearl Harbour and Poland were in the future.

On June 22nd, 1932, General Araki, the Japanese Minister of War, in anticipation of the true report which would be made by the Lytton Commission on Japanese aggression in Manchuria, declared before the Supreme Military Council that the resolutions of the League of Nations and all statements made by Japan concerning

CHRISTOPHER, Conflict in the Far East   20

Manchuria prior to the establishment of Manchukuo could no longer be considered binding on Japan, adding that Japan would not withdraw her troops into the railway zone as required by the League resolution and as promised by her own agreements. He further stated that Japan would not recognize the competence or authority of the League of Nations Inquiry Commission to recommend solutions of the Manchurian affair.

Here we can see the result of America's patience and appeasement. As soon as Japan felt that the United States would not do more than talk and make diplomatic protests, and that she was strong enough to challenge world efforts to halt the aggression in Manchuria, she flouted both America and the League.

On July 16th, [1] Grew, the Ambassador to Japan who replaced Forbes, notified Stimson of the results of the findings of the Lytton Commission as learned in confidence from General Frank R. McCoy, American member of the Commission. He said that the Commission was "unanimous in finding that Japan's actions in Manchuria were based upon two false premises: (1) the argument of self-defence and (2) the argument of self-determination in Manchuria". He said that the Japanese arguments would not hold water. "The Commissioners have proved to their satisfaction that the blowing up of the railway and every subsequent incident in Manchuria since September 18th, 1931, were carefully planned and carried out by the Japanese themselves." It was his opinion that the setting up of the puppet state of Manchukuo, instead of pacifying the Far East, would lead to future war. The Commissioners held that Japan's action ran contrary to her obligations under the Nine Power Treaty, the Kellogg Pact and the Covenant of the League of Nations, and that she should have consulted with other signatories of these treaties before taking any action. They felt that Japan's guilt was made perfectly clear in their conferences with the Japanese, quite apart from any talks with the Chinese. They had advised Japan to discuss and to delay recognition of Manchukuo, but Count Uichida had answered "unequivocally that Japan had made up its mind to recognize Manchukuo and that he could not consider any counter arguments nor enter into any discussion of the matter."

---

[1] *Op. cit.*, pp. 93—5.

Grew had advised Stimson against protesting the recognition of Manchukuo by Japan on July 7th. He now re-affirmed this and gave as his reason: "The press, which at present largely represents the point of view of the military, would under present circumstances be quite capable of magnifying such representations by the United States in a manner out of all proportion to their significance and an outburst might well occur which would afford the military a pretext for earlier action than the more conservative members of the Government may desire. That this risk exists is the opinion of every member of my staff." [1]

Here again, we see clearly that appeasement was the order of the early thirties. The desire to appease was almost universal, and especially among responsible officials and diplomats. America had sunk to such a low point that her diplomats were even advising against mere protests against aggression. Certainly if she did not even consider it wise to protest, she would not take more drastic action.

Japan cannot have been unaware of this reaction on the part of the Powers. For these reasons she knew that there would be no restraining influence and that hence she had a *carte blanche* to do as she pleased. At first she feared world opinion, and especially American opinion, but when she realized that America would do nothing more than talk, she became utterly contemptuous and scornful of America, and of her international obligations, as well as of the rights of the peoples of the world to freedom and justice.

It is not, therefore, entirely just to blame Hoover, Stimson or Grew for their attitudes and reactions. These seem to have been universal among the Western Powers in that period. In the final analysis it was what the people wanted; otherwise the statesmen could not have carried out such policies for long because of the pressure of the voters. It was the spirit of the age. We wanted freedom and justice for ourselves and would like others to have them but we were not then willing to fight for these things for ourselves or for others.

On August 13th, [2] Grew informed Stimson in a dispatch that

---

[1] *Loc. cit.,* p. 95.
[2] *Op. cit.,* pp. 99—100.

the Japanese had taken a speech of Stimson's, made before the
Council for Foreign Relations, and twisted it out of all proportions,
using it to inflame the Japanese public against America. He compared it to the deliberate build-up in Germany for the war of 1914.
He said Japan was inflaming the public against all Foreign Powers
and especially against America, to strengthen the hand of the
militarists, in the face of foreign, and especially American, opposition.

Grew said that Japan was in serious difficulty, that the internal
economic and financial trouble might become desperate at any time.
He said he had been told recently that Japan had been refused
loans by England, France and Holland, and could not get financial
help from abroad. The farmers were in a serious position and
industry was operating at a low level. Grew feared that when the
public learned of the true situation and of the tremendous amounts
of money being squandered in the Manchurian affair they might
take drastic action, that there was no telling what they might do.
He said that the militarists realized this and were trying to build up
an anti-foreign public opinion, by making it appear that America
was trying to thwart Japan's attempt at self-preservation. Grew
felt that the militarists were using the old expedient of diversion
of attention from internal affairs by foreign military activity. He
warned that the Japanese military machine was built up for war,
and was well trained, had never been defeated, was extremely
self-confident and would welcome war. He closed this cogent
dispatch with the admonition: "I am not an alarmist but I believe
we should have our eyes open to all possible future contingencies.
The facts of history would render it criminal to close them". [1]
Yes,—Pearl Harbour resulted.

America's dilatory policy soon began to bear fruit. As a result
of Stimson's desire to be reasonable and friendly to Japan he made
statements, which today in the light of what transpired later seem
unwise, if not indefensible. These statements were used and twisted
by the Japanese to drive a wedge between the Powers and to make
it seem that Stimson, at least, was in favor of their actions in
Manchuria, or that he did not strongly disapprove. They used his

---

[1] *Loc. cit.*, p. 100.

statements to suit their own purposes, and their use was not consistent. As we have just seen, they reacted violently to his speech of August 8th, to stir up anti-American feelings in Japan.

We now come to one of the queerest and most anomalous situations to be found in relations between two Powers of approximately equal standing in world affairs. The Japanese Assessor handed out to the members of the Lytton Commission what purported to be a French translation of a statement made by Stimson to Debuchi. It is necessary to quote the statement and the reply in *extenso* to get the nuances and to realize just how near the nadir America had descended in her foreign policy.

"I understand perfectly that Japan has special and vital relations with Manchuria and as a consequence I faithfully respect the rights and interests of Japan in that region; and I certainly have no ambition to make America a rival of Japan in Manchuria. However, as I intend to be faithful to the spirit of both the Kellogg Pact and the Nine-Power Treaty, I find myself obliged to say things which sometimes may not be very agreeable to your country; I hope that you will understand this. Moreover, my last speech was simply in explanation of the happenings affecting the fundamental spirit and the application of the Kellogg Pact: I did not intend to make use of the occasion to attack Japan. Consequently I was particularly careful about using the word 'aggressor' which I am told has been so severely criticised in Tokyo. I especially preceded it with the indefinite article in order that I might express myself in the abstract." [1]

This remarkable document was wired back to Castle by Johnson without comment, except to say that it was unsigned. [2] It was answered immediately by Castle.

"With reference to the document handed to the members of the League Commission by the Japanese Assessor, the statements attributed to the Secretary differ in varying degree from the Department's record of the statements made on August 10th to the Japanese Ambassador by the Secretary, with the consequence that the distorted version which was supplied to the Commission gives the impression that the attitude of the Secretary is more lenient toward Japanese operations in Man-

---

[1] *Op. cit.*, pp. 100—101.
[2] *Op. cit.*, pp. 101—102.

churia and more strictly an expression of the Secretary's personal opinion than is actually the fact.

"In summing up his views on the Manchurian situation, the Secretary of State mentioned to the Ambassador his sympathy with Japanese rights in Manchuria, with which he asserted he had no desire to intervene. Further, the Secretary said he knew that there was no desire on the part of the United States to intrude or become a political rival of Japan in Manchuria. Whatever his own views might be, he said he had no intention of saying anything in his speech of August 8th for the purpose of annoying Japan; that on the contrary his preparation of the speech had been very painstaking in order to make certain that nothing was said in the speech which might justly cause irritation. However, the Secretary very seriously pointed out to the Ambassador his real position; namely that the speech of August 8 was a statement of his views and those which in his opinion were the views of the people of the United States toward the Briand–Kellogg Pact; that he and the people of this country felt that this pact was of the utmost importance to the United States and to the civilized world and that in the event it came to a question between permitting the destruction of that peace treaty on the one hand and annoying Japan on the other, he would unhesitatingly, even though it caused regrettable annoyance to Japan, take his stand for the preservation of the treaty. The Secretary also called the Ambassador's attention to the fact in the press he had noticed that Japanese discussion had been aroused by an alleged statement which he had not made and he pointed out the fact that instead of the words 'The aggressor' he had used the words 'an aggressor'.

With regard to the foregoing information please transmit it to General McCoy orally and confidentially, and state that the Department has no objection to his communicating it orally and confidentially to the other members of the League Commission if it is his opinion that they should receive this information.

Much could be said about this "Alice In Wonderland" type of diplomacy. One can see of course that Stimson was made a foolish dupe by the crafty Japanese and used to serve their own ends. But what is even more striking is the weak denial by Castle and the fearful and secret method used to notify the Commissioners. One feels that the denial was so weak as to be purposely damaging to Stimson; it is almost *Lese-Majeste*. Obviously Stimson was away from Washington, since Johnson addressed the telegram to the Acting Secretary of State, and it was answered by Castle, Acting Secretary. It almost seems that Castle was being personally disloyal to Stimson, and making the case even worse for him than it actually was. Why did he instruct Johnson to be so careful, to transmit the message 'orally and confidentially' to McCoy, and to authorize him to do likewise, in the event he thought the other Commissioners should receive the information? One would have thought Castle would have called in the press and made a public denial before the world and called on the Japanese Ambassador for a public statement. Certainly there must have been discord between Castle and Stimson. How can a country have a consistent foreign policy if there is no agreement between the President and his Secretary of State, between a Secretary and his Assistant, between Congress and the administration?

On September 3rd, Grew sent to Stimson a telegram in which he expressed it as his firm conviction that Japan intended to see the Manchurian incident through unless stopped bij superior military force and that there was nothing America could do about it, "although internal economic pressure and moral pressure from outside may in time compel modifications in Japanese policy".

On September 15th, Japan released the information that she had formally recognized Manchukuo as a sovereign state.

On November 21st, Matsuoka [1] called on Hugh Wilson [2] and Norman Davies [3] in Geneva and informed them that (1) Japan will not be diverted from her purpose in Manchuria, (2) that there was danger in the hostility of Japanese public opinion to America, and that (3) Japan would leave the League if her dignity were hurt. We have come a long way since the destruction of a few yards of rail on the night of September 18th, 1931, to the point where we are being threatened by Japan fourteen months later. But is was a development implicit in the diplomacy of America and the lacadaisacal attitude of the League. Our buzzards were coming home to roost.

---

[1] Head of Japan's delegation to the League of Nations.

[2] American Minister in Switzerland and alternate delegate at the disarmament conference.

[3] American delegate at Geneva disarmament conference.

On January 5th, 1933, Japan attacked Shanhaikwan. The Ambassador came in and told Stimson that it was "a local incident, provoked by a minor outbreak of Chinese against the Japanese there ... and that unless there was further provocation in Jehol by Chang Hsueh-liang the matter would be controlled. He said that in any event Japan had no territorial ambition south of the Great Wall". The Ambassador was reminded by Stimson that a year ago he had been given similar assurances by him that Japan had no territorial ambitions in Manchuria. The Ambassador became flustered and admitted that that was so, but said that the situation had changed; at any rate he could now assure Stimson that the Japanese had no ambitions in North China. He told Stimson that no Japanese Cabinet which advocated a compromise in Manchuria could survive and that the Shanhaikwan incident must be regarded as a closed incident. [1] Stimson advised Japan to get out of the League and out of the Kellogg Pact.

On January 18th, [2] President-elect Roosevelt issued a public statement in which he said: "I am willing to make it clear that American foreign policies must uphold the sanctity of international treaties. That is the cornerstone on which all relations between nations must rest."

On February 20th, [3] Japan announced a decision by the Government to secede from the League of Nations if that body were to adopt the report of the Committee of Nineteen. In informing Stimson of this, Grew said Japan was ready to fight if any nation tried to interfere in any way with her schemes. He said occupation of North China was likely to eventuate if the League applied active sanctions. He said Japan was ready for war with either or both the United States and Russia.

Here was, indeed, a council of despair. Don't do anything to anger Japan or she will swallow North China. Don't interfere or she will go to war against you. If you do nothing, she will do whatever she likes anyway.

On February 25th, [4] Stimson sent an important statement of

---

[1] F.R.U.S., *op. cit.*, p. 107.

[2] *Op. cit.*, p. 109.

[3] *Loc. cit.*

[4] *Op. cit.*, pp. 115—16.

American policy to the Minister in Switzerland to transmit to
Drammond.

"... I have the honor to state the views of the American
Government as follows:

In the situation which has developed out of the controversy
between China and Japan, the purpose of the United States
has coincided in general with that of the League of Nations,
the common objective being maintenance of peace and settlement of international disputes by pacific means. In pursuance
of that objective, while the League of Nations has been
excercising jurisdiction over a controversy between two of its
members, the Government of the United States has endeavored
to give support, reserving to itself independence of judgment
with regard to method and scope, to the efforts of the League
on behalf of peace.

The findings of fact arrived at by the League and the understanding of the facts derived by the American Government
from reports made to it by its own representatives are in
substantial accord. In the light of its findings of fact, the
Assembly of the League has formulated a measured statement
of conclusions. With those conclusions the American Government is in general accord. In their affirmations respectively of
the principle of non-recognition and their attitude in regard
thereto the League and the United States are on common
ground. The League has recommended principles of settlement.
In so far as appropriate under the treaties to which it is a party,
the American Government expresses its general endorsement
of the principles thus recommended.

The American Government earnestly hopes that the two
nations now engaged in controversy, both of which have long
been in friendly relationship with our own and other peoples,
may find it possible, in the light of the now clear expression
of world opinion, to conform their policies to the need and
the desire of the family of nations that disputes between nations
shall be settled by none but pacific means."

On February 27th, Stimson received Debuchi and they rehashed
the same old stuff. Stimson reiterated his friendliness for the
Japanese Government and people, and stated that he only blamed
a small group of militarists for the events in Manchuria. Stimson
made excuses for the harsh or unfriendly things he had said against
Japan and her actions, in effect apologizing again to Debuchi. The
Ambassador said he still believed in his people and that sooner or

later the moderate elements in Japan would win out. Stimson joined him in this hope. Debuchi told Stimson that he appreciated what he had done for Japan, and hoped they could be friends after Stimson went out of office. Stimson reciprocated his wish.

Since this was only a few days before Stimson went out of office, it may be looked upon as an official farewell. In looking at his memoirs written years later, one finds no rancor, no suspicion, no apparent awareness that Debuchi had duped him. Stimson went out with his banners waving, still believing in the Japanese. Could he have been right? and all these events have been merely coincidental, without preconception or a carefully laid plan? The findings of the Lytton Commission do not bear out such an idea. The documents do not bear it out. What can we say then? Stimson and the Hoover Administration made a mistake that cost us a major war, Stimson, partly, perhaps, because his hands were tied, because he did not have a proper Assistant Secretary, because he could not make the policy and enforce it. But in all honesty and fairness to a great old man, it must be admitted that it does not seem that his policy would have been very different, even if he had had the full power over foreign relations. Can we say then that Hoover was to blame for the catastrophe? or the League? or the individual Great Powers? This is too much over-simplification. It was nobody's and everybody's fault. The statesmen were children of their day, of their time. They could not use 1940 style diplomacy in 1931. The Japanese, were, of course, primarily responsible. They tried a shoe for fit, and finding it fit, proceeded to walk, waiting to be stopped. It reminds one of an old story told in West Texas. The Indians on the plains caught a white man and were about to kill him, but they were intrigued by some contrivance he had slung over his shoulder. They motioned to him to show them what this was before they put him to death. He sat down and strapped on his ice skates and began demonstrating their use, going in circles about the Indians, but always widening the circle until all at once the Indians realized that he had got away, since he was too fast for them to catch and was too far away for them to stop with a bullet. The Americans (Frenchmen, and Englishmen) were like the Indians; by the time they quit being lulled, they realized that the Japanese were too far to stop. They did not want to do anything other than talk, to stop the Japanese, and the Japanese, realizing this, stalled, until they had solid accomplishments to present as *faits accompli*. They took advantage of the indecision and lack of unity among the Powers to gain their objective. It was daring and it succeeded

The successors of Hoover and Stimson made no attempt to alter their policy. On March 11th, Hull sent a reply to a letter written by the Secretary General of the League, to Stimson, as Secretary of State, on February 25th, enclosing a resolution passed by the League to appoint an Advisory Committee, and informing the Secretary that at the first meeting of the Committee they had issued an invitation to America to co-operate in its work. In his reply Hull stated:

> "...I am happy to inform you that the American Government is prepared to co-operate with the Advisory Committee in such manner as may be found appropriate and feasible. As it is necessary that the American Government exercise independence of judgment with regard to proposals which may be made and/or action which the Advisory Committee may recommend, it would seem that appointment by it of a representative to function as a member of the Committee would not be feasible. However, believing that the participation by a representative of this Government in the deliberations of the Committee would be helpful, I am instructing the American Minister to Switzerland, Mr. Hugh R. Wilson, to be prepared so to participate, but without right to vote, if such participation is desired."

On March 13th, Hull issued a statement to the press in which he repeated the instructions, and added:

> "This procedure, if adopted, will not give to the representative of this Government a position of membership on the Committee.... It does not in any way impair the right of independence of judgment and freedom of action of the United States. The representative of the United States cannot take any action binding this country."

American foreign policy was nice and safe, for Japan, just as it had been under the previous Administration. Hull disavowed Wilson before he ever had an opportunity to do anything. America was setting up a scarecrow, a dummy member of the Committee.

And with this crowning anti-climax we close our period, knowing that between it and the embargoes of July, 1941, there intervened nothing, on American part, except swallowing in humility such things as the sinking of the Panay, while making huge profits from American sale to Japan of steel scrap and oil and raw materials for the building of the Japanese war machine. While she sent these things to Japan and prepared her for the great day when the American fleet in the Pacific would be immobilized and almost destroyed at Pearl Harbour, her national honor smirched as never before—and, is it vain to hope never again?—America had oatmeal boxes set beside cash registers in drugstores, cafes, and groceries all over America, showing a bloodspattered Chinese mother holding a mutilated baby, and beneath the picture a legend asking for pennies to help war-devastated China.

Yes, America sent scrap to make bombs and shrapnel for Japan to ravage China, and she sent pennies to China to heal the wounds which those instruments of war inflicted. This was American policy for nearly ten years after the Kwantung Army first broke loose on the night of September 18th, 1931.

ADDENDUM

The non-recognition of territories organised by aggression was made a part of our diplomatic policy by Stimson. This has been louded as one of the great diplomatic achievements of the 20th century by no less a person than Toynbee.

Stimson used a letter to Senator Borah, Chairman of the Senate Foreign Relations Committee, to set forth the background of American policy in China and to give official sanction to the non-recognition theory. The letter is reprinted as an addendum, without comment except for italics by the present author.

"You have asked my opinion whether, as has been sometimes recently suggested, present conditions in China have in any way indicated that the so-called Nine Power Treaty has become inapplicable or ineffective or rigthly in need of modification, and if so, what I considered should be the policy of this Government.

This Treaty, as you of course know, forms the legal basis upon which now rests the 'Open Door' policy towards China. That policy, enunciated by John Hay in 1899, brought to an end the struggle among various powers for so-called spheres of interest in China which was threatening the dismemberment of that empire. To accomplish this Mr. Hay invoked two principles (1) equality of commercial opportunity among all nations in dealing with China, and (2) as necessary to that equality the preservation of China's territorial and administrative integrity. These principles were not new in the foreign policy of America. They had been the principles upon which it rested in its dealings with other nations for many years. In the case of China they were invoked to save a situation which not only threatened the future development and sovereignty of that great Asiatic people, but also threatened to create dangerous and constantly increasing rivalries between the other nations of the world. War had already taken place between Japan and China. At the close of that war three other nations intervened to prevent Japan from obtaining some of the results of that war claimed by her. Other nations sought and had obtained spheres of interest. Partly as a result of these actions a serious uprising had broken out in China which endangered the legations of all of the powers at Peking. While the attack on those legations was in progress, Mr. Hay made an announcement in respect to this policy as the principle upon which the powers should act in the settlement of the rebellion. He said

> 'The policy of the Government of the United States is to seek a solution which may bring about permanent safety and peace to China, preserve Chinese territorial and administrative entity, protect all rights guaranteed to friendly powers by treaty and international law, and safeguard for the world the principle of equal and impartial trade with all parts of the Chinese Empire.'

He was succesful in obtaining the assent of the other powers to the policy thus announced.

In taking these steps Mr. Hay acted with the cordial support of the British Government. In responding to Mr. Hay's announcement, above set forth, Lord Salisbury, the British Prime Minister expressed himself 'most emphatically as concurring in the policy of the United States.'

For twenty years thereafter the Open Door policy rested upon the informal commitments thus made by the various powers. But in the winter of 1921 to 1922, at a conference participated in by all of the principal powers which had interests in the Pacific, the policy was crystallized into the so-called Nine Power Treaty, which gave definition and precision to the principles upon which the policy rested. In the first article of that Treaty, the contracting powers, other than China, agreed

> 1. To respect the sovereignty, the independence and the territorial and administrative integrity of China.
> 2. To provide the fullest and most *unembarrassed opportunity* to China to develop and maintain for herself *an effective and stable government.*
> 3. To use their influence for the purpose of effectually establishing and maintaining the *principle of equal opportunity* for the commerce and industry of all nations throughout the territory of China.
> 4. *To refrain* from taking advantage of conditions in China in order to seek *special rights or privileges* which would abridge the rights of subjects or citizens of friendly states, and from *countenancing action inimical to the security of such states.*

This Treaty thus represents a carefully developed and matured international policy intended, on the one hand, to assure to all of the contracting parties their rights and interests in and with regard to China, and on the other hand, to assure to the people of

China the fullest opportunity to develop without molestation their
sovereignty and independence according to the modern and
enlightened standards believed to maintain among the people of
this earth. At the time this Treaty was signed, it was known that
China was engaged in an attempt to develop the free institutions
of a self-governing republic after her recent revolution from an
autocratic form of government; that she would require many years
of both economic and political effort to that end; and that her
progress would necessarily be slow. The Treaty was thus a
covenant of self-denial among the signatory powers *in deliberate
renunciation of any policy of aggression* which might tend to *interfere* with that development. It was believed—and the whole history
of the development of the 'Open Door' policy reveals that faith—
that only by such a process, under the protection of such an
agreement, could the fullest interests not only of China but of all
nations which have intercourse with her best be served.

In its report to the President announcing this Treaty, the American Delegation, headed by the then Secretary of State, Mr. Charles
E. Hughes, said

> 'It is believed that through this Treaty the 'Open Door' in
> China has at last been made a fact.'

During the course of the discussions which resulted in the Treaty,
the Chairman of the British delegation, Lord Balfour, had stated
that

> 'The British Empire delegation understood that there was
> no representative of any power around the table who thought
> that the old practice of "spheres of interest" was either advo-
> cated by any government or would be tolerable to this con-
> ference. So far as the British Government was concerned,
> they had, in the most formal manner, publicly announced that
> they regarded this practice as utterly inappropriate to the
> existing situation.'

At the same time the representative of Japan, Baron Shidehara,
announced the position of his government as follows:

> 'No one denies to China her sacred right to govern herself.
> No one stands in the way of China to work out her own great
> national destiny.'

The Treaty was originally executed by the United States,
Belgium, the British Empire, China, France, Italy, Japan, the
Netherlands and Portugal. Subsequently it was also executed by

Norway, Bolivia, Sweden, Denmark and Mexico. Germany has signed it but her Parliament has not yet ratified it.

It must be remembered also that this Treaty was one of several treaties and agreements entered into at the Washington Conference by the various powers concerned, all of which were interrelated and interdependent. No one of these treaties can be disregarded without disturbing the general understanding and equilibrium which were intended to be accomplished and effected by the group of agreements arrived at in their entirety. The Washington Conference was essentially a disarmament conference, aimed to promote the possibility of peace in the world not only through the cessation of competition in naval armament but also by the solution of various other disturbing problems which threatened the peace of the world, particularly in the Far East. These problems were all interrelated. The willingness of the American government to surrender its then commanding lead in battleship construction and to leave its positions at Guam and in the Philippines without further fortification, was predicated upon, among other things, the self-denying covenants contained in the Nine Power Treaty, which assured the nations of the world not only of equal opportunity for their Eastern trade but also *against the military aggrandizement of any other power at the expense of China.* One cannot discuss the possibility of modifying or abrogating those provisions of the Nine Power Treaty without considering at the same time the other promises upon which they were really dependent.

Six years later the policy of self-denial against aggression by a stronger against a weaker power, upon which the Nine Power Treaty had been based, received a powerful reinforcement by the execution by substantially all the nations of the world of the Pact of Paris, the so-called Kellogg-Briand Pact. These two treaties represent independent but harmonious steps taken for the purpose of aligning the conscience and public opinion of the world in favor of a system of orderly development by the law of nations including the settlement of all controversies by methods of justice and peace instead of by arbitrary force. The program for the protection of China from outside aggression is an essential part of any such development. The signatories and adherents of the Nine Power Treaty rightly felt that the orderly and peaceful development of the 400.000.000 of people inhabiting China was necessary to the peaceful welfare of the entire world and that no program for the welfare of the world as a whole could afford to neglect the welfare and protection of China.

The recent events which have taken place in China, especially the hostilities which having been begun in Manchuria have latterly been extended to Shanghai, far from indicating the advisability of any modification of the treaties we have been discussing, have tended to bring home the vital importance of the faithful observance of the covenants therein to all of the nations interested in the Far East. It is *not necessary* in that connection *to inquire into the causes of the controversy* or attempt to apportion the blame between the two nations which are unhappily involved; for regardless of cause or responsibility, it is clear beyond peradventure that a situation has developed which *cannot,* under any circumstances, *be reconciled with the obligations* of the covenants of these two treaties, and that *if the treaties had been faithfully observed such a situation could not have arisen.* The signatories of the Nine Power Treaty and of the Kellog-Briand Pact who are not parties to that conflict are not likely to see any reason for modifying the terms of those treaties. To them the real value of the faithful performance of the treaties has been brought sharply home by the perils and losses to which their nationals have been subjected in Shanghai.

That is the view of this Government. We see *no reason for abandoning the enlightened principles* which are embodied in these treaties. We believe that this situation would have been *avoided had these covenants been faithfully observed,* and no evidence has come to us to indicate that a due compliance with them would have interfered with the adequate protection of the legitimate rights in China of the signatories of those treaties and their nationals.

On January 7th last, upon the instruction of the President, this Government formally notified Japan and China that *it would not recognize any situation, treaty or agreement entered into by those governments* in violation of the covenants of these treaties, *which affected the rights* of our Government or its citizens in China. If a similar decision should be reached and a similar position taken by the other governments of the world, *a caveat will be placed* upon such action which, we believe, *will* effectively *bar the legality* hereafter of *any title* or right sought to be obtained *by pressure or treaty violation,* and which, as has been shown by history in the past, *will eventually lead to the restoration to China of rights* and titles of which she may have been deprived.

In the past our Government, as one of the leading powers on the Pacific Ocean, has rested its policy upon an abiding faith in the future of the people of China and upon the ultimate success in dealing with them of the principles of fair play, patience, and mutual goodwill. We appreciate the immensity of the task which lies before her statesmen in the development of her country and its government. The delays in her progress, the instability of her attempts to secure a responsible government, were foreseen by Messrs. Hay and Hughes and their contemporaries and were the very obstacles which the policy of the Open Door was designed to meet. We concur with those statesmen, representing all the nations in the Washington Conference who decided that China was entitled to the time necessary to accomplish her development. *We are prepared to make that our policy for the future.*

Very sincerely yours,   (Signed) Henry L. Stimson"

LITERATURE

Bau, M., *The Foreign Relations of China*.

Bland, J. O. P. and E. Backhouse, *China under the Empress Dowager, being the history of the life and times of Tzŭ Hsi*, London 1910.

Borg, D., *American Policy and the Chinese Revolution 1925—'28*, New York 1947.

C.F.R., *Survey on American Foreign Relations 1928—'36*, 2 vols.

"China today" Series, *The Puppet State of Manchukuo*, Shanghai 1935.

China Year Book, Shanghai.

Clyde, P. H., *International Rivalries in Manchuria 1689—1922*, Ohio 1928.

Couling, S., *The Encyclopedia Sinica*, Shanghai 1917.

Cressey, G. B., *China's Geographic Foundations, a survey of the land and its people*, New York 1934.

Dennett, T., *Americans in Eastern Asia*, New York 1922.

Etherton, P. T. and H. H. Filtman, *Manchuria: Cockpit of Asia*, London 1932.

F.R.U.S. (*Papers relating to Foreign Relations of the United States*), 1929, 1930, 1931; Japan 1931—1941.

Griswold, A. W., *The Far Eastern Policy of the United States*, New York 1938.

Hornbeck, S. K., *The United States and the Far East, certain fundamentals*, Boston 1942.

Hudson, G. F., *The Far East in World Politics*, Oxford 1937.

I.P.R., Publications, New York.

Japan Year Book, Tokyo.

Johnstone, W. C. Jr., *The United States and Japan's New Order*, Oxford 1941.

Lansing, R., *War Memoirs of ... Secretary of State*, New York 1935.

Latourette, K. S., *Chinese History and Culture*, New York 1943.

————, *The Development of China*, New York 1927.

Lattimore, O., *Manchuria Cradle of Conflict*, Baltimore 1932.

League of Nations Report of the Lytton Commission, Geneva 1932.

MacNair, H. F., *China*, Berkeley—Los Angelos 1946.

————, *China in Revolution*, Chicago 1931.

————, *Selected Readings in Chinese History*, Shanghai 1929.

Manchurian Year Book 1920—'33, Tokyo.

Morley, F., *The Society of Nations, its organisation and constitutional development*, Washington 1932.

Morse, H. B. and H. F. MacNair, *Far Eastern International Relations*, Chicago 1931.

Murdoch, J., *A History of Japan*, 2 vols., London 1925—'26.

Pollard, R. T., *China's Foreign Relations 1917—'31*, New York 1933.

Pratt, Sir John, *War and Politics in China*, London 1943.

Quigly and Blakeslee, *Far East, International Survey*, New York 1935.

Reischauer, R. K., *Conflicts inside China*, Boston 1936.

Steiger, G. N., *A History of the Far East*, New York 1936.

Stimson, H. L., *Far Eastern Crisis*, New York 1936.

———— and McG. Bundy, *On Active Service in Peace and War*, New York 1947.

Toynbee, A. J., *The Annual Survey of International Affairs*, Oxford 1933.

Vinacke, H. M., *A History of the Far East in Modern Times*, New York 1946.

Wellington Koo, *Memoranda presented to the Communists 1932*, 1940.

Willoughby, W. W., *China at the Conference*, 1935.

————, *Foreign Rights and Interests in China*, Baltimore 1936.

————, *Sino-Japanese Controversy and the League of Nations*, Baltimore 1935.

Woo, T. C., *The Kuomintang and the Future of the Chinese Revolution*, London 1928.

Yakhontoff, V., *Russia and the Soviet Union in the Far East*, London 1932.

Young, C. W., *The International Status of the Kwantung Leased Territory*, Baltimore 1931.

————, *Japan's Special Position in Manchuria*, Baltimore 1931.

————, *Japanese Jurisdiction in the S.M.R.*, 1929—'31.

INDEX